AF541215

Kathakali

The Dance-Drama of Malabar

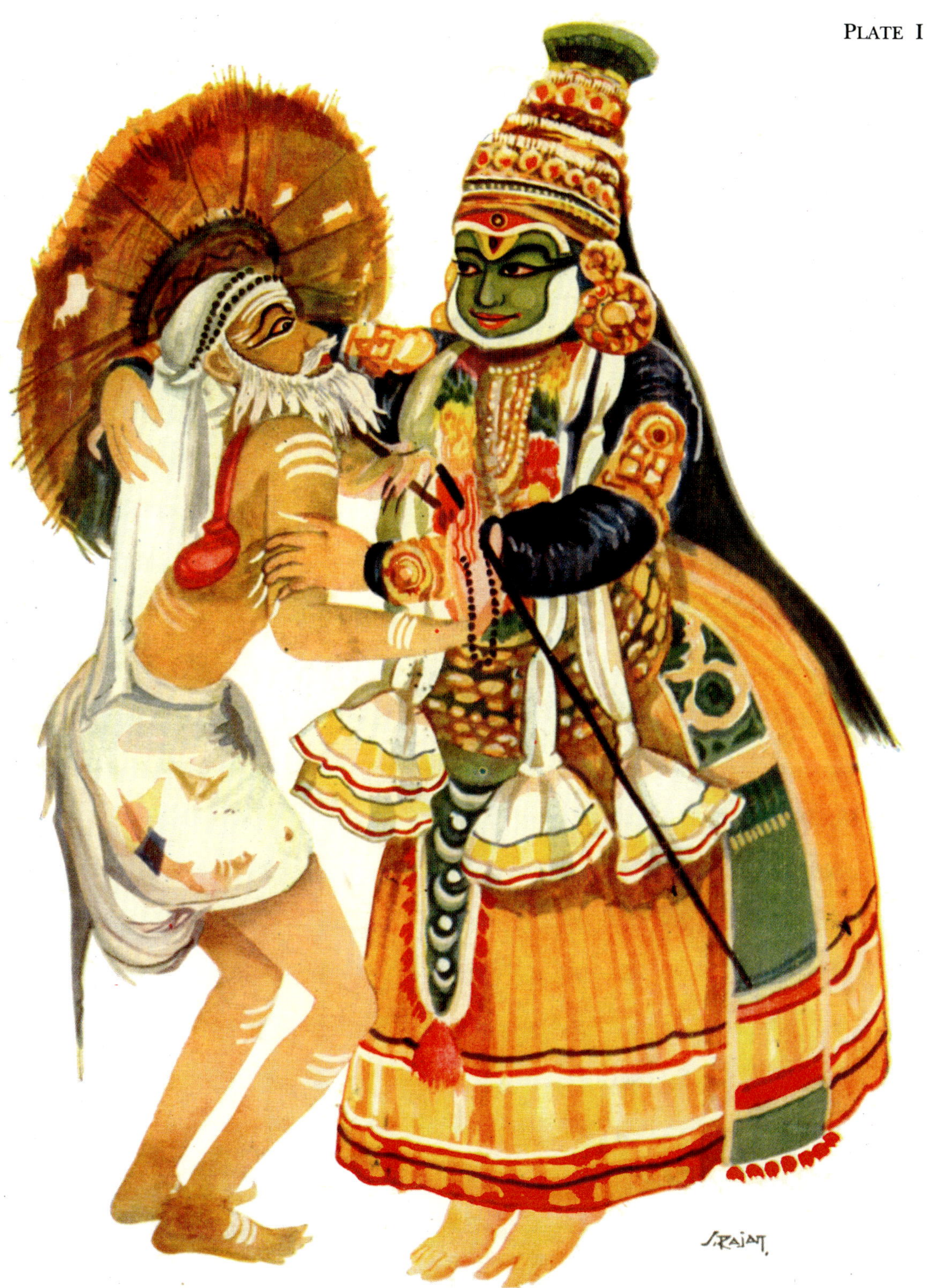

Kriṣṇa welcoming Sudhāma, the poor Brahmin devotee (p. 46 and 103).

Kathakali

The Dance-Drama of Malabar

K. Bharatha Iyer

DEV PUBLISHERS & DISTRIBUTORS

New Delhi

Published by:

DEV PUBLISHERS & DISTRIBUTORS

2nd Floor, Prakash Deep,
4735/22, Ansari Road,
Darya Ganj,
New Delhi-110002
Phone : 011-43572647, 9810236140
e-mail: devbooks@hotmail.com
website: www.devbooks.co.in

ISBN 978-81-920752-1-1
This edition 2011
Originally published in 1955 by
Luzac & Co. Ltd, London
This edition published with permission
from copyright owners.

Printed in India

CONTENTS

APPENDICES

LIST OF ILLUSTRATIONS

FIGURES

PLATES

AUTHOR'S PREFACE

Though it would not be correct to say that Kathakali was a dying art during the first quarter of this century which witnessed a marked decline in traditional values, its popularity was steadily on the wane. A considerable section of the people of Malabar had begun to look down upon it as the relic of a less civilized past. It was at such a time that the Kerala poet, Vallathol Narayana Menon, established the Kerala Kala Mandalam (Kerala Academy of Arts) with the object of promoting and popularising Kathakali. Apart from lack of enthusiasm, this project met with misleading and uncharitable criticism. A similar fate overtook the author and his friends when they invited the poet and his Kathakali artists to Rangoon in 1935. An overwhelming section of the Malayalis who constituted the Committee formed for the promotion of Kathakali, were frankly apprehensive that the exhibition of this 'old-type dumb-show' would go towards lowering the prestige of the Malayalis.

Kathakali has now received wide recognition due to the efforts of several Indian and European dancers, most of whom are internationally known and the appreciations of this art-form voiced by various foreign writers. The Malayalis are now no longer apologetic about it; rather, they are a little too aggressively conscious of its merits. This deepened interest is certainly a major gain, for no art, however great can thrive in an atmosphere of increasing frigidity. But as yet no effort has been made to properly canalise this interest. The world-wide recognition which Kathakali has received has had one baneful effect, which we hope is but a passing phase and, therefore, need not unduly worry us. Lured by the success of "modern" Indian dancers, several Kathakali artists have left their native stage and have become "modern" dancers. Having enjoyed the less strenuous and more glamorous life of the modern stage, they are loath to return to their traditional calling. A great deal of what they have learnt through years of careful training and discipline has gone into cold storage, for what they require in their new role as "modern" dancers, aspiring for international fame, is after all very little. Watching the developments of the last four decades and having witnessed the plays staged at the Kerala Kala Mandalam in the thirties, when reputed masters like Kunju Kurup, Ravunni Menon, Kavalappara Narayanan Nair, Vechur Raman Pillai and Kunjan Panikkar appeared in important roles assisted by talented pupils like Kalamandalam Krishnan, Madhavan, Ananda Shivaraman and great musicians like Venkichan Pattar, Venkitakrishna Bhagavatar, Moothamana Nambutiri and others, the conclusion that there has been a fall in quality and that a first rate performance is at present but an occasional one needing careful planning ahead, is inescapable. What appears to be of prime importance at the moment is the promotion and preservation of the highest standard. To facilitate this, a Board of reputed connoisseurs of the art and wellknown Kathakali artists and the formation of a State controlled institution somewhat on the lines of the Imperial Russian Ballet run under the direction of the Board would seem to be an urgent necessity. I hope that the Travancore-Cochin Government which has a special responsibility in the matter, would consider this suggestion in earnest for the preservation of this magnificent heritage.

In the ensuing pages a close-up view of every aspect of this unique dance-drama is presented. Its evolution and crystallization into a highly developed art-form is traced against the particular geographical position of Kerala and the distinct cultural and social life of the people. The meaning and purpose of the Kathakali conventions, the symbolism underlying its stage practices, the ritualistic and religious character that pervades the play, its definite artistic intention and how that is achieved through a combination of the several elements of the drama, such as the strange make-up, the extraordinary drumming, the song, dance and the mime, are dealt with in this survey. The enumeration and description of the various movements and *mudras* of Kathakali are outside the scope of this work for they are best learnt from a teacher and are of little help to the reader. Instead, attention is focussed on how these actually function on the living stage as an effective means of communication, lending meaning to the canons in the texts and how they emerge as a rich and coherent pattern of boundless and universal significance. No longer can it be said that Indian *Natya* is not functioning in some of its highest forms as envisaged in the ancient texts or that such an achievement is but the memory of a golden past. This work, it is hoped, will help to bring this accomplished dance-drama however remote it may appear at first to those unfamiliar with it, within the common field of their experience and to recreate in a more intense and intimate way the experience of those who have already witnessed it.

This book was completed in October 1946 and was with the publishers ever since. Owing to the phenomenal rise in the cost of production, the publishers felt that it would not be financially prudent to proceed with a publication so purely Indian in character and on a subject so little known at the time. I am grateful to the Royal India & Pakistan Society (London) for their keen interest in my venture and for their kind offer to sponser the publication of this book which unfortunately could not materialise as they were unable to find the necessary funds. I am deeply grateful to Beryl de Zoete for her generous appreciation recorded in her book *The Other Mind* and for her efforts to expedite the publication of this book. My indebtedness to Dr. Ananda Coomaraswamy for finding time to read through the Ms. and for recording his high appreciation, is indeed great. Had not death claimed him so suddenly this book would have been the richer for an introduction from his incomparable pen.

In the writing of this book I have received considerable help from several of my esteemed friends and it gives me great pleasure to acknowledge my indebtedness to them. The superb art of the wellknown artist Kunju Kurup and his warm friendship have been a source of great inspiration to me. I am deeply grateful to M. Mukunda Raja, ex-Secretary of the Kerala Kala Mandalam and a reputed connoisseur, for his critical examination of the text, for suggestions, for help in securing illustrations and above all for his continued interest and encouragement; to Prof. K. R. Pisharoti and to Miss Alice Boner for suggestions;

to Manhar R. Vakil, Barrister-at-Law for his suggestions and for kindly reading the proofs; to the scholars of the Rama Varma Research Institute (Cochin) for their commendation of this book to the late Cochin Government; to Kala Mandalam Krishnan, Madhavan, Krishnan Kutty of Bombay and to Kunju Kurup for dancing and posing for the special illustrations required; to S. Rajam, wellknown artist of Madras, who took the trouble of going over to Malabar to prepare the colour plates and the several sketches and whose sincere interest in the success of this venture has been a source of great encouragement; to Thalor Venkiteswara Iyer whose several sketches were helpful to S. Rajam; to S. Chavda, wellknown Bombay artist, for preparing special illustrations; to S. Jepson and Alexander Janta for the loan of their photographs so generously placed at my disposal and to Miss. Alice Boner and Michael H. Brown for permission to use extracts from their writings which appear in the appendix to this book. I have taken care to acknowledge the source of the illustrations and if there are any omissions or errors, they are purely accidental. Finally I wish to record my thanks to the printers Messers. E. J. Brill (Leiden) and the publishers who have cooperated in the production of this handsome volume.

January 1955. K. BARATHA IYER

CHAPTER I

THE SEED-BED

Kathakaḷi is a traditional art and also the art of a people. It possesses many unique features which distinguish it from any theatrical art known to us. Since those features are largely the product of environment an attempt is made in this and the two succeeding chapters to acquaint the reader with the influences, geographical, historical and intellectual, which helped to shape it.

The home of Kathakaḷi is Keraḷa [1], better known as Malayāḷam or Malabar. It is a compact cultural and linguistic area comprising the State of Travancore-Cochin and the Malabar District of Madras State. Situated at the extreme west coast of the southern littoral of India, Keraḷa lies cradled between the Arabian Sea and the Western Ghats. Its narrow southern extremity dips into the Indian Ocean. Skirted by languid back-waters, its palm-fringed western coast presents a dream-like panorama of gleaming light, strange shadows and quivering reflections. All along the east it is bounded by the Ghats whose deep jungles are the home of the tiger, the python and the elephant. Viewed in this setting, Nature, it seems, has intended for this land a certain degree of isolation from the rest of the mainland. This geographical situation has deeply influenced the social, cultural and political evolution of Keraḷa which in many respects took a turn distinct from that taken by her neighbours.

---

[1] Keraḷa is also known as Bhārgava-kṣhetra after the Brahmin warrior-sage Bhārgava (Parasu-Rāma) an *avatar* of Viṣṇu. To expiate his sin of matricide he created it by the power of his austerities and offered it to the Brahmins as a gift. Standing at Gōkarna, so the legend says, he hurled his fiery battle-axe into the Indian ocean; the waters receded to the point where the axe fell. The land thus re-claimed was made over to the Brahmins under whose fostering care it developed. The land was theirs by this right and they exercised sovereignty over it: an instance of the combination of the *Regnum* and the *Sacerdotium*. Nowhere else in India have we a region so largely under the authority and moral leadership of the priestly class as in Keraḷa.

Keraḷa lies in the monsoon belt and for fully six months in the year there is the festival of the rains. Dark, massive clouds march over the heavens in serried ranks, gleaming with vivid flashes of lightning and looking like a fantastic cavalcade of be-jewelled elephants. Thunder rattles like the remorseless thudding of Śiva's drum. The sky in a frenzied orgy pours out a deluge, the storm sweeps in violent fury, abating only to rise in a diabolic tempo; nature dances wildly like Śiva the destroyer. At long last the scene changes; the cloud curtain lifts and a brilliant sun from a turquoise sky beams, warms and bakes. Drenched by copious life-giving showers and warmed by the sun, the soil seethes with quickening life and Nature swells with exuberance.

Everywhere, the landscape is of a luxuriant emerald, broken by the deep blue of the sky and the gorgeous colours of the flowers. The plains are studded with vast stretches of paddy, waving with golden corn and sandwiched between gardens where the feathery coconut, the lean, tall arecanut palms and the soaring teak, tower over the jack, mango and plantain trees, rich with fruits. Pepper, nutmegs, cardamom and other fragrant spices, grown here so abundantly, carried the fame of the land to distant countries of the Old World long before the time of Hippocrates (460-357 B.C.). In the wake of a mounting demand for these spices, men from the West roamed over unchartered seas, tramped dangerous wilds and inhospitable deserts in search of this land of spices; these epochal movements deeply affected the course of history. A considerable maritime activity ensued between the Malabar ports [2] and those of Greece, Phoenicia and Rome. Later, the monopoly

---

2 Muzuris, Naura, Tyndis, Nelcynda, Becara and Belit were the major ports. Of these Muzuris (modern Crangannore) figured as the most important emporium of trade frequented by the vessels of the nations of the West. Ancient Tamil chronicles sing of the fine large vessels of the Greeks arriving at Muzuris, laden with gold for exchange for pepper and other spices of the land. To secure the pepper trade the Romans are believed to have stationed a cohort at Muzuris. Pliny refers to Muzuris as "*primum emporium Indiae*". Tiru-vanci-Kulam (included in Muzuris or Crangannore) was the capital of the *Ceras* and existed as an independent kingdom in the middle of the 3rd cent. B.C. (vide Edicts of Aśoka). Roman writers and Tamil poets speak of the high degree of its civilisation at the beginning of the Christian era; it included the coast territory between Gokarna and Comarin and the kings were known as Ceraputras or Keralaputras. The town was of great extent and strongly fortified. Amongst the notable edifices were the king's palace, a temple of Viṣṇu, a Buddhist Chaitya and a Nigrantha monastery. In the 8th cent. an Armenian merchant Thomas Cana settled down at Crangannore in the South Street and brought a colony of 400 Christians from

of the Indian trade passed into Arab hands and for centuries nations of the West lost direct touch with India. The price of spices and especially of pepper rose high during the Middle Ages and after, and attempts were made by European traders to re-establish direct trade relations with India. In 1498 Vasco de Gama sailed direct to India and reached the pepper ports of Malabar. This opened up a new and historic epoch of momentous consequence for India as well as for the entire East and that story is still unfolding itself.

Thus the western sea-board of Malabar with its belt of sleepy lagoons remained for a long time the most conspicuous gate-way of India. Many strange influences filtered through. The Cross of Christ was planted on Indian soil first [3] in Malabar. According to local Christian tradition St. Thomas was the earliest evangelist to arrive; and much of the missionary work of St. Xavier is also associated with this land. After the second sack of their temple at Jerusalem the Jews, a much persecuted race, sought asylum at Muzuris. They too, like the early Christians, enjoyed the patronage and protection of the ruling chiefs. The sea-faring Arabs who came later settled down in the coastal regions. The Muslims of Keraḷa known as Moplahs are said to be descended from these Arab traders. Thus the Jew, Christian and Muslim met here [4]. In the mystic setting, as it were, of their new homeland they forgot old rivalries and for over a thousand years they have lived side by side in amity and have ever been treated kindly by the sons of the land. To-day they are an integral part of the society and inherit and share a common culture and way of life, unmistakably *Malayāḷi* in tone and texture.

Baghdad, Nineveh and Jerusalem. Philip Baldes describes Cranganore as a thriving centre of Christianity with a noble college of Jesuits, a stately library belonging to it, a church of Franciscans, a college of Chanotte—resort of the Christians of St. Thomas, with a school for the education of their youths. In the sack by Lopa Soares in 1504 the town was burned and looted and much that was ancient and thriving disappeared. Till the arrival of the Portuguese the Jews thrived; the charter of Bhaskara Ravi Varma conferred on the Jews valuable privileges and the head of the community was raised to a Nāṭuvāzhi (Governor). The Portuguese persecuted and compelled them to leave the town in 1565 when the Hindu ruling power had weakened. Extract from *Cochin State Manual*—C. Achyuta Menon.

[3] According to tradition in 52 A.D.

[4] Reminiscent of those days, a church, a synagogue and a mosque still stand side by side at the ancient settlement in Cranganore.

The original inhabitants of Keraḷa are believed to be Dravidians. The great majority of the people belong to this ancient race whose magnificent cultural achievements form so integral and vital a factor in Hindu civilisation and culture. Āryan penetration into this purely Dravidian region marked the beginning of a fruitful contact which later gave birth to a distinctive phase of Hindu culture. Many institutions of the land and particularly Kathakaḷi are the product of this synthesis of the two great cultures. In the rest of India, Kṣatriya clans set up sovereignty; here a Brahmin oligarchy, at all times numerically small, exercised unhindered political over-lordship for many centuries. Their incompetence to wield the double sceptre of spiritual and temporal power led ultimately to the adoption of a republican device. From about the 2nd century B.C. [5] the Brahmin aristocracy and the representatives of the people met generally once in twelve years on the banks of the Bhārata river at Tiru-nāvāi and elected as sovereign one of the princes from the neighbouring kingdoms of either the *Colās* or *Pāṇdyās*. The nominee styled as *Perumāl* became the military and administrative head of a republican council in which was vested all sovereign power. This institution worked very well for some centuries until it gave way to personal ambition and one of the *perumāls* set up a dynastic rule of benevolent despotism. The court of the *Perumāls* became the centre of intense intellectual activities. There, Hindu, Buddhist and Jain scholars and theologians met and stimulated the spirit of enquiry. Vivid glimpses of the life of those days can be had from the great Tamil classics, *Śilappadhikāram* and *Mani-mekhalai.*

With the break-up of the *Perumāl* power which occurred about the 4th century A.D. (?) the Nāyar militia led by war-lords emerged into prominence. The Nāyars have always been the most powerful community next to the Brahmins. They "were in fact magnates of the rulers of Keraḷa and exercised as much authority over their inferiors as their rulers did over them" [6]. Circumstances shaped them into a military caste and they gloried in arms and warfare. Soon *kaḷaries* or military colleges sprang up all over the land. Under expert teachers young men were

5 The first Council met in 113 B.C. Cf. *Samgha-Kali* by Appan Thampuran. (in Malayāḷam).

6 See *Cochin Castes and Tribes*—L. K. Anantakrishna Iyer.

put through a long and arduous course of physical training and massage [7] which imparted to their body and limbs a steely strength and extraordinary pliability which enabled them to perform miraculous feats of strength and skill [8]. They were trained to wield weapons with skill and were taught the subtle strategy of the game of offence and defence. The ballads of the land sing in glowing terms of the adventurous and tense life of the valiant knights and of their loves and blood-feuds. They picture an age of heroism and chivalry.

The rise of the Nāyars into a military caste is from a historical point of view the return to power of the indigenous element, but this in no way resulted in a conflict with the Brahmins of Keraḷa (called Nambūtiris) who have ever remained the first citizens and leaders of society. The Nambūtiris have long been subject to the social custom which required that only the eldest male member of the family (i.e. the head or would-be head of the family) should marry within the caste. The others married Nāyar women [9]. This long established practice drew the powerful Nāyar caste into intimate social relationship with the Nambūtiris and altogether eliminated every chance of conflict between the two. The Nāyars are a matriarchal group; in their family set-up woman is the centre-piece, a position which secured for the Nāyar woman a social status, freedom and economic privilege that seems to have no parallel in Hindu society elsewhere.

Amongst the various peoples of the land the Nambūtiris, as has been said, occupy a privileged position. They have exerted a powerful influence over the life and culture of the Malayāḷīs. These refined and aristocratic Brahmins exist and move in a different world and are in certain respects a distinct group from the Brahmins of the rest

---

7 Some of the *kaḷari* practices were adopted by the Kathakaḷi actors to gain strength, agility and pliability. The technique of Kathakali fighting scenes are also influenced by the *kaḷari* method of offence and defence.

8 The Portuguese poet Camoens, Duarte Barbosa (in his *Descriptions of the Coasts of East Africa and Malabar*) and Johnston (*Relations of the Most Famous Kingdoms*) quoted by L. K. Ananthakrishna Iyer in *Cochin Castes and Tribes* speak in high terms of Nayar valour and skill in weapons.

9 The children born of these out-of-caste unions were only entitled to maintenance and not to any share in the family estate. This proved economically beneficial to Nambūtiris as it checked fragmentation of their family property. The position has of late changed owing to the legalisation of such 'unions'.

of India. Their chief interest is in guarding a way of life that has all but disappeared except in isolated instances elsewhere and the cultivation of a great body of traditional knowledge. The Nambūtiris have remained a landed aristocracy from ancient times and consequently a leisured class. Rarely has this privileged position of assured affluence been abused by the community in the past. As a class they have lived a dedicated and disciplined life; but that was never at the expense of the refined enjoyments of the arts of life. Devotion to religious practices and rites, so pronounced a feature of their daily life, has not bred in them a dry asceticism spoiling the sense of relish and enjoyment. Behind an apparent outward simplicity, almost ascetic in severity, they remain aristocrats with fine tastes. Their love of poetry and the arts and sciences are well known; but they have fine epicurean tastes too. For the delights of the table they show an undisguised weakness; their feasts held on the slightest pretext are justly famous for many exquisite delicacies. No less famed are they for their evident love for amorous pleasures, a predilection that has found ample utterance in a branch of Malayaḷam literature (also well reflected on the Kathakaḷi stage) bearing the stamp of Nambūtiri genius. Again, as a class, they are distinguished for their sense of humour and wit; these features are found highly developed in the Keraḷa theatre (notably in the *Prabanḍham kūttu*). The Nambūtiris when they converse use picturesque and emphatic hand gestures and facial expressions. This habit is too evident a characteristic to be missed. As a body they stood aloof from the sweeping current of modernity [10] that has all but completely de-cultured the modern Indian. Had the Nambūtiris too chosen early to exchange their great traditional culture for modern "mis-education" many noble institutions of the land and Kathakaḷi too would have degenerated beyond redemption.

The love for Sanskritic studies which the Nambūtiris have cultivated and elevated into a creed, permeated and influenced every caste and class and helped to make Keraḷa a stronghold of learned studies [11].

---

10 Vast changes are taking place in the community; a fall from the traditional ideals is also discernible.

11 This love for Sanskrit studies is shared by the Harijans or 'depressed classes': from their ranks have risen many scholars throughout the centuries. The Christians of Keraḷa too are lovers of Sanskrit.

To the spheres of philosophy, poetry, drama, astronomy, astrology and medicine the contribution of Malabar scholars is very considerable [12]. The astounding achievements attributed to the credit of the Keraḷa astrologers and physicians would sound almost incredible but for the fact that such feats are none too rare even in these days. Strange as it may seem, some of the most difficult cures are effected by the physician, the astrologer and the *mantravādi* (chanter of *mantras*) working together. The belief in the curative and magic value of ritual ceremonies still remains as an operative force.

Hinduism, with its creeds and beliefs, is of course the religion of the land; but Malabar has stamped its colour on it. The religious outlook of the people is characterised by a sense of moderation and an awareness of the need for synthesis. This largely accounts for the absence of keen sectarian rivalries. Śaivaite and Vaiṣṇavite feuds which disturbed the religious life of the people of the neighbouring Tamil country, with which Malabar always remained in intimate cultural contact, were never allowed to divide her people. Mostly her religious practices are highly ritualistic and the rituals reveal intimacy with Tāntric cults. The belief in magic, sorcery and witch-craft and their practice, help to maintain contact with unseen and mysterious forces. *Mantravādis* who can win the favours of benevolent powers and subdue the most malevolent spirits with incantations of terrific potency are important elements in the social scheme. The world of mystery and twilight is seen and felt.

The *Bhagavati* cult with its many picturesque and refined rites is the cult of *Durga* with more softened shades. This *Devi* very often manifests through the *veliccappād* [13] or oracle. During ritual worship or when the deity rides out in ceremonial procession, he appears with drawn sword. A blood-red sash is tied over his white cotton dress and he wears anklets that jingle at every movement. His tense features and wildly flowing hair make him appear a mysterious figure. When the drums pound and the conches blow he begins to sway and then dances

---

12 In the 8th cent. A.D. intellectual activities in Keraḷa seemed to have reached the zenith as is evidenced by the great movement of Hindu renaissance in full swing at this time which was led by the Keraḷa philosophers and teachers, notably by Sankara.

13 He is the descendant of the "ancient dancing priest". In *Bhagavati pāṭṭu, Tiyāṭṭu* and *Pāna* which are ritual plays, the *Veliccappād* gets "possessed" and dances.

like one possessed. From time to time he roars in a stylized voice.

In the midst of these frenzied acts he waves his sword wildly and cuts his forehead. The red, warm blood oozing out from the cuts bespatters his body and garments. The worshipping crowd is put into a tense devotional mood. He is now the goddess; the worshipper and the worshipped are face to face and they speak to each other. The *veliccappād* (literally light-revealer) is thus an agent who keeps clear the life-line of faith. The many mysterious magic rites and tāntric rituals preserved in Keraḷa belong to the most ancient order. The offering of *Kuruti* (a compound of lime and turmeric dissolved in water that looks like blood), one of the rites practised, is perhaps a sublimated and symbolic process of blood sacrifice. The belief in the magic quality of spilled blood has found utterance on the Keraḷa stage from its earliest days and is enshrined as a major spectacle in Kathakaḷi dramas.

No less significant is *Kaḷam Ezhuttu.* On special occasions vivid pictures of deities are drawn on the temple floor. The figures are traced first in outline with white powder. Brilliant and deep colours (of powder) are then applied. The floor space covered by these drawings is sanctified and becomes a temporary shrine. The figures drawn are then "en-livened" by a special rite called *jīva-pratiṣta.* Then ritual worship is conducted accompanied with song and drumming. These coloured floor-drawings preserve an ancient pictorial tradition which has undoubtedly influenced the Kathakaḷi scheme of facial painting. The influences of this pictorial tradition are also noticeable in the Malabar murals which form a distinct school of Indian painting with many zonal peculiarities.

The supremacy enjoyed by the serpent is evidenced by the *Sarpa-Kāvūs* or serpent shrines found in every Malayāḷi home where quaint rituals are performed to propitiate it [14]. Wandering minstrels move

---

14 The wrath of the serpent is very much dreaded. Persistent skin diseases that do not easily respond to medical aid and repeated death of children occurring in a home are attributed to the wrath of the serpent. In such cases elaborate and expensive rituals are performed.

Viṣa vaidya (treatment for snake-bite) is a highly developed science—a traditional science still practised for the alleviation of human misery. The physicians who take to this art are prohibited from receiving any fees in return for their services. Their profession should be *niṣkāma karma.* They believe that desire for money is a corrupting influence that will mar their efficiency or skill in cures.

among the people and sing the great story of the snake tribe and kindle their faith. The high priests of the serpent cult are the Nambūtiri Brahmins of *pāmpumekkāṭ* (the house of the serpent grove). By *māṇtric* power they exercise an astonishing control over the snake

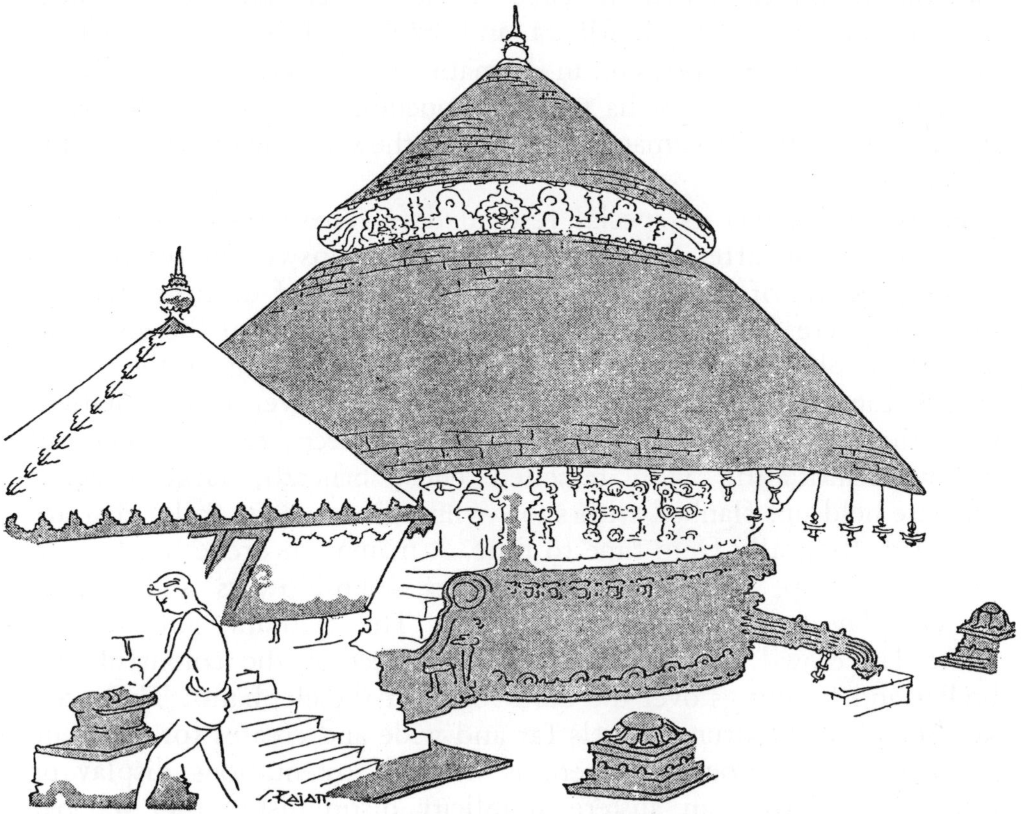

Fig. 1. A typical Keraḷa Temple (at *Irinjalakuda*).

tribe. All these, give us glimpses of an unfamiliar world of mystery and of unknown forces which is nevertheless a reality to the people at large.

In a survey of this nature we cannot ignore the Malabar temples which play so large a part in the religious and cultural life of the people (Fig. 1). These temples offer an austere contrast to the great South Indian ones which have towering pyramidal structures and pillared halls, all richly carved and ornamented. While within the massive structures of the latter, amidst magnificent setting, the *Deva-*

dāsi (*Bayadere* of the temple) sang and danced gracefully, in the spacious court-yards and *Kūttambalams* (temple theatre) of Keraḷa a dramatic dance-art of epic proportions evolved its stately form. The same impulse and inspiration, which elsewhere in India flowered into the architectural magnificence of the rock-cut temples or which covered wall-spaces as at Ajānta and Bāgh with forms of infinite beauty, here found expression in dramatic art. The body and the limbs were used as dynamic media to weave unending rhythmic patterns of significant forms. Here, man made himself the supreme material for his artistic expression.

Every temple has its special festival days. These festivals come in quick succession after the monsoon, as man's answering response to nature's festival of rains. Day and night the sound of drums penetrates the atmosphere. These drums announce the procession of the gods and stir the people to a new life. The gods come out riding lordly tuskers in gay caparison and glowing with gold and silver ornamentation. Over them tower stately umbrellas of deep green, red, crimson and yellow, scintillating with tasselled ends; beneath, large peacock fans are held up, flanked with snow-white *cāmara* (yak tails) that are waved rhythmically from time to time. A mammoth orchestra, four to five lines deep, with drummers, pipers, horn-blowers and cymbal players play for hours as if possessed. The brilliant sun and the white-clad crowd help to intensify the effect of the colourful umbrellas and trappings over the dark forms of the elephants. The incessant sound of the drums travels far and wide and creates for the scene a "charged background". There is little of ostentatious display or ornate effect; only an austere simplicity distinguishes the Malabar temple festivals and makes them impressive spectacles.

Those who think of India as a land of oriental splendour, of colourful costumes and rich jewellery will realise how deceptive that description is, so far as Keraḷa is concerned, if they ever happen to be within her borders. The atmosphere is one of restraint, dignity and poise. Men and women drape themselves in immaculate white and the use of jewellery is sparing. This prevailing white adds to the colours used a rare poignancy of expression, as in the case of the colours applied within the white border lines (*cuṭṭi*) of the Kathakaḷi facial painting. The Malayāḷi loves the open air and garden setting; his simple dwelling is set in a garden. Gregarious living in streets is foreign to his way of life. His great national festivals are Ōnam and Tiru-vātira; these have little religious significance. Shorn of all costly pomp and characterised by simple intense enjoyments, these are long periods of communal rejoicings during which the homes are happy with family reunion and the courtyards are brilliant with gay flower patterns. Girls gather in groups and break out into song and dance (*Kai-koṭṭi-kaḷi*) whose unwearied merriment and sweet delights sustain them for hours. The men indulge in more vigorous games not the least important of which is the *Ōṇa-tallu,* a sort of boxing and martial game over which the chieftain of the locality presides and distributes prizes to the participants [15].

The Malayaḷi has many distinct tastes and preferences. The elephant, to which reference has already been made, is his pet animal. Volumes of enchanting tales could be written about the Malayaḷi and his elephant pet. Here too as in other cases, the Nambūtiris and princes have set the fashion. They rear them with loving care, call them endearing names, to which they respond with touching affection and intimacy. This intimacy recaptures for us the whole atmosphere of the old times when the elephant was such a pronounced feature of Indian art and literature. To decorate these noble beasts the Malayāḷi has devised simple but effective trappings. The great silk umbrellas of variegated colours which stand on red lacquered handles, the picturesque peacock fans and immense *cāmarās* fixed to silver or gold handles and above all the gold and silver cover for the head and trunk; these are vividly decorative.

There is one particular characteristic of the Malayāḷi which can hardly be suppressed without impairing the subtle shades of the picture. That is his inordinate love of poetry. In this too the Nambūtiri Brahmins have led the way. The most conspicuous and important branch of Malayāḷaṃ literature is its poetical works. It is not only in the number of acknowledged poets and the still larger number who take to composing poetry as a learned pastime that this great love of poetry is revealed, but above all in the national passion for reciting poems, (*akṣara-slōka)* a game which often commences as soon as three or four meet. This develops into great competitions; an enlightened intellectual amusement yielding aesthetic pleasure, now alas! going out of fashion at

15 These practices are becoming rare and are dying out.

the touch of modernism and the advent of the card table [16]. To put every communication into verse-form was the fashion until quite recently. Every prosaic and commonplace thing was vivified into verse. "Poetry is a superior amusement" to a very large section of the people. This love of poetry has deeply influenced the tone and temper of Kathakaḷi.

The Malayāḷi very often employs the word *rasa* or *rasika* in referring to things or individuals. *Rasa* is flavour and the *rasika* is one who has the capacity to enjoy the flavours. By the term *rasika* the Malayāḷi denotes not only the lover of the beautiful (as the Sanskrit rhetoricians would have it) but any one who has a healthy sense of humour and wit, any one who enjoys the pleasures of life, anyone who can create an atmosphere of cheer and happiness around him. Such a one is welcomed everywhere. To be called a *rasika* is indeed a matter of distinction. The Malayāli's ideal is the *rasika.* The word is indicative of the Malayāli attitude towards life and things. By and large the people of Keraḷa are a race of *rasikas* and their theatrical arts, primarily the *Kūttu* and the Kathakaḷi, are intended for *rasikas.* This trait has influenced the theatrical arts of Keraḷa in several ways and facilitated their constant and continued development. In practice *Natya* was recognised as the fifth Veda. The stage was linked to the temple and provision was made for the up-keep of the artist and his family [17]; in fact an artist caste was created to ensure the continuity of the tradition.

The reader who goes through the following pages will find that almost every feature and shade in the picture presented above, of the land and its people, has directly or indirectly affected the Kathakaḷi drama. It is redolent of the soil and the people.

---

16 *Akṣaraślōka* is a game in recitation intended to test one's extensive knowledge of poetry and memory power. Any number can join in the competition. It commences by one reciting a śloka; the next one has to recite another which should commence with the first letter of the third line of the verse sung by the first. In the same order others have to continue. The one whose wit fails is defeated and retires from the game.

17 Temple lands were settled in perpetuity on artist families; in addition, they are entitled to rations issued daily from the temples.

CHAPTER II

THE KERAḶA STAGE — A HISTORICAL RETROSPECT

Kathakaḷi (story-play) or Āṭṭakatha (danced-play) is but the name given to a finalised phase of the Keraḷa theatre which crystallized into a pantomime dance-drama. To appreciate the formative forces which ultimately developed into this distinct drama it is necessary to notice only a few landmarks of the Keraḷa stage still extant, with which this form of dramatic art is related.

A rich variety of dances, dramatic spectacles and dance-dramas are prevalent in Keraḷa [1]. Of these the *Mutiēttu* seems to be one of the oldest: it means wearing the crown [2], an act symbolic of victory. The most popular theme found enacted is *Dārika Vadha* (slaying of the demon Dārika), a story connected with the Bhagavati or Kāḷi cult. The enactment is a votive offering, a religious rite that follows special ritual worship in the temple. The performance is completed in two acts: in the first one, Śiva receives the sage Nārada who voices the many grievances of the world against the misdeeds of the demon Dārika who was possessed of invincible might. Śiva promises to bring about his destruction by sending Kāḷi. In the next scene, Dārika appears and challenges Kāḷi. The scene of challenge is an elaborate affair. Kāḷi and Dārika mount war chariots from where a long and spirited verbal

---

1 Ritual and cult plays such as Bhagavati Pāṭṭu, Tiyāṭṭu, Pāna, Kaṇiyār Kaḷi, Tūkku, Kāḷi-āttam, Daivāṭṭam etc.

Non-ritual but religious like Cākkyār Kūttu with its important sub-divisions Prabandhaṃ, Nāṅgyār-Kūttu and Kūṭiyāṭṭam, then Krishnāṭṭam, Taṭṭil-me-kaḷi and the Rāmayana Shadow Play.

Secular ones like Mōhini-āṭṭam (a localised version of the Tanjore school of dancing), Korati-āttam, Kai-koṭṭi-kaḷi, Tuḷḷal, Pāṭakam, Kōl-kali, Kalyaṇakkaḷi, Parisa-muṭṭuṃ Kaḷi etc.

2 The headgears are of enormous size. The make-up of the characters is also very bizarre and symbolically significant.

exchange follows, which accentuates provocation, leading to intensity of passion. A great but leisurely fight ensues which lasts for hours during which the two combatants move about in the whole temple compound, for the stage is everywhere in the depiction of this cosmic event. When a blood-red sky over-head announces the annihilation of darkness, Dārika is slain by Kāḷi. It is an impressive though ghastly scene. The abdomen of the fallen demon is ripped open, the avenging goddess drinks his blood and adorns herself with the garland-like entrails of the *Asura.* The play is simple in theme, structure and in the technique of staging. The opposing forces of light and darkness, the scene of provocation and challenge, the ghastly death scene, the bloody meal and the conveniently expanding stage are all met with in the more developed Kathakaḷi. This and other similar cult plays, distinguished by a bizarre make-up, magic and religious associations connected with the Bhagavati cult, disclose pre-Aryan strains.

Cākkyār Kūttu. The art of the Cākkyārs is a more comprehensive and developed one. They are a community of dramatic artists and story-tellers whose origin [3] is as singular as their devotion to their caste-heritage. They claim descent from the story-telling *Sutās* referred to in the *Mahābhārata.* Whatever be the validity of the claim they seem to have practised their profession for nearly two thousand years [4]

---

3 Cākkyārs belong to the Ambalavāsi (temple-dweller) caste, an intermediate caste between the Brahmin and the Nāyar. The services of the Ambalavāsīs are dedicated to the temple. The Cākkyārs form a separate sub-caste within this fold; they are the temple artists. When a Nambūtiri woman is suspected of adultery she is at once placed under "suspension" till her guilt or innocence is proved. A trial is conducted by competent judges drawn from recognised members of the Nambūtiri society. When the guilt is proved she is out-casted. The judges decide the "period" which is the interval between the date of her offence and the date she is out-casted. Any issue born during this "period", if a male, becomes a Cākkyār and if a female a Naṅgyār. The Cākkyār caste is believed to have originated in this way. What is of particular significance here is that the issues of this "period" are not branded and punished. Their status in society is fixed next to the Brahmins and the vocation which has been prescribed as their caste-*dharma* is *Natya,* a calling of considerable standing and merit. *"Ottilleṅgil kūttu"* means that having been deprived of the right to learn the Vedas (*Ottu*)—not being Brahmins—their right or vocation is *Kuttu* or *Nātya* i.e. theatrical art. I think this saying and its adoption recognise that *Nātya* is the fifth Veda, a claim which the ancient traditions admit.

4 The Cākkyārs, it seems, were practising their dramatic art in the early centuries of the Christian era. This is evident from a reference in the *Silappadhikāram,* a Tamil

and are the world's most ancient order of dramatic artists still extant. In addition, they enjoy the distinction of being the only Sanskrit stage artists left. *Kūttu* covers both *Prabandhaṃ-kūttu* also known as *Vāk* (word) as well as *Kūtiyāṭṭam.*

Prabandhaṃ Kūttu is the name by which the story-telling art of the *Cākkyār* is known. His rendering is highly dramatic and is characterised by elegance of style, erudition and a profound sense of wit and

---

classic whose date is assigned to the 2nd cent. A.D. (?). A Cākkyār from Parur near Tiruvancikuḷam, where it is believed the poem was composed, is mentioned as having executed a Śiva Tāṇḍava dance before King Cenguttuvan while he was encamped at the Nilgiris. The description of this dance resembles in a remarkable way the theme of a Kangra painting which Dr. Coomaraswamy has reproduced in his *Indian Drawings,* where the *Mūla-prakriti* or Pārvati—the consort of Śiva—is depicted as seated looking at her form in a mirror as if absolutely unaffected by the cosmic dance. The *Śilappadhikāram* describes the dance as follows: When Śiva danced, his anklets jingled, the *damaru* (drum) in his quick moving hands sounded, his red eyes reflected a thousand indications (moods, ideas etc.) and his whirling *jaṭa* swept the four quarters. And Uma sat—not even her anklets, bangles, or be-jewelled belt whispered, neither her bosom nor her ear-drops or coiffure moved.

This Tamil work which is often called an epic bears ample testimony to the high degree of development of the theatrical art of South India at so early a period and is a certain indication of the esteem and widespread appreciation it enjoyed. Several kinds of dances and dance spectacles then prevalent are listed. The accomplished courtesan skilled in dancing and music was a notable social institution. The moving story of this great Tamil epic is centred round the most celebrated *danseuse* of the time, Madhavi by name. According to long established custom she made her *debut* at a great gathering of the elite of the city of Kaveripumpattinam, the capital of the great Coḷa country. The king himself as the supreme patron of the arts presided and as was customary presented Madhavi with 1001 gold coins and in recognition of her great skill, the fresh leaf garland that he was wearing. The confidante of Madhavi took this garland to the aristocratic quarters of the city and offered the love of her mistress to any one who would purchase the garland for 1001 gold coins. Kovalan, the hero of the poem, happening to pass by and hearing the announcement promptly paid the amount. He was led to the presence of Madhavi whose exceeding beauty and great skill in dancing and music captivated him. He fell in love with her so deeply that he neglected his faithful wife, his parents and his duty. From this infatuation of Kovalan the story moves to its tragic climax.

According to the popular version of this story, which is found enacted on the Tamil stage, Madhavi was invited to dance at the marriage festivities of Kovalan and Kannakai (the son and daughter of two merchant princes of the city). She agreed to dance on condition that the person around whose neck the necklace she flung at the conclusion of the dance, chanced to fall, should be surrendered to her as her man. She asked for no other fee. It seems, this strange condition was accepted. The necklace fell around the neck of the bridegroom Kovalan whom she claimed. From this the tragic sequel developed.

humour. The stories told are drawn from the *Purāṇas* and are based on the presentations made by well known Sanskrit poets and dramatists. In this performance the *Cākkyār* employs *Vācikābhinaya* (speech or spoken word) to the utmost effect. Many gestures are used to re-inforce the words. There is no music except the occasional drumming on a huge

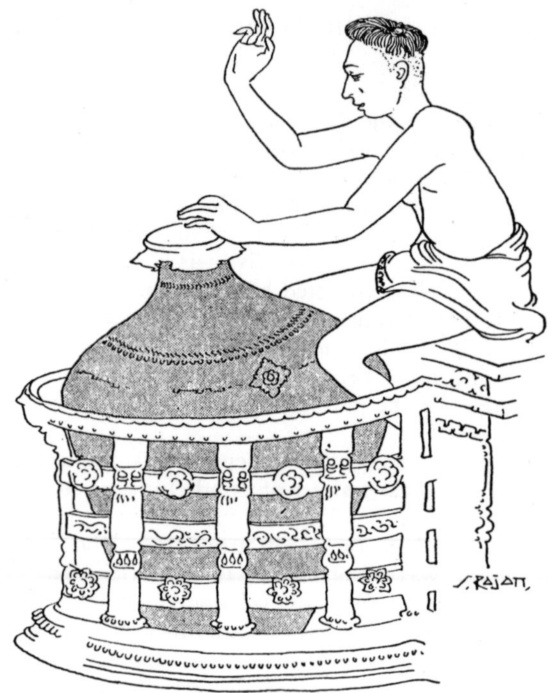

Fig. 2. Miḷāv, the giant copper drum of the Cākkyārs.

copper drum [5] (Fig. 2). There is hardly any dancing except a few conventional steppings and gestures.

Kūṭiyāṭṭam is the most significant phase of the *Cākkyār's* art and the one most intimately connected with this enquiry. The term signifies joint or combined acting, as a number of actors, male and female (*Cākkyārs* and *Naṅgyārs*), take part in this drama. On the *Kūtiyāṭṭam* stage only Sanskrit dramas are enacted. But the enactment has certain

[5] This drum has almost its exact counterpart in the Chinese theatre judging from the illustration in Mr. Arlington's *Famous Chinese Plays.* Compare Fig. 2 with the one facing page 47 of his book.

distinctive features which do not belong to the classic Sanskrit stage [6]. These peculiarities can be regarded as belonging to older traditions obtaining on the Keraḷa stage, which, it is presumed, had its separate individual existence. A notable reformation of the Keraḷa stage is believed to have taken place by about the 8th century A.D. Kula Śekhara Perumāḷ, the reigning monarch, was a playwright [7] and actor of repute. In his Brahmin minister Tōlan [8] he found a great collaborator both in the administration of the state and in his artistic and learned activities. These two are credited with having reformed and re-vitalised the presentation of Sanskrit plays. By meticulous elaboration *Kūtiyāṭṭam* assumed cyclopaen proportions, offering limitless possibilities for aesthetic enjoyment. That the enactment of a seven-act play should take as much as a couple of months and the staging of a single act as many as eight to nine days, apart from other considerations, is a sure indication of the paramount role of the theatre in the cultural life of the times.

The actual staging of an act—which alone is attempted in recent times—is preceded by a four-day introduction [9]. This is in no way related to the theme of the drama, yet, it functions as a very necessary prelude by virtue of its rich entertainment value. In this introduction the *Cākkyār* takes life and its ends or purposes (*puruṣārthas*) as the

---

6 Facial make-up, costumes, centrally situated oil lamp, scenes of fighting, the blood scene and the torch-lit procession of certain characters, are some of the peculiarities the Kūtiyāṭṭam and Kathakali have inherited. We have no evidence to believe that most of these peculiarities belonged to the Sanskrit stage.

Representation of death is not prohibited by the *Nāṭyaśāstra.* How to represent death on the stage attributed to such causes as sickness, snake-bite, injury by weapons is described. Cf. Chapter VII slokas 86-90, Chapter VI sloka 65, say that the Furious Sentiment is created by striking, cutting, mutilation and by such special acts of cutting off the head, the trunk and the arms.

7 Kula Śekhara wrote two plays in Sanskrit: *Tapatī Samvarana* and *Subhadra-Dhanaṃjaya.*

8 Tōlan wrote a guide to *Nātya* known as *Aṭṭa-prakāra,* designed to help the actors.

9 The first two days are taken up with the *Stāpana* and *Nirvacana* (preliminaries) of the play by the *Sūtradhāra.* The *Puruṣārthas* commence only on the third day. In this the *Vidūṣaka* is the sole actor; the scene is laid in the Village of Illiteracy, led by the priest, who befittingly is innocent of all knowledge of *Mantra, Tantra* and *Vidya.* The discourse takes the form of a discussion amongst the villagers. The dialogues are intensely dramatic and the *Vidūṣaka* makes it doubly so by his extraordinary skill in miming many characters.

theme. These *puruṣārthas* are classified under four main categories[10] and are treated in the form of a trenchant social satire. They are (1) *Vinōda*—enjoyment of pleasures, (2) *Vañcana*—deception with all its subtle shades, from statecraft to pilfering, self-deception, the guiles of the courtesan, etc., (3) *Aśana*—satisfaction of the palate or the lure of eating and feasting, and (4) *Rājaseva*—service under the crown and its consequences[11]. The *Cākkyār* discourses on these aspects and interests of life with a fluency and brilliancy of speech as attractive as it is enlightening. But his approach is also that of a consummate cartoonist. Wit, humour and sarcasm are some of the sharp missiles which he uses; they are backed by the extraordinary power of his acting and the very lively words he employs. The audience is gripped, entertained and moved to giggles and laughter. Social evils, the grievances of the people, the man who transgresses the moral law and propriety, the despot and villain, even the literary bore and the unskilled poet are subjected to his close examination and unsparing criticism. In doing this the *Cākkyār* recognises no law other than the standard and ideals of the people (*dharma*) and no restraint other than the sharpness of his tongue. In this way, even kings, poets, administrators and other important members of society are mercilessly castigated for their misdeeds, in their very presence and with impunity. For whatever is said on the stage—the *Cākkyār* says it in *Deva-sadas* (assembly of the gods) and in *Brāhmmaṇa sadas* (assembly of Brahmins) he enjoys perfect immunity granted to him by a sacred convention. Not only that, his observations are not to be questioned or interrupted. If that is done, the *Cākkyār* will take off his *muṭi* (head-gear) and walk out of the stage and then the votive offering of *Kūttu* will come to an abrupt end. That would be a sacrilege—amounting to profanation of a sacred ritual—and the interrupted *Kūttu* can only be revived after expiatory ceremonies[12]. This convention of the Keraḷa stage is a most emphatic recognition of the sanctity of the artist's role.

At the end of this very long introduction the *Kūṭiyāṭṭam* takes

---

10 As opposed to the real and serious *puruṣārthas* which are *Dharma, Artha, Kāma* and *Moksa* (duty, prosperity, pleasure and spiritual freedom).

11 The conversation in this last section cleverly leads to the scene of the drama to be enacted.

12 All this applies equally to the *Prabandhaṃ Kūttu* of the Cākkyārs.

place. The performance is of course a votive offering enacted in the temple theatre[13]. Since the language of the play is Sanskrit, the *Vidūṣaka* interprets the Sanskrit verses in Malayāḷam. This innovation was made to bring the drama nearer to the people at large. Music is practically absent in *Kūṭiyāṭṭam.* The verses are chanted by the characters in a monotone; though the chanting has little musical quality it induces in the listeners the feeling that they are listening to voices from a supernatural world. Dancing is assigned a very minor role. The faces of the actors are painted but the patterns and colouring are not so well developed in comparison with the Kathakaḷi plastic masks. The distinctive feature of the play is *abhinaya.* The *Cākkyārs* through centuries of devotion to their vocation had evolved a superb technique of *abhinaya.* But for them, this most significant phase of Hindu histrionic art would have been lost and the development of Kathakaḷi made impossible. To this day, they have guarded their art jealously; it is their *Veda.*

The text of the play undergoes a three-fold presentation at the hands of the *Cākkyār;* first *āṅgika* (gestural interpretation), then *vācika* (words or speech) and lastly again in *āṅgika.* On the *Kūṭiyāṭṭam* stage both *āṅgika* and *vācika* exist side by side; though separate and independent, they complement and amplify each other. The process is rather a long-drawn-out one. Kathakaḷi has borrowed from *Kūṭiyāṭṭam* many stage practices including its very distinguished technique of *abhinaya.* Kathakaḷi artists have improved upon it in several ways and they have now a style distinct from the *Cākkyārs.*

Kriṣṇāṭṭam marks another stage in the development of the Keraḷa theatre. Mānaveda, a member of the royal family of the Zamorins of Calicut, organised this play. He wrote the text of the play in Sanskrit

---

13 The *Kūttu* is staged only in the temple theatre (*kūttambalam*), a well constructed wooden structure—which is a feature of the important Keraḷa temples. The raised dais or stage is covered by a wooden pavilion, the ceiling of which is richly carved and painted with floral and other decorative motifs. The pavilion stands on four lacquered pillars (brilliantly coloured) and surmounted by *amalaka* capitals. The auditorium is in two tiers, the higher one is intended for Brahmins and royalty and the lower one for other high castes. The green-room is just behind the stage having access through the door in the partition wall. The stage is open on three sides, only the rear side is covered by the partition wall of the green-room. The four walls of the theatre are made up of wooden railings, leaving open interstices allowing light and air.

using the Kriṣṇa legends as his theme. This drama was first staged in about 1650 A.D. The performance of this play is always a votive offering and is completed in eight nights. In course of time this purely lyrical drama tended to become more exclusive—it is found enacted only in certain specific localities—and remains closely associated with religion [14]. Pantomimic acting is the basic language or technique of expression; but this idiom reached its full maturity only in Kathakaḷi. Certain characters of the play wear wooden masks while others have their faces painted. These paintings have none of the richness and variety of the Kathakaḷi plastic masks; even the *cuṭṭi* is found, but it is incipient and is a thin wiry line. This type of drama is interesting for the contrary strains it embodies both in structure and technique and on these grounds would justify the assumption that it was born on the Keraḷa stage at a time of transition.

The foregoing survey of the stage practices of the land is intended only to show that the elements of the art of Kathakaḷi are discernible in various degrees of development and in differing assortments in the many types of cult-plays and other theatrical entertainments found in Keraḷa. The mimed story-play is an ancient Indian theatrical legacy. The *Rāmanāṭṭam* which is believed to have developed later into Kathakaḷi was born into that tradition: its peculiarities are just the traditional peculiarities of the Keraḷa stage or developments therefrom.

Rāmanāṭṭam. A Raja of Koṭṭārakkara dramatised the story of Rāma in eight plays and had it staged at his court in the latter half of the 17th century A.D. [15]. It proved to be the inauguration of a new move-

14 The actors observe fasting on the days of performances and the pious section of the audience also observes fasting on the day "the birth of Kriṣṇa" is enacted. The spectators, it is believed, gain religious merit by witnessing these performances.

15 The popular theory that *Rāmanāṭṭam* came into being because of the refusal of the Zamorin to lend his *Kriṣṇāṭṭam* troupe to the Rāja of Koṭṭārakkara stands discredited amongst a section of Keraḷa scholars. The subject is still not free from controversy; whatever be the final verdict it need in no way affect this enquiry. The *Kriṣṇāṭṭam* in almost every respect is a less evolved type than the Kathakaḷi.

Those who believe that *Kriṣṇāṭṭam* influenced the birth of *Rāmanāttam* date it from the latter half of the 17th cent. A.D. while a few others ascribe it to the latter half of the 15th cent. Some critics are perplexed as to how this unique Kathakaḷi art could have grown within less than three hundred years and are straining to push back its date. But there is one difficulty to be faced; there is no Kathakaḷi drama older than the *Ramanāṭṭam* plays which at any rate cannot be placed earlier than the latter

ment. Its staging at the commencement could not have been spectacularly very different from the current stage practices of the land. Among the changes and reformations that followed, not the least important was the adoption of the language of the people. So far the language of the learned stage was Sanskrit. Though the language of the new play was a highly Sanskritised Malayāḷam [16], still it was Malayāḷam and this helped to make it popular. This signalised the birth of a people's theatre.

One school of thought believes that at first the *Rāmanāṭṭam* players spoke, sang and wore wooden masks; if so, all this changed. The wooden mask, if at all used, was thrown over as the "superstition" of the past and the plastic mask was developed. Great changes took place in the costuming too. Much more than these, speechless acting or pantomime was raised to its highest possibilities. A number of other changes in stagecraft as well as in the technique of presentation were effected [17]. Music, instrumental and vocal, became integral elements of the drama. Dancing was introduced in full measure and its fullest possibilities were utilized to enlarge the scope and appeal of *abhinaya.* In course of time, a perfect synthesis of these elements was achieved which made the drama a well-balanced structure. In saying all this we have anticipated events. *Rāmanāṭṭam* was changing into Kathakaḷi in this pro-

---

half of 15th cent. What is important to remember in this connection is that the art of Kathakaḷi or rather its chief elements are very much older than any Kathakaḷi literature, being a continuation of older traditions. The events subsequent to the staging of *Rāmanāṭṭam* led to a marked development and reformation which crystallised into a distinct form known as Kathakaḷi. If this perspective is kept clear the problem about age need not worry us unduly. Modern Keraḷa scholars have been more concerned with Kathakaḷi literature and have made a predominantly literary approach to Kathakaḷi. But Kathakaḷi is primarily a theatrical art form and has to be viewed as such in its traditional setting, i.e. in the context of the earlier cult-plays and other theatrical entertainments of the land.

16 The language of the new drama was a rhythmic blend of Sanskrit and Malayāḷam already evident in the *Campu* literature. This ushered in a new literary medium of expression whose melodic beauty and richness of diction gained for it many adherents. An increasing number of poets took heartily to this blend and a remarkable literary revival followed, the momentum of which has not yet weakened.

17 The intelligent and active participation of a long line of princes and Nambūtiris have contributed richly to make Kathakaḷi what it is. Some of them wrote plays, acted in them and maintained their own troupes. *Veṭṭam, Kallaṭikōṭan, Kapliṅgāṭan* and *Kōṭṭa* were some of the leading schools, that were engaged in the reforming activities.

cess. The possibilities of this new theatrical experiment attracted other playwrights[18] and lovers of the theatre. When new plays based on themes from the *Mahābhārata, Bhāgavata* and *Śiva Purāṇa* were dramatised and staged, the name *Ramanāṭṭam* had to give way to a more general one. The nomenclature changed into *Āṭṭakatha* (mimed play) or Kathakaḷi (story-play). There are now over 112 plays and more are being written. These form a noble body of literature and are noted for their musical, poetic and dramatic qualities.

This new drama in course of time danced its way into the hearts of the people. While it remained associated with religion there was no prohibition against staging it outside the temple premises. This too contributed to make it popular. But it should be remembered that the Kathakaḷi stage never set out to cater to the unlearned or to the ones who did not share a common tradition with the actor. Like all great art, it is both religious and popular, but its popularity is free from any subservience to "uncultivated taste". The continued patronage of the princes secured for it the advantages of a court art but that was never at the expense of its truly popular qualities. It not only remained at the temples and the courts but travelled over the highways and byeways, from village to village and house to house, gaining in course of time the distinction of a national art. It is an art that remains "in the highest sense for the people".

---

18 The most notable of the playwrights are the Rājās of Koṭṭārakkara and Koṭṭayam, Kartika-tiru-nāl and Asvati-tiru-nāl of Travancore and Vidvan Koyil Thampuran. Amongst a galaxy of talent it would be difficult to pick and choose but it would be easily admitted that Unnayi Varier and Irayimman Thampi are outstanding.

CHAPTER III

PSYCHOLOGICAL BACKGROUND

Kathakaḷi is conducted like a ritual and everything connected with it is invested with religious significance. Kathakaḷi actors have a tradition concerning the stage which gives it a highly symbolic significance. The stage [1] represents the world that has come into being [2] in space by the primal act of the Creator. The thick blazing wick of the oil lamp [3] set towards the stage and the thinner one facing the audience symbolise the sun and the moon. Sound is heard in the drumming which first vibrates "*Pṛaḷaya, Pṛaḷaya dimuṛdala*" announcing the end of the Great Deluge and the coming of the 'New Age'. The curtain is *rajani* or *tamas* (the darkness that divides). Behind it a couple of dancers execute an invocative dance called *Tōḍayaṃ.* They stand for *Māya* and *Sakti* [4]. The dancers remain unseen by the spectators, just as these forces work beyond the ken of human perception; their activities represent *līla,* the endless play of cosmic forces. There is no background for the stage, for life emerges from the dark, unknown void and there can be no background to the sport of the gods which transcends time and space. In this endless process of the advent of gods and mythological heroes, there is only an un-veiling or falling off of the

---

1 The Kathakaḷi stage and auditorium are just one piece of level ground; only the giant bronze lamp separates the two and marks off the stage.

2 This acquires significance in the light of what the *Nāṭya Śāstra* says in respect of the origin of the drama. The dramatic art was fraṃed by Brahma at the end of the *Kṛtā Yuga* or at the very beginning of the *Tretā Yuga* i.e. for the "world about to be". It seems that it is the birth of this "world about to be" (co-eval with the birth of the drama too) that is sought to be expressed in the symbolism concerning the stage explained above. This symbolical significance is known to most of the senior actors of the present day but in slightly varying versions. The above version follows the one given to me by Kunju Kurup.

3 This single lamp with its two points of light is all the lighting for the stage and the auditorium.

4 Formerly it was the practice to have the *tōḍayaṃ* danced by two female characters: *Māya* (Illusion) and *Śakti* (Primal energy or Creative power).

veils that obstruct vision. Therefore, the curtain is not fixed but held up by human agency (two men hold it up) and it falls away the moment reality approaches. The musical prelude with rhythmical drumming and singing symbolises the development of sound into language. Light, life and letters having been manifested, prayers are offered to the gods and the *gurus* (teachers). The next stage in the structure of the play is *Purappād* (literally going forth), signifying the grand pageant of life on earth; what follows is the depiction of the world in its various phases and moods [5]. Invariably a great and revered mythological character is introduced [6]; connected with the theme of the play, he sets the pageant in motion. The themes are the legends that take us back across vast stretches of time, covering several geological ages. They deal with the times when the *devas* and the great gods sought fellowship with virtuous men and mighty kings (of whom some fought with and some against the *devas* themselves), when ever-young celestial maidens were sent to tempt great heroes, when *riṣīs* endowed with invincible spiritual prowess remained a mighty challenge to the *devas* and demons turned the three worlds into a raging inferno. What is unravelled is a world of might and power where light and darkness, good and evil, wage a titanic conflict, in which great aspirations, noble endeavours, massive achievements, loves and hatreds, struggles, failures and victories tell their imperishable tales: in short, the world in all its varied phases. What is seen on the stage is a world of dreams and they are dreams of our deepest longings. How much the magic effect of the make-up, drum-rhythms, light-waves and the technique of acting contribute towards the generation of this feeling is dealt with elsewhere.

A peep into the green-room will only deepen the sense of mystery and religious awe. It is reached through a causeway of darkness where

---

5 This all-comprehensive nature of the drama is stressed by Brahma who according to tradition created *Nātya*. The dramatic art "represents the true and essential nature of the world." "I made this play as following the movement of the world whether in work or play ... replete with diverse moods, informed with the varying passions of the soul, linked to the deeds of all mankind . . . ." See *The Mirror of Gesture*—Coomaraswamy & Duggirala.

6 It is a ceremonious introduction under a colourful canopy, with peacock fans held on either side (these are emblems of high rank such as royalty and divinity) and with the sound of the conch.

silent, half-clad figures move about like apparitions. In the feeble light of the oil lamps a greater part of it remains in semi-darkness with islands of soft light here and there throwing into relief strange, tense figures tracing weird designs on the faces of inactive, sometimes slumbering men (Pl. III fig. 2). A whole array of fantastic garments is seen suspended like festoons in dreamland; more lie heaped up in deep boxes that might well have come out of the Egypt of the Pharaohs. An animated silence hangs over everything like a spell and nothing but the gentlest whisper or gesture is heard or seen. The green-room is the sanctum of *Sri Pōṛkkali* or *Durga* the patron deity of the Kathakaḷi stage. Though invisible, everyone believes in the immediate presence of the deity in the green-room. Therefore its austere atmosphere is never allowed to be disturbed. A visitor does not refuse any service to an actor while in the green-room, no matter howsoever high placed he be. There is none too low to ask for a service and none too high to refuse it in the presence of a deity to whom this art is dedicated and which is a form of worship.

The actor is an initiate; he has been disciplined from childhood under the rigorous tutorship of his *guru* and patron to conduct himself as a wholesome and adequate vehicle to portray the *līla* or sport of the gods. He is seldom allowed to forget that his calling is a sacred one. Even the paint, costumes, head-dress, anklets, stage, musical instruments and light are all deified and he salutes these as he does the *devās* and the *gurus*. From the moment he enters the green-room till he washes off the paint he conducts himself as a devotee in a shrine.

The divine origin and association of dance and drama are constantly kept in view; *Nāṭya* is the fifth *Veda*. The belief that the gods are present to witness the performances and are pleased with the exhibition of their deeds, is sedulously fostered. In certain temples Kathakaḷi plays are enacted at the expense of worshippers as votive offerings. The deity at Caṃprakulaṅgara (near Palghat) is well known as 'Kathakaḷi-mad'. No troupe passes that village without staging a play as a votive offering, for bad luck and misery, it is believed, would dog its steps if this sacred convention is disregarded. The actors are treated as honoured guests of the deity. When the performance takes place, the doors of the inner shrine, generally closed at night, are kept open. The Great Host is present in the auditorium. It is a *deva-sadas* (assembly of the gods) and therefore Brahmins and other high castes alone can take their seats; others must stand. The deity's interest is so personal and intimate that the story to be enacted is made known to the priest who officiates at the evening worship. The announcement made by him is accepted with all the force of a divine command. Where so intimate and living a bond as this exists, art is sacred and thrives on a plane far removed from that of the secular arts.

Acting, in the true sense of the term as understood in India, is not mere impersonation, however clever or illusionistic the effect. The actor is compared to a *yōgi,* meaning thereby that he is one who treads the path of *yōga* (union) or mental concentration, whereby the subject and the object, the worshipper and the worshipped, the actor and the acted become one. Keraḷa legends emphasise this aspect. In the temple at Tiru-vilva-mala (in Tr.-Cochin State), where the presiding deity is Rama, episodes from the *Rāmayaṇa* are the favourite plays enacted. Once when *Khara vadha* (slaying of the demon Khara by Rama) was enacted, Khara burst on the scene with a highly provocative challenge to Rāma. He mocked, sneered and proudly boasted of his great prowess. In mounting rage he raised war cries that sounded like monsoon thunder, creating a tense, electric atmosphere of blood and fury. The dreaded and vicious demon appeared, ready to destroy everything before him; the audience cowered, weighed down by the sense of an impending doom and the *asura* (demon) towered over all, Fury incarnate. "You worm, come to battle with me!" sneered the demon. He was no longer an actor simulating a role; he had become Khara himself. Suddenly, the doors of the inner shrine flew open and a column of bright flame blinded everyone for the space of a split second. When the audience recovered from their consternation Khara was missing! The enactment of this particular play was discontinued in the temple from that tragic day [7].

Kathakaḷi dramas are never enacted by day-light. The shades of night are the proper setting for the mythological heroes, demons and *devas.* In that eerie, mysterious, setting they become realities. The elaborate facial masks from which all semblance of the merely human is eli-

---

[7] A similar incident is associated with the temple at Tiruvalla in Travancore-Cochin State.

minated, the fantastic costumes, archaic jewellery, glittering head-gears that symbolise supernatural opulence, the charged silence of the actors, the inexpressibly beautiful gestures and dancing-eyes that form the medium of communication—which more than anything else suggest the language of a super-world—and the different manners of walking and dancing, all these heighten the sense of the supernatural and the marvellous. The actors on the stage are no longer men simulating a divine or diabolic entity; they are the very thing itself. Acting is no adequate term for their embodied acts and passions. Every time a play is staged the fabled heroes, demons and *devas* come to life.

CHAPTER IV

HOW THE ACTOR IS FASHIONED

The actors are drawn from the higher strata of society, generally from the Nāyar caste. This in itself ensures a certain level of cultural and traditional background helpful to the calling [1]. The actor's vocation is regarded as a serious one and the aspirant is disciplined in its ways from quite an early age. Training commences between the ages of ten and twelve. On an auspicious day at the astrologically specified hour, after going through the prescribed ritual ceremonies to obtain the blessings of the gods, the elders and the *guru,* the young aspirant enters the arduous path of discipleship. The attitude of reverence to the art and the *guru,* that takes root in the pupil from the day of initiation, is steadfastly cultivated and becomes a sacred creed with advancing years. The teacher's interest in the pupil is very intimate, something more than personal, for in the latter he seeks continuity for his dedicated art. The pupil lives with his teacher; he is for all practical purposes a member of his family and entourage. Affection and devotion make their relationship a sacred one. It is not merely the class lessons that shape the student; he is always near his teacher sharing fully in a far richer life. The art and traditions of the *guru* grow into the pupil. Mostly, the young artist has the patronage of some wealthy and influential connoisseur whose loving care and attention are devoted to his perfect shaping as an artist. He provides for his training, directs it and encourages him with many tokens of affection and takes legitimate pride in the achievements of his protégé.

In this mimetic art the body is the sole means of expression. To fulfil its high function it is drilled into a perfect medium. First the body is prepared by a rigorous course of physical exercises and daily

---

[1] A good literary background both in Malayāḷam and Sanskrit, a capacity to appreciate poetry and familiarity with the vast mythological literature are the essential general equipments of the actor.

massage with medicated oils which are calculated to ensure suppleness and grace and to develop the expressive capacity of the various parts of the body (Pl. II and Pl. III fig. 1). Eyes, brows, chin, lips, head and neck have seperate exercises. Everyday after the preliminary exercises [2], the pupils go through a three-hour practice known as *colliāttam* (Pl. IX figs. 2-4). While one person sings the text and keeps time, the master teaches and directs them. The lessons are repeated for a couple of hours in the afternoon. They learn to act all the roles and then only are they allowed to specialise. The exercises, the massage [3], the careful training and the severe discipline imposed are necessary to fashion the pupil into a skilled artist. As Nietzsche has said: [4] "It is no small advantage to have a hundred Democlean swords suspended above one's head; that is how one learns to dance, that is how one attains freedom of movement." A Kathakaḷi artist at sixty rarely thinks of retiring. He maintains the same lightness in his spring, the same buoyancy in his movements and the same fluidity in his lines as in his thirties. Those who have seen great masters like Kunju Kurup, Ravunni Menon and Kavalappara Narayanan Nair would have realised what adherence to traditional discipline had made of them and still can do to others. To the Kathakaḷi artist a smooth, supple and sinuous frame is more essential than the "body-line", "waist-line" or the "looks" of a dancer [5]. The elaborate plastic mask, the costumes and ornaments are such as to cover bodily defects of this kind. Outward symptoms of age like wrinkles or sagging muscles and a growing waist-line which are a perpetual nightmare to dancers and actors generally do not disturb the Kathakaḷi actor or affect his art as long as he retains skill in action.

The very many movements and gestures of this mimetic art are

---

2 Every day the pupils start their morning lessons with a course of eye-exercises in which the various movements of the eyes, eye-brows and eye-lashes are taught. The following are some of the basic movements in the exercises: 1. circular, the eye-balls travelling from right to left and in the reverse order, 2. up and down, 3. diagonal (also in the reverse direction), 4. square, 5. zig-zag, 6. vibration, 7. progression and 8. regression.

3 The actors keep fit and get charged with fresh energy and youthful vigour by undergoing yearly, during the rains, a course of massage with medicated oil—an effective system of rejuvenating treatment developed by the Keraḷa physicians.

4 See Havelock Ellis—*Dance of Life*—chapter on Art of Morals.

5 This does not imply that a well-formed figure is not an asset or that it is despised.

precise and are learnt from a teacher only after years of training. Nothing is left to chance and no actor consequently sinks below the level assured by the technique. One who has mastered the technique and follows the path, attains a freedom beyond the laws and "From the very moment in which he dominates his body which serves him as an instrument he may express (one feels tempted to say) something beyond expression" [6]. At the same time there is no room for the actor to shift the interest from the drama to himself. Neither tradition nor discipline allows him to degenerate into a "toy-maker", "to tickle aesthetic society into one more quiver and giggle of art debauch".

The *debut* of an actor is an event of ceremonial importance and this usually takes place under the patronage of some distinguished connoisseur when he has undergone training for an year or two. Thereafter, he acts as an under-study and appears in minor roles; his appearance in the major roles of the drama is entirely dependent on the degree of skill he attains.

Kathakaḷi artists have enjoyed the regard and respect due to their high calling. They are respected as teachers who spread the message of the *purāṇas.* A senior member of the troupe is always addressed as *Aśān* (*guru*—teacher) by everyone including leading members of society. The continued patronage and association of the princes and Nambūtiris, some of whom considered it an honour to appear on the stage and were themselves artists of high order, ensured for the Kathakaḷi artist a privileged status. The worthy example set by leading members of society attracted to the stage the Tamil and Tuḷu Brahmins of Keraḷa who have distinguished themselves as actors and musicians.

The leading houses of the land organised and maintained their own Kathakaḷi troupes; no expense and trouble were considered too much. The pride and pleasure of possessing a first rate troupe [7] of accomplished artists was all that mattered. This tradition of patronage is happily still extant. The continued devotion and patronage of the aristocracy of Keraḷa have helped in a great measure to preserve this art from neglect and decay.

---

[6] *Story Plays in Living Tradition*—G. Boner.

[7] A troupe consists of nearly 30 men, including actors, make-up men and musicians.

NOTE

To be known as "*Kathakali-brāndhan*" or "Kathakali-mad" is no reproach, but an enviable distinction; the term has acquired wide currency. Some of the "Kathakali-mad" have gone to excessive lengths in their zeal for the art, spending a good deal of their time, resources and capacities in perfecting the drama. I am told of an argument that developed between two meticulous, fastidious "Kathakali-mad" brothers belonging to a well known Nambutiri family on what may seem to us a comparatively minor matter. The point in dispute was, as to how many times Kīcaka should emit the cry "*Gwa-Gwā*" in a particular context in the drama of *Kīcaka-vadha* (The wild, wicked and demoniac types of characters in Kathakali emit certain sounds which vary in volume, pitch and significance; they are indicative of moods). The brothers were unable to agree among themselves and this ultimately led to a family dispute in which the other members took sides and caused much public discussion and sensation at the time.

Perhaps it would be appropriate to remember here the names of a few master artists who have lent distinction to the art: They are Bāli Othikkan Nambutiri, Nalan Unni, Parasu Pattar, Eswara Pillai, Kochu-Narayana Panikkar, Ittirarissa Menon, Kavingal Kunju-Krishna Panikkar, Kesava Kurup, Sankaran Nambūtiri (guru of Uday Shankar), Vechoor Raman Pillay and Kavaḷappāra Narayanan Nair.

Amongst the living actors special mention is deserved by Kunju Kurup. His reputation as a master-artist has stood high for the last four decades. Though over 65 he still maintains his great reputation. He is perhaps the best link with the great traditions of the past. Another well-known actor is Ravunni Menon. Kalamandalam Krishnan is today a great favourite. Kuñjan Panikkar also belongs to the "old guard" and is a gifted and sprightly actor.

CHAPTER V

THE ORCHESTRA

There are various musical instruments in Keraḷa which are specially intended for out-door performances. Kathakaḷi artists had only to pick and choose from these to form their orchestra. And how well the quaint orchestra serves the artistic intentions of the Kathakaḷi stage is soon realised when we expose ourselves to a "demoniacally clever and incessant drumming that shakes up" our dormant solar plexus [1]. Most important are the drums. They are of two kinds: the *Maddaḷa* (a large *Mṛidaṅga*) and the *Ceṇḍa,* a cylindrical drum peculiar to Keraḷa. The *Maddaḷa* is fastened to the waist by a cotton belt and remains in a horizontal position (Fig. 30, page 86). It is played on both sides simultaneously, with the palm and fingers. A cotton suspender running over the shoulder and chest of the player keeps the *Ceṇḍa* in position; it remains suspended vertically in front of the figure of the player who has to remain standing, as it cannot be played while it rests on the ground or when held horizontally. Only the top side is operated and that is done by a pair of sticks that have slightly up-turned ends; sometimes it is played by a stick held in one hand and by the palm and fingers of the other hand. These two modes of operation yield varying shades of sound, volume and pitch. Generally the *Ceṇḍa* is loud and powerful; tempestuous and violent rhythms are natural to it but it also yields softer shades of sound. It is not used when women characters (other than ogresses or *rākṣasīs*) act; for tender or softer drum accompaniments the *Maddaḷa* is played, but is much toned down. The drumming in which both the *Ceṇḍa* and *Maddaḷa* join is often wild and elemental, taking in its gamut the many variations of the monsoon thunder storms down to the gentle patter of dripping water from tree and roof. Whether it pleases unfamiliar ears or not, it can most unfailingly stir and quicken

---

1 As was the experience of Dr Jung; see "Dreamlike World of India"—*Asia Magazine,* January 1939.

our heart-beats. In its wild abandon, it can stir us most powerfully and lift us, in spite of ourselves, into a strange new world. In its deafening hammer strokes that generate monstrous rhythms we hear the angry sweep of a mountain storm and feel the mighty tremors of the earth. In such moments it is like angry, cosmic vibrations and remorseless like the thudding of Śiva's *damaru* as he dances the dance of destruction; verily we feel that the worlds are crashing around us. It is impossible to describe adequately the effect of the drumming. In fact it is the life of the play, an inexhaustible power-house, as it were, radiating energy and strength. Always spirited, and intensifying the dramatic, it creates a "charged atmosphere"—an adequate and credible background—for the strange events of a super-world developing on the stage. The drum variations are a commentary on the hand gestures and other movements of the actor-dancer. With the drum-beats how much they gain in intensity!

The gong on which the chief singer keeps time while singing, actively re-acts to the tempo of the song and action. The beating is so controlled as to regulate the sound to the requirements of the situation; it may be a short and crisp thud or a lengthening note. A pair of cymbals, whose clanging is sprightly and spirited, completes the instrumental set. At times a deep-sounding conch is used to intensify the dramatic effect. Its lengthening, swelling boom has a marvellous capacity to impart a feeling of solemnity to the occasion where it is needed [2].

The orchestral group is on the stage, in full view of the audience; the singers are behind the actors and the drummers stand to the right. The whole group is led by the singers. There are two (sometimes three) singers, a principal and an under-study; the latter repeats the lines sung by the former. Kathakaḷi is a musical drama. Its songs are composed in the musical modes of the old Karnatic school [3] of music, in what is called *sōpāna rīti,* which is the temple or hieratic style, as distinguished from chamber or concert style of singing. The melody

2 The arrival of Kriṣṇa at the court of Duryōdhana as the messenger of the Paṇḍavās on the eve of the great battle of Kurukṣetra, the meeting of Kriṣṇa and Sudama and the occasion when Viṣṇu assumes his cosmic form, are some of the instances where the conch is used to intensify the dramatic effect, or to create an air of solemnity.

3 Mr. Mukunda Raja tells me that the ex-Maharaja of Mysore, a reputed connoissuer of Indian Music, told him that the Kathakali style of singing was the original or early style of Karnatic vocal music. The *Ślokas* or verses of the drama are composed in Āryan or Sānskrit meter and the songs in Dravidian meter.

modes selected are choice ones suitable for a dance-drama. The rendering of these classical modes has acquired a distinct style which is primarily determined by the needs of a dance-drama where the singer and the actor are different persons and where the latter has to interpret the song, word by word, through acting-dancing. The melody mode or *rāga* of each song is determined by the *bhāva* (mood) that is expressed. The singer leads the actor; what he chooses to omit from the text is not acted. He is thus the sole director of the show. The grace-notes and flourishes so characteristic of Kathakaḷi singing, are helpful to the *abhinaya* process which requires time to translate into gesture-vocabulary the literary equivalents. Every line of the song is repeated till it is acted or gestured word by word; the emphasis in the presentation perhaps varying each time on the different words to make the picture impressive. Good singing invariably reacts on the actor, for *rāga* and *bhāva* are closely related and *rāga,* when well rendered, inspires the right expression of *bhāva.* When such is the case, the actor surpasses himself; his rendering acquires a sparkling vibrancy and persuasive charm. The acting and the dancing then achieve a rare unity with the tonal quality of the melody and the animating passions. Consequently the audience experiences a new relish, a poignant sense of beauty. "The voices of the singers, the sound waves of the drums, cymbals and gong carry the rhythm of the acting" [4] and these go on throughout the night without interruption, creating an immense rhythmic pattern that sustains the unfolding spectacle.

NOTE

This chapter would seem incomplete if it did not take note of the names of the great singers and drummers who have enriched the presentation of the drama. Amongst the singers the fame of Mānu Bhagavatar, Gopala Krishna Bhagavatar and Sivarama Bhagavatar is legendary. They are all deceased. Amongst the living ones Venkita-krishna Bhagavatar, Nilakantan Unnithan and Kesavan Nair are well known. Amongst the Maddaḷam players the fame of Chittan Pattar, now deceased, has never been rivalled. His nephew Venkichan Pattar, now over 70, is still a wizard of the drum. He has no equal and this reputation has stood very high during the last half century [5]. The pride of place that Maddaḷam now occupies in the Pancha-Vādyam (Kerala Temple Orchestra) is very largely due to him. I am indebted to my friends Mukunda Ṛaja and Kunju Kurup for this information in respect of Venkichan Pattar. Of the *Ceṇḍa* players Cheenu Pattar, Subrammanya Iyer, Kuṭṭan Marar and Kakkoor Kunjan Marar are some of the stalwarts of the past. Amongst the living Ceṇḍa players the fame of Mootha-mana Nambutiri stands high.

4 G. Boner.

5 He too has passed away.

CHAPTER VI

THE PLAY BEGINS

Rhythm starts the show and it remains predominant throughout. At sun-set a vigorous drumming (*kēḷi-koṭṭu*) that carries its message far and wide in the hushed silence of the evening, announces the show and puts the people into a mood of expectancy. With subtle speed, whispers wing their way and everyone seems to know the particular drama to be enacted, the star actors and the role assigned to each. The story is well known to all and the stage can give no element of surprise in this respect. Much more important than the story is the technical means or *abhinaya*[1]. It is the quality of the *abhinaya* and the quality of the spectator that complete the drama and create *rasa* (flavour). Kathakaḷi is rich in elements of popular entertainment but its *Nāṭya-dharmi* technique (conventions and stylized movements) has an intellectual basis which requires that the audience should be a learned or initiated one.

The show is an open-air all-night function. The location for its enactment may be a temple compound or the courtyard of a private residence. The stage is about 16 feet square; it is a sacred and sanctified spot protected against the intrusion of evil spirits. A *panḍāl* decorated with fresh leaves and flowers covers this space. Generally the stage has no dais; it is just a portion of the level ground of the court-yard and is covered by rough mats. The eager and devotedly expectant audience even overflows on to the stage. "Attracted by the fire (of the lamp) and the weird call of the drums, grey shapeless crowds draw together and hang in trance-like emotion on the small stage, where colourful events of all the three worlds are unfolded"[2]. The open auditorium remains

---

1 *Abhinaya* is a comprehensive term covering every aspect of the dramatic technique viz. acting, dancing, gestures, songs by the actor, his make-up and the expression of psychic states. In a much narrower sense, in which it is widely used, it denotes acting-dancing or miming.

2 See Alice Boner—*Kathakaḷi,* June 1935. Journal of the Indian Society of Oriental Art.

for the most part, as it were in twilight, for the single lamp on the stage can spread but a soft glow on it. The spectators are in touch with the surrounding shades of night and over them is the immense starlit vault of heaven. The tall, massive, shining metal lamp is the only lighting. Fed by an abundant supply of coconut oil, the two thick clusters of wicks—the thicker one facing the stage and the other the audience—create a small magic sphere of light. The area close to the lamp is brilliantly lit against the surrounding darkness. The lamp is the focal point of the actor. This oil-fed lamp has a distinct personality and function in the drama. It vivifies and subdues; an effect that can hardly be achieved by the most scientific lighting scheme. The dancing flame of the lamp now leaping, now flickering, pulsates with a live and intelligent energy, reacting to the rhythmic cadences and moods of the play (Pl. XIX).

At about 8-30 P.M. the drumming commences as a rhythmic prelude. The sound waves are incessant, vibrant and compelling; a good deal of drumming also takes place before the first scene of the play; we are gripped and taken into a fairy world, where at the merest touch or wish, magic casements open out in never-ending succession and soon we become involved—deeply involved—in the happenings of this different world. At the conclusion of *Suddha Maddaḷa,* as this first rhythmic prelude is called, two men come on to the stage and hold up a curtain. It is about 12 feet in length and 8 feet in width; it is generally made up of rectangular pieces of satin or silk of different bright and deep colours, and a large full-blown lotus is very often found embroidered in the centre. Invocatory verses in honour of the deities are sung and prayers are offered for the successful conclusion of the play. Two dancers execute a devotional dance (*Tōdayam*) behind the curtain. This is followed by the *Purappād* [3] (setting forth or commencement). This is a pure dance prelude by a *pacca* (green type) character and his mate. They are a divine pair and their august presence is indicated by a ceremonious introduction. With a flourish of drums and the sound of the conch, the curtain is lowered half way, revealing the two dancers under a colourful canopy. Two peacock fans and *cāmarās* (fly whisks) are held up by their sides. They appear like a celestial pair partially obscured by cloud curtains. Their eyes and brows begin an

[3] In the *purappād* sometimes companion characters also appear.

enchanting dance, punctuated with graceful bodily flexions. The footwork, hand gestures and eye-movements are very elegant and sparkling; the rhythmic co-ordination established between these and the drumming is perfect (Figs. 3-6).

Then a song from the *Gīta Gōvinda* (*Mañjutara*) is sung and it is followed by a skilled display of drumming (*Meḷappadaṃ*), whose rhythmic accents stir the spectators' sense of expectancy. This gives an opportunity to the drummers to exhibit their skill.

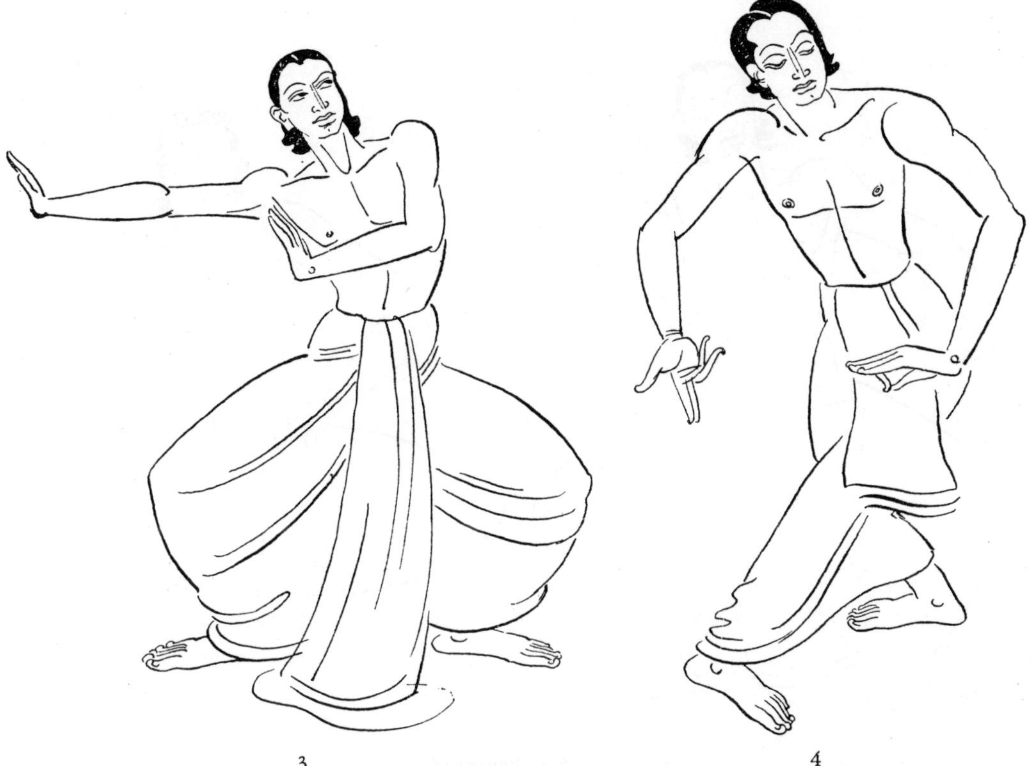

3 4
Figs. 3-4. *Purappād* (sketches by S. Chavda, Bombay).

The first scene of the drama sometimes opens with the hero and the heroine in a pleasure garden[4]. Lest the reader forget, it is as well to state here that the garden comes into being, not through the aid of any clever scenic effect, but by the magic power of the artistry of the actor.

4 Love scenes of this nature are present in most of the plays; they do not always appear at the commencement of the story.

That the hero and the heroine should meet in a garden setting, where spring spreads her inflaming enchantments, feeds the pain of reckless passion and leads to the raptures of amorous dalliance, has become a

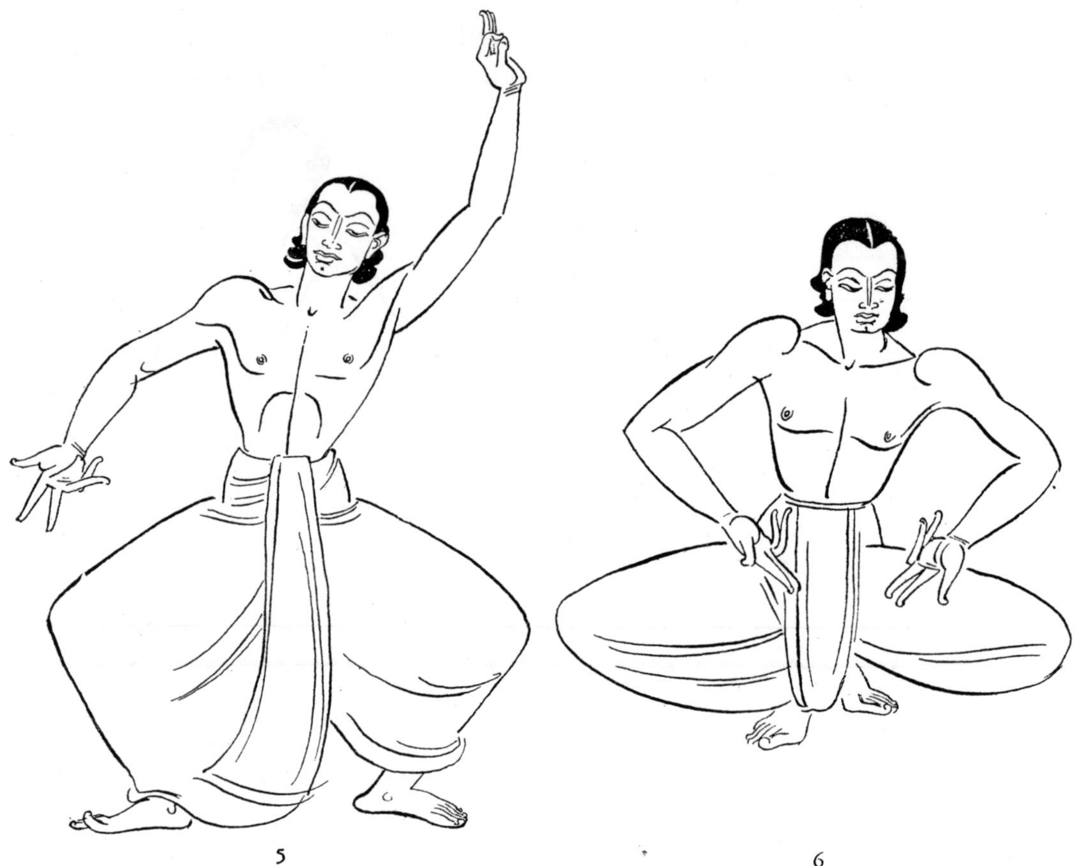

Figs. 5-6. *Purappad.*

Figs. 3-6 poses by Krishnan Kutty.

convention of the Kathakali stage. Their conversation leads to the opening scene of the play.

The story that follows is one drawn from the vast storehouse of Hindu mythology (*Purāṇas*) [5], peopled with gods and goddesses, titans and human heroes, and is rich in warm human feeling and appeal. The story enacted may perhaps have nothing to do with the gods. A moving

[5] The *Purānās* are not merely mythological tales, they are also profoundly symbolic.

romance like that of *Naḷa-Damayanti* may be the text of the play; or it may be the story depicting the heroic austerities and penance of Arjuna, undertaken, to win from Śiva, the mighty weapon of *Pāśu-pata,* wherein, the great god, in the guise of a hunter, engages himself in mortal combat with his devotee, to test his fitness, till Parvati intervenes to quiet the on-rushing torrent of fury and destruction in which the combatants were becoming submerged; or the episode selected may be one connected with the deeply human drama of poverty wherein Sudāma, the poor Brahmin devotee of Kriṣṇa, is faced with the problem of feeding his wife and hungry family of many children. But his eyes see not the miseries of the children and his ears hear not their piteous wailings; he sees in everything only the ever radiant form of Kṛiṣṇa (Pl. XV). Eventually, how Kriṣṇa helps the destitute family and makes the poor Brahmin blessed, is the theme of this popular drama. The adventures of Bhīma, the Indian Hercules, who sets out for distant lands in search of a miraculous flower, in order to satisfy the womanly whim of his beloved spouse Draupadi, form the theme of another drama. The story for another is supplied by the clever ruse of the gossiping saint Nārada, in decoying the powerful and haughty demon-king Rāvana, which kept him tied as a prisoner to the tail-end of the monkey-king Bāli, in which position he remained for long, shorn of all pride and humbled to the dust. It has all the thrills of a diplomatic manoeuvre to bring about the destruction of an enemy and all the subtle and vivid humour of a comedy that such a situation creates. An altogether different theme, like that of king Rugmāṅgada (Pl. V), the very soul of piety and truth, who submits to the extreme demands of the temptress Mōhini (Pl. IX fig. 1) in order to honour his plighted word—a story of great pathos, forms the subject of another drama. Yet another play is built round the romance of Kriṣṇa and Rukmini. Rukmini falls in love with Kriṣṇa but is forced to keep her love a secret, owing to the bitter antipathy of her brother towards her lover. The brother decides to marry her to Śiśupāla. How the young princess, friendless and helpless, manages to send word of her love (Pl. XVI) and of the impending marriage, how Kriṣṇa arrives at the last moment, boldly waylays the princess while she is on her way to the temple and abducts her before the gaping crowd of warrior-suitors (all aspirants for her hand), are the main incidents of the play. A more stirring drama is the *Sacrifice of*

Dakṣa, depicting the immolation of the insulted Sati in flames, the great wrath of Śiva sweeping over the worlds and the destruction that follows when everything goes into smouldering ruin. The incident of Kriṣṇa acting as a messenger to the court of the Kurus on behalf of the dispossessed and wronged Pāṇḍavās and trying in vain to avert the mighty battle of Kurukṣetra, is another story that creates tense situations. In another play, the theme is the fatal infatuation of the wicked Kīcaka, for the lovely Pāṇḍava queen who lived in disguise as a maid-servant at the court of Virāṭa. So too the several episodes of the *Rāmāyaṇa,* the *Mahābhārata* and the *Bhāgavata* supply the themes for other equally well-known plays.

Employing one or other of these dramas the performance goes on throughout the night. The drumming and the singing continue all-night and there is no break in these or in the rhythmic web spun ceaselessly. The voice of the singers and the sound of the drums, cymbals and gongs carry forward the rhythm of the acting and dancing. The performance progresses like a serious sacred rite impelled by the force of some mysterious power, a power found reflected in the concentrated, monstrous energy, animating the singers, drummers and actors who appear possessed. Rhythm remains predominant; the initial as well as the sustaining urge and strength of the performance. Like the ceaseless waves of the ocean, it ever surges forward, now gentle, now rising, at times swelling, turbulent and overwhelming. This rhythmic pulsation simultaneously manifests itself through the drumming, singing and the gestures and movements of the actor.

The story that has commenced with the opening scene in the garden, moves on with rhythmic sweep, until the climax of passion—very often fierce passion—is reached. This takes place in the early hours of the morning when the major figures of the drama are drawn in hostile array (they represent the idealised principle of Good and Evil). A mighty conflict between the forces of light and darkness ensues and the principle of unrighteousness, the *Asura* or the villain, is slain, at times with all the gruesomeness of a bloody scene. As the sound waves die down and the lamp flickers, at the conclusion of the final act, which raises us to the climax of emotional fervour, we are taken back into a grey world of prosaic realities, a foretaste of which comes with the quickening light of the morning.

NOTE

The songs are in the form of dialogues and are meant to be acted out fully. So too are the *Daṇḍakās,* which are descriptive songs, indicative of phychological attitudes of dramatic intensity or narratives of particular situations. They cover incidents of the story too. Difficulties of time are bridged over by *ślōkās* (verses) that are only announcements not intended to be acted; there are situations where such *ślōkas* have to be acted.

CHAPTER VII

ĀHĀRYĀBHINAYA

Hindu histrionic art is known by the Sanskrit term *Abhinaya.* Interpreted literally it means *educare* [1a] or leading the play towards the audience. Embodying so significant a conception, it covers every aspect of the process by which that object is achieved and is the synthesis resulting from the combination of four separate and fully developed dramatic elements. They are *Āhārya, Vācika, Āṅgika* and *Sātvika. Aharyâbhinya* denotes the decorative elements of the play, like facial make-up, costumes and jewellery. *Vācikâbhinaya* refers to speeches and songs by the actors. *Aṅgikâbhinaya* means bodily movements, hand gestures, eye-movements etc. *Sātvikābhinaya* is the expression of psychic states and is intimately associated with emotional conditions and manifests itself in tears of joy, horripilation, change of colour, change of voice, trembling, fainting, motionlessness etc. In a woman in love it shows itself in instinctive amorous gestures, bashfulness or in a sense of confusion (*vibhrama*) that arises out of excess of joy. *Sātvika* is a very subtle force. A play in which *Satvikābhinaya* finds full expression is considered by the *Nāṭyaśāstra* as very superior.

The Kathakaḷi stage presents the strange mythological personalities of the three worlds [1b] who are endowed with super-human qualities, mental and physical. Further, they are not so many individuals as symbolic personalities. To present them convincingly is a problem that would test the ingenuity of any producer. They can only be 'realized' through suggestion or symbolic representation. The extra-ordinary preparations that commence in the green-room, even before the fall of the day, and which continue till the early hours of the morning like a sacred rite; the fantastic assemblage of colourful costumes and jewel-

---

[1a] The actors educate the "spectator by stimulating in him the latent possibility of aesthetic experience." *The Mirror of Gesture.*

[1b] The upper world of the *Devas,* the middle world of the human beings and the nether world of the *Asuras.*

lery, the resplendent head-gears and the paints, show, with what skill and care an actor is transformed into a *deva,* a fearsome demon, a disgusting gnome, a charming temptress, a graceful golden swan, a great serpent king, the fiery discus of Viṣṇu or an avenging man-lion.

The make-up which is a very striking feature of the drama and which creates in no small measure the deeply sensitive and dynamic atmosphere so characteristic of the Kathakaḷi stage has a history as old as the beginnings of the Keraḷa stage. A study of the cult-plays and folk dance spectacles would reveal that the Kathakaḷi art of make-up is but the finalised phase of experiments carried on from a remote past. Here, the traditions appear to be non-Aryan and probably pre-Aryan and have little in common with the classic Sanskrit stage. Amidst these paints and costumes we are in an unfamiliar world that may seem fantastic, even grotesque to some, but they have a definite symbolical significance and contribute so very much to the extraordinary atmosphere of the Kathakaḷi stage, that their importance can hardly be overstressed.

The characters of the drama are not so many individuals but expressions of principles or qualities. Broadly they fall into three principal categories: *Sātvik, Rājasik* and *Tāmasik.* Other intermediary types emerge in proportion to the preponderance of one or other of these qualities. All these types (basic and intermediary ones) are brought on the Kathakaḷi stage under five principal classes. They are *Pacca* (Green), *Katti* (Knife), *Tāṭi* (Beard), *Kari* (Black) and *Minukku* (Polished). All these types are distinguished primarily by the facial make-up, the colour scheme and pattern of which differ in each case. The function of the make-up is to create a significant form, a form that possesses competency to express the character or qualities of the type it represents. The art is thus in no way different from that of the painter. The make-up artist achieves this by a skilful use of lines, dots and colours and by an aesthetic application of the law of contrast. The outline of the pattern on the face is first traced in black by the actor himself. Thus the actor is in a special way responsible for the pattern on his face, which must of necessity accord with his facial features. There is therefore no dead uniformity in these facial make-ups, for patterns, though of the same type and colours, vary in the quality of the lines.

The colours used are white, green, vermilion, red, black and yellow; mostly they are deep and radiant. Colour is first ground into an exceedingly fine paste by the addition of coconut oil; when applied to the face it maintains a smooth and glistening effect. The soft light of the oil lamp, the twilighted zone and the darkness beyond are admirable foils to accentuate the colour effect. The patterns reveal that the colours used are selected for their sensitiveness to communicate ideas and their transforming qualities. Their charged intensity is harnessed within assigned surfaces, bounded by radiant white borders and their purposive force and significance are unmistakable. "The deeper the nature of the thought we wish to express, the more it ought to be steeped in the fire of colour" is an ancient Indian belief; this feeling fully permeates the colour scheme of the Kathakaḷi make-up and here, more than elsewhere, colour exists as the language of symbolism [2]. A more brilliant and effective arrangement of colours, with due regard to their tonal values and their capacity to express ideas, could hardly have been devised. Types that have mixed qualities are suggested by the skilful apposition of the relative colours. The combinations arising from this process are varied.

Pacca (Green). Where the face is painted predominantly in green, the type is called *Pacca.* This colour symbolises inner refinement, poise, heroism and moral excellence. *Sātvik* or beneficent and virtuous characters like *devas,* and celebrated mythological heroes, come under this type (e.g. Indra, Rugmāṅgada, Naḷa, Arjuna, Kriṣṇa, etc. (Pl. V). In harmony with these qualities their movements and bearing are dignified, graceful and aristocratic. The face is first marked off with a white *cuṭṭi.* Starting from the centre of the chin the *cuṭṭi* rises on either side of the face along the jaw bones in a sweeping bow-shaped curve and tapers at either extremity. The inward side of the *cuṭṭi* is

---

2 The *Nāṭyaśāstra* stresses the efficacy of facial colouring to express states and sentiments and to enhance the beauty and communicative capacity of gestures and glances. Cf. Chapter VIII ślōkas 159-165. The Kathakali facial colour scheme and make-up and the reddening of the eyes appear to be a logical development, though to our knowledge there is nothing on the Sanskrit stage (except in the *kūtiyāṭṭam* of Kerala) to parallel this. In the *Nāṭyasāstra* the sentiments are allied to particular colours e.g. erotic with light green, terrible with black, furious with red and yellow with the marvellous etc. Cf. Chapter VI ślōkas 42-43.

terraced: the repeating lines forming a constructional gradient imparting monumental grandeur to it. This ridge serves as a brilliant white frame to the coloured pattern within and is in itself a work of exquisite beauty (Pl. III fig. 2 and Pl. IV). The *cuṭṭi* paint is a mixture of rice-paste and lime and is applied while it is wet, with great care and precision, so as to ensure the correct rhythmic curve, shape and size. As the paint dries it becomes a strong and solid frame-work [3]. Another white border-line in a double arch, sweeps the span of the forehead, marking the upper limit of the facial pattern. The area within this is then painted predominantly in green. The prevailing green is broken by the brilliant coral red of the lips, the deep, black border-lines of the elongated eyes and the neatly pencilled eye-brows. The green over the forehead is vivified by a trefoil *vaiṣṇava* mark in white and red. There are other charming variations in the details of the trefoil mark.

While the patterns and paints over the face are of the utmost significance in demarcating the types, the head-dress and the costumes worn by the various types are for the most part very similar, so much so, that what applies to one can in general be considered as applicable to other types except in the *Minukku*. Important variations are noticed in the relative descriptions below.

The forehead above the painted portion is covered by the Indian-red ribbon of the head-gear. The gilded head-gear which completes the make-up sits like a crown of shining splendour on the head of the super-human figure into which the actor is transformed. Every head-gear is a perfect work of art. Its extremely rich effect and regal splendour invest the wearers with supernatural majesty. Though there are many charming variations in the details of the patterns of the head-gears, generally the head-gear is a crown of superimposed domes ending in a bud-shaped finial and with an enormous halo-like disc at the back. Wrought in light wood and pith and gilded all over, it is encrusted with a brilliant mosaic of red and green. The several tiers of the crown are set with tiny metallic tassels. The differences in the types of characters are also emphasised by the head-gears; for instance, a demoniac character wears a bigger and flamboyant one, which is more spectacular and imposing than the one

---

3 An unfortunate modern tendency is to make the ridges with strips of paper, an easier method, but certainly a far less skilful one and lacking in beauty.

worn by the *pacca* type. The make-up of Krisṇa is a pleasing variation of the *pacca*; but not in the colour scheme of the facial painting. This is effected by a change in costume. The head-gear is a beautiful coronet decked with peacock plumes, the jacket is of deep blue, over which is an enormous garland of flowers (*vana-māla*) and the skirt is in vivid yellow (Pl. I and Pl. XVI).

Katti. In this the green back-ground is broken by a red patch—an up-turned moustache—running close to the upper cheek bones, the border-lines of which are picked out in radiant white. At the tip of the nose and on the forehead, close to the root of the eye-brows, two white balls called *cuṭṭi* flowers are affixed (Pl. VI and Pl. XVIII). Their protuberance and peculiar position impart to the facial expression a strange but fascinating savagery. This type as well as every other fierce character wears a pair of *dhumsṭrās* (two large canine teeth, on the upper row, near the corners of the mouth) which when bared, over the lower lip, heighten the demoniac effect. Seized by anger the *Katti* characters bare these savage fangs and growl or emit shrill cries or roar. Their glances hurl defiance. They assume an arrogant majesty in movement and demeanour. The *Katti* make-up symbolises demoniac types or a race of titans, like Rāvaṇa, Śiśupāla and Kaṃsa, who revelled in their might, were ambitious and arrogant and were a law unto themselves. Nevertheless, they were great in valour, fond of the pleasures of love and possessed certain cultivated tastes and high accomplishments. The retention of this green pattern attests to these graces and virtues. But evil and aggressive propensities get the better of them, as symbolised by the fiery red patch and the savage knobs, which with startling effect, transform the configuration and expression of the face of the *pacca* type, of which this is a significant variation. A more demoniac class in this category is indicated by a larger *katti*; the up-turned and fiery moustache is larger and runs up close to the eyes; over the eye-brows and running into the fore-head are a pair of red patches as complements to the lower ones.

Tāṭi. The wearers of beards are classed under one major type *Tāṭi*; they are distinguished as red, white and black beards, according to the colour of the beard worn. In this as well as in the succeeding types the white *cuṭṭi,* so prominent a feature of the *Pacca* and *Katti* types, is absent.

Red-beard. This shows a marked change from the *Katti* both in the pattern and in the colour scheme. Blazing red and deep black, shot with a dash of white, are employed with great skill to effect a change that is truly astounding. All softer graces and every indication of restraint are lacking; the elongated eye-lines, the arched eye-brows and the vivid red lips [4] which enhanced the *Pacca* and the *Katti* faces are absent. Instead, around the eyes a patch of deep black appears, giving to the red and circular eyes a fiendish look. The enlarged lips painted in lurid black beget a beastly expression. On either cheek a weird pattern is executed in white pith. It is a double row of white bristles running up from the upper lip to the eye-brows and throwing into bold relief the black around the red fiery eyes. The rest of the face, mostly the lower half, is painted red. The red and black, emphatically demarcated by brilliant white, lend to the colours an acute and fierce intensity. The white balls affixed to the tip of the nose and the forehead are bigger than those of the *Katti.* All restraint has disappeared with the elimination of the white *Cuṭṭi* frame-work and in its place is a flaming red beard which in its semi-circular sweep emphasises the massiveness of the visage. The head-gear that crowns the figure is larger and its halo-like disc more spectacular, with a fringe of fiery red wool surrounding the rim. The red fur-coat that covers the body is enormous and the bulge of the skirt more pronounced. The ornaments worn echo the same fierce sentiment and add to the volume and burliness of the figure. What emerges is an embodiment of elemental, untamed passions, massive and overpowering (Pl. VII and Pl. XXII) [5]. Generally this type represents vicious and vile characters and power-intoxicated beings like Duśśāsana and Bakāsura. The great

---

4 The lips, eyes and eye-brows are painted in different ways, which change their expression and shape, so as to bring out the character of the various types.

5 The citizens of Ekachakra, in order to save themselves from the wild and indiscriminate slaughter caused by the demon Baka who preyed on them, arrived at an agreement with him whereby they undertook to deliver to him once a cart-load of food, two bullocks and a human victim. This went on until Bhima, moved by the wailings of an aged couple forced to part with their young son whose turn had arrived, agreed to take his place. Arriving at the demon's cave, Bhima instead of delivering the food, sat down to make a leisurely meal of it. The enraged demon rushed on Bhima and in the great and cruel fight that ensued, Baka was killed and the citizens of Ekachakra were rid of the terror.

monkey generals of the *Rāmāyaṇa* like Bāli and Sugrīva, though not wicked, are included in this category, because they are fabulous animals and typify all the brute force and undisciplined violence of wild life. The behaviour and style of *abhinaya* of the Red-beard express more clearly what the exaggerated physical proportions and weird facial mask seek to symbolise. The Red-beard's glances are invariably furious and his gestures are emphatic, aggressive and haughty. His dancing is tempestuous and earth-shaking. His cries roll like thunder or are the graduated grunts and growls of a savage beast and he mocks and sneers a great deal and his laughter is often boisterous and extremely derisive [6].

White-beard represents a higher type of being. The best example of this class is the great monkey general Hanuman, the son of the Wind God, celebrated alike for his piety and devotion to Rāma and for unrivalled strength (Pl. XXI fig. 2). Though pious and virtuous, he is but a giant monkey. The animal is well suggested in the make-up. The upper half of the face (from the nostrils) is predominantly painted black and the lower half in red, demarcated by white border-lines. On the chin is a rosette in white with red heart, the lips are coloured black and a moustache-like pattern in white is traced on the upper lip. The nose is painted green [7]; above it and on the forehead are two ovals in red. The white cuṭṭi-like pattern on either side of the cheeks, forming a loop in red spots, branches off in a curve over the forehead, to the end of the eyebrows. The white, woolly beard and the enormous white fur-coat, complete the suggestion of a great monkey. The head-gear is a distinctive type, somewhat like a Chinese hat, ending in a bud-like finial and adorned with tassels.

Black-beard. Aboriginal hunters and dwellers of the forests come under this category. The face is painted in deep black and is broken up by bracket-like patterns drawn around the eyes, in white border-lines and coloured in red within. White bristles are stuck to the ridges. The flaming red of the lips vivify the black around. On the tip of the nose is a *Cuṭṭi* flower. The beard worn is black and a crown of peacock

---

6 There are different kinds of laughter in Kathakali which depend on the type of character and the occasion. The *Pacca,* and the *Minukka* smile gently (*smita*) and never indulge in loud laughter. The other types such as the *Katti* and *Tādi* indulge in loud laughter which is vulgar, violent and full of ridicule.

7 Symbolic of his *Sātvik* or upward tendency.

feathers rises over the figure like an expanding lotus capital (Pl. VIII).

The hunter carries a large bow with arrows in a quiver and a sword. He has a queer somewhat puzzled look about him. His glances are quick and suspicious and he creates the impression that his ears are ever alert and have almost a visual gift. An unsophisticated child of the wilds, he symbolises the simple joys, fears and thrills of wild life with which he is in perpetual conflict.

Kari, the all-black, is the most grotesque and bizarre figure on the Kathakaḷi stage, just as the Red-beard is the most impressive. Vile *rākṣasīs* (ogresses), like Śūrpanakha and Simhika, belong to this category. The face is painted in lamp-black with weird patterns in white. This type wears *dhumsṭras.* The costumes are wholly black. Two enormous and grotesque breasts, attached to the breast-plate, add to the feeling of disgust the type evokes. The head-gear is of the same kind as that worn by the black-beard.

Minukku (Polished), by its very simplicity, is in sharp contrast to all the elaborate class of make-ups hitherto described. This colour scheme stands for gentleness, restraint, poise and high spiritual qualities. Brahmins, *riṣis* and all women characters other than *rākṣasīs* belong to this category. The face is painted in delicate flesh colour obtained by the mixture of yellow and red. The eyes and eye-brows are pencilled in black and elongated: the lips are vivid red. There is no loud orchestration of colours or complex patterns and no flamboyant effect is aimed at. Every face shines as it were with the subtle glow of an inner light; a quiet spiritual halo surrounds these forms and makes them radiant. The costumes and ornaments of the male characters of this class, viz. Brahmins, *riṣis,* etc., are unostentatious and in keeping with the subdued colouring. The bulging skirt, the big over-coats and the great head-gears are absent. Male characters of this class wear a white or slightly coloured waist-piece. *Riṣis* are distinguished by grey or black beards and by head-gears that resemble *jata-makutās* (Pl. XVII).

Women characters [8] of the drama form a separate class under the *Minukku* type (Pl. IX fig. 1). They are modelled with a delicate touch. Over the light, golden yellow of the face, powdered mica is sprinkled;

---

[8] Woman characters of the play are impersonated by men.

this imparts to the face a brightness and an etherial glow. A delicate sense of refinement is discernible in the sensuous curve of the elongated eyes and eye-brows. The hair is gathered into a knot near the top of the forehead, a little to the left. A light coloured veil, ornamented with a border of gold or silver, covers this knot and head and falls over the back to the waist, like the end of a sari. The body and the arms are encased in a tight-fitting red jacket, admirably fitted to enhance the effect of the gold coloured ornaments. Over the chest is a gilt breast plate with red breasts fixed to it; red and white scarves which flow over the shoulders cover them. A white sari pleated with folds and adorned with an ornamental belt covers the lower half of the body. Ornaments like ear-rings, necklaces, armlets and bangles are worn. The palms and edges of the feet are dyed in *henna* red. These women characters have an air of repose and tenderness that is easily felt against the prevailing exuberance and expansive movements of the male characters, and acts as a foil to the almost shocking vitality of the demoniac types. Their poses, gestures and movements are tender, gentle and graceful. Their important role in the drama is the delineation of the amorous and the pathetic: women in love and women in distress—the two themes around which the great stories of the world are built—are invariably the roles in which they appear.

The foregoing descriptions are confined to the principal types; within these are many picturesque and significant variations, such as the make-up of Garuda (eagle mount of Viṣṇu), Hamsa (swan), Takṣaka (a serpent king), Sudarśana (fiery discus of Viṣṇu), Narasimha (man-lion, a manifestation of Viṣṇu) and Bhadra-Kāli.

The costumes and ornaments of the male characters, except those of the *Minukku* (Brahmins, *riṣis* and women) and the *Kari* class already described, are almost identical. Generally speaking, the most noticeable amongst these is the enormous skirt—somewhat like a cross between the Camargo and the Romantic skirt of the ballet dancer—a drapery that may seem rather queer in male characters in view of the association of the skirt with women. That it is in no way an imitation of the feminine skirt is evident. It is made up of broad ribbons—probably an adaptation of the primitive drapery made up of the bark of trees. Skirts made of the ribbon-like tender leaves of the coconut palm are used by male characters appearing in certain ritual and other dance spectacles in vogue in Keraḷa. A deep red and triangular piece of cloth called *munti,* ornamented with crescents and stars, hangs down in front, skilfully emphasising the colour and volume of the skirt (Pl. VIII, Pl. XIII and Pl. XXII). This seemingly cumbersome costume is both a clever device as well as a welcome convenience. Its functional qualities are appreciable. By its rhythmic sway the skirt imparts a certain ceremonious grace and majesty to the movements of the actor. Further, it adds volume, giving the much needed balance to the over-sized figures whose heads are crowned with large head-gears. The ample space it provides, offers facility to the leg movements of the actor-dancer which are of the utmost importance in this masculine art. The body and arms are covered in a tight-fitting jacket of deep red. Red and white scarves with ends like full-blown lotuses, glide around the neck down to the waist; their sinuous undulations trace graceful patterns in sympathy with the movements of the actor-dancer and his swaying skirt. So also the streaming hair, falling over the back to the waist, enriches the symphony of movements.

The head-gear lends height to the figure in proportion to the bulk added by the overcoats, ornaments and skirt. The circular disc attached to it is an artistic and structural necessity. A merely peaked head-gear crowning these voluminous and enlarged figures would certainly create a structural void, upset their balance and impair in no small measure the beauty of their movements. The circular and ample skirt, the almost oval face with boldly sculptured features, the head-gear with a sweeping circular disc, which repeats the rhythm of the skirt below—no better setting could have been devised for the many angular hand and leg movements of the actors.

The more massive forms of the Red-beards and White-beards are obtained by the use of large fur-coats, bigger head-gears and more voluminous skirts that fit in with the bold features of the painted mask. Armlets, wristlets, epaulettes, breast-plates, necklaces, ear-rings and bangles are some of the ornaments used to adorn these figures. In addition, all actors wear tiny bells or jingles on their legs.

Most of the male characters wear long silver nails on the fingers of the left hand. They impart a sleekness and tapering elegance to the fingers, qualities which in turn enhance the beauty of the *mudras* (finger poses) and hand movements. In the case of the demoniac characters they look like formidable claws to cleave, clutch and strangle.

Another very remarkable feature of the Kathakaḷi make-up is the practice of reddening the eyes of all the characters by the application of *cuṇḍa poov* (flower of *Solanum pubescence*). The crimson eyes always remain in vivid contrast to the colour scheme of the face and are consequently turned into a sensitive and vibrant medium of expression. In a system of histrionics in which expressions of the eye occupy so paramount a role, it would have been rather fatal to have left the eyes "un-prepared". These *aruṇa-nayanās* (red eyes) appear exceedingly lovely and bright in the *Pacca* and *Minukku* faces. Seen in conjunction with the colour scheme of each type, they acquire a power of expression and significance differing with each. Strange as it may seem, the red eyes accord with some of the varying moods of the characters. In the love scenes they appear *madāruṇa* (red with passion, or intoxication). Similarly they become significant in a character swayed by anger or in one piteously weeping in a pathetic situation. In the demoniac characters the red eyes, set within the deep black patch around, gleam like balls of fire, fierce and flaming (Pl. XXII).

A few simple colours, a few simple costumes and some picturesque but tinsel ornaments are put to intensive effect. By supreme artistry and a highly developed colour sense, that fully exploits the symbolic value of colours, a feeling of the marvellous is created and sustained. The charged silence of the actors proves an inexhaustible means to heighten this effect. We are irresistably attracted by the marvel moving on the stage; its every gesture interests us deeply, to the exclusion of everything else and we are transported to a plane of consciousness where the mind, free from any distractions, is actively engaged in experiencing the strange events of the drama. Even one witnessing the spectacle for the first time will soon realise what a powerful force Kathakaḷi *ahārayābhinaya* is to create *rasa.*

The transformation of a human being into a *deva* or *asura* takes hours of patient labour, especially the facial painting. While that is being done, the actor lies flat on his back and sometimes goes to sleep. In the many hours of inactivity that follow, he is consciously or unconsciously storing up emotional tensions which help to transform him into a god or demon. In that seeming immobility—a restful interlude—

preparatory to an extraordinary activity, he gathers within himself those very qualities which the outer habiliments and paints seek to envisage. As each costume and ornament is put on, the new personality possesses him more and more. At last, he takes up the sacred head-gear. With eyes fixed on the living flame of the lamp, which is symbolic of divine presence, he prays devotedly, salutes the head-gear and places it on his head; he gains a new grandeur and stature and his transformation into a mythological hero is complete [9]. He is that and no longer himself and he steps out in an "elevated mood". The actors no longer walk in the usual way [10] but with heavy stamping steps, expressing an accentuated rhythmical tension; this is so both when they come out of the green-room and return to it from the stage. The several stylized manners of walking, even the position of the feet which touch the ground with their outer edge only, suggest super-worldly origin [11]. The finished product that comes out of the green-room is not only a transformed being but a splendidly colourful figure. For example in the *Pacca* type the headgear is a mass of shining gold, scintillating with green and red mosaic, the face glows with the radiant white *cuṭṭi* and the deep green, red and black of the plastic mask, the body is encased in a red jacket, which is vivified with gold coloured jewellery and many coloured scarves, and the purity of the white skirt is thrown

---

9 The Attic as well as the Chinese theatre had recourse to parallel conventions in make-up. The Greek players used cothurni of various heights, according to the importance of the actors, for exaggerating their height. The mask rendered in conventional form was an indication of age, station and prevalent mood. The colour of the hair indicated age, a snub nose low birth, the married and the un-married women were distinguished by the way the hair was dressed. Cf. Allardyce Nicoll's *The Development of the Theatre*: Harrap & Co. In the Chinese theatre, jewels convey a woman's social status; a face painted red indicates sacred or royal personage; black, an honest but uncouth personality; white, a treacherous, cunning, but at the same time a dignified one; a white patch on the nose, a villain or comedian. Devils have green faces, gods and goddesses yellow, mixed colours indicate a variety of characteristics. See *Famous Chinese Plays* by Arlington & Acton.

10 "Movements and gaits that have been prescribed by the rules for a character which has entered the stage should be maintained by the actor without giving up the (particular) Temperament till he makes an exit." *Nāṭya Śāstra,* Chapter XXVI verse 116-117 (Translation by M. M. Ghosh).

11 "They are like creatures who walk the earth as guests, though possessing also other means of motion. This manner of being in contact with the ground seems to be an expression of power and might." G. Boner. *Story Plays in Living Tradition.*

into bold relief by coloured bands and the *munti.* Each type is a symphony in colours making us believe that "colour is the language of the gods". The Kathakaḷi make-up is itself a great art; much of the atmosphere of the super-world on the stage is created by it. Once its symbolic significance is understood it will satisfy and fascinate even the most fastidious modern taste. The forms it creates abide in the mind of the spectator [12] as unforgettable visions or symbols of divine powers. They are derived from super-human prototypes [13]. The Kathakaḷi make-up re-affirms the truth that "the soul of a thing is its form."

---

[12] Narayaṇa Bhattaṭṭhiri, reputed Sanskrit poet and philosopher of Keraḷa and a devotee of Krisṇa, was once asked by a friend why he had ceased attending Kathakaḷi shows, of which he had been a great enthusiast. He replied that his love for the art had not abated a bit but he had to forego the pleasure of witnessing them for a special reason. After seeing a show, he said, he found it difficult to forget the form of the Lord in the Kathakali guise; whenever he sat in contemplation the figure of the Lord appeared to him in the typical Kathakaḷi make-up. It was difficult to envisage Him in any other form, or in His formless aspect, while this picture persisted.

[13] Kapliñgat Nambutiri, the author of many Kathakaḷi stage practices, is said to have been much exercised over the problem of making-up the actors in the form of mythological characters. At last, one night he escaped into the solitude of the sea shore where he prayed to his *Iṣṭadevaṭa* for light and sat in deep contemplation. Looking out into the sea he saw the forms of the gods, demons and other mythological personalities appearing over the waves from the waist upwards. The Kathakaḷi characters are modelled after this divine vision; they are the forms in which the gods and demons, etc. revealed themselves to human eyes. Corroboration of the legend is sought in the practise of draping almost all characters in the billowing, wavy skirt which symbolises the foamy, heaving, sea surface over which all the forms appeared. The differences in the types are of course stressed in the make-up from the waist upwards.

CHAPTER VIII

VĀCIKĀBHINAYA

Pantomime was developed as a distinctive feature of the Hindu stage from ancient times. Even "the Vedic sacrifice was essentially a *mimesis*", though the purpose of dancing in it was something far more serious than entertainment, as Dr. Coomaraswamy has pointed out [1]. On the Sanskrit stage even the literary drama, however superb, did not hold sway to the exclusion or subjection of *āṅgikâbhinaya.* Supreme moments of the drama found expression in *mimesis* (acting-dancing). Plays like the *Śakuntaḷa* of Kāḷidāsa provide internal evidence of the importance given to this method of staging. In what is considered the greatest love scene in Sanskrit dramatic literature—the meeting of Duṣyanta and Śakuntaḷa—it will be noticed that the heroine does not speak a word. Her love, too deep to be expressed in words (an overwhelming experience to the simple unsophisticated maid brought up in a forest hermitage in the company of anchorites and the deer), is intended to be mimed. The *Nāṭyāchāryas* of the Kathakaḷi stage took the view that the spoken word was a needless burden on the actor and that it was imperfectly equipped to discharge the function it was called upon to bear in the drama. They therefore developed a more powerful vehicle of expression. The body was put to the fullest use to express ideas, thoughts, feelings and emotions through mime and dance. This method has certain decided advantages. Movement is more eloquent in expressing innate impulses and feelings than words, and the charged silence of the actor gives intensity to his expressive movements, which would not be the case when he is also expected to concentrate on his words or declamation. In silent-acting or mime the experience is much more intense and effective. Perhaps that is why when the "Progenitor and Death are engaged in opposing sacrifices, the latter is defeated because of what on his part was 'sung to the harp' or enacted

[1] Cf. *The Mirror of Gesture,* f.n. on p. 16—Coomaraswamy and Duggirala.

(*nṛtyate*) or done vainly (*vṛthā*)" [2]. Sacrifice that was sung to the harp was nothing in comparison with sacrifice that was *mimesis*. Obviously this method has certain advantages: it helps for example to retain the sense of the marvellous. Spoken words would mar this feeling by bringing down the beings of a super-world and mythological heroes to a very familiar plane. Further, the infinite suggestiveness of the gesture language makes it akin to poetry and artistically a more satisfying medium for the drama. Words are prose, but movement is poetry.

While eliminating *vācikābhinaya* from the functions of the actor, it was nevertheless retained on the stage as the chief directive force. The singers who sing the text of this musical drama are on the stage and the actors are only interpreting the songs word by word in gesture language and dance. A perfect union is established between the song, the instrumental music and the miming of the actor. Since the body was to become the sole medium of dramatic expression, it was but natural that it should be subjected to minute observation; every little movement natural to the *angas, upāngas* and *pratyaṅgas* (limbs, parts of the body and features), its relation to emotions and its communicative capacity were studied. So too the movements of birds and animals in love [3] and fight [4], of storm-tossed trees, the twinkling of the stars, the drooping of the lotus at sun-set, the soft, confident clinging of the tendrils, the peacock dancing in rapture, all these have gone into the fashioning of this medium. Instinctive and natural movements (*Loka-dharmi*) [5] were added to the conventional (*Nāṭya-dharmi*). Thus all

2 *The Mirror of Gesture.*

3 Those who carefully watch the *patiñjāṭṭam*—the slow-moving love-scene in Kathakali—will inevitably be reminded of the leisurely love making of doves characterised by many gentle, tender and patient dalliances.

4 Something more than the worst human passions have gone into the portrayal of the demoniac characters. The oppressive overwhelming fury, the freezing grin, snarl and sneer and the weird cries characteristic of these types, must have been distilled from the wildest of wild creatures.

5 *Abhinaya* or the histrionic art is the harmonious combination of the realistic (*Loka-dharmi*) and the conventional (*Nāṭya-dharmi*). Gestures that are natural and instinctive, ornaments that are ordinarily used such as ear-rings, garlands, necklaces and costumes familiar to us in everyday life, tears and laughter that appear on the stage in the realistic manner, are *Loka-dharmi.* The various stylized *hasthas* or *mudras* (hand gestures), the several types of gaits (as distinct from ordinary walking) and similar conventional movements of the limbs, the plastic masks built on the face, the reddening of the eyes, the peculiar costumes like the enormous skirt and the resplendent head-gears, the simulation of weeping, etc. belong to the *Nāṭya-dharmi* technique.

abhinaya is the harmonious blending of these two modes. The studied movements that emerged out of this process are very many and relate to almost every part of the body and the limbs. They are codified in the texts with meticulous care. The suppressing of the *vācika* led to a remarkable development of *āṅgikâbhinaya* with an extensive vocabulary of its own; it became an independent language that needed no words.

NOTE

The more enlightened critics of the Western drama have realised how unsatisfactory the purely literary drama is, and in their search for the dance-drama, they have envisaged something resembling Kathakali, at least outwardly.

Terence Gray in a provocative treatise asks.... "But, are words the only or the essential medium of dramatic art? Is drama necessarily a matter of the manipulation of words?" He answers that words "become a strikingly inadequate medium for the expression of emotion... Casting into the mould of words the chaotic up-welling of sudden and over-whelming emotions is not possible, much more so at the time of experiencing them, and so this is dramatically unsound and wrecks the carefully built up cumulative effect of the play. Consequently the audience does not experience the most vital revelations and fail in the fullest possibilities." Gray laments that the experiments in the art of the dance-drama conducted in the West which showed great promise at the commencement have not been sustained. The full-length play *Sumuru,* produced by Max Reinhardt, and *L'Enfant Prodigue* were staged in London without the spoken word, but these, he regrets, perished without offspring. He bemoans that in none of the forty odd theatres of the West-End the art of the theatre is practised seriously and says that the dance-dramatist is yet to be born. "For the great moments of the drama words are inadequate, at such moments the character should express himself in mime and dance." *Dance-Drama-Experiments in the Art of the Theatre* by Terence Gray.

CHAPTER IX

ĀNGIKĀBHINAYA

The term *āṅgikâbhinaya* denotes studied movements of the *aṅgas* like the head, breast, hands, waist and feet, of *pratyaṅgas* like the shoulders, shoulder-blades, arms, thighs, knees and elbows, and *upāṅgas* such as the eyes, eye-lids, pupils, cheek, nose, teeth, tongue, heels, toes, fingers, palms, face and lips. Of these, *hastas* (hand gestures) and eye movements are of particular importance; *hastas* are the words of the sign-language; the facial expressions, particularly the eye-movements, enforce their significance. The eye-expressions, as it were, ensoul the forms created by the *hastas.* Other movements such as those of the eye-brows, nose, cheeks, legs and shoulders are mostly ancillary; therefore the function of hand gestures and eye-movements will alone be noticed in detail.

Gesture has always played an important role in the transmission of the thoughts and emotions of man. Even now the practice of gesture remains a universal feature. Many of the natural gestures are found to be common to mankind and their meaning therefore is understood by all. The natural inclination to gesticulate functions vigorously when we are gripped by emotion or when we desire to emphasise or illustrate a thought, feeling or idea, which thus gains a visual form with rhythmic content. This wide-spread and persistent practice is perhaps largely due to the consciousness of mankind of the inadequacy of words to give adequate expression to what is intimately felt.

In India, where everything is sublimated through association with religion, it is no matter for surprise that so natural and human a characteristic should be regarded as a religious symbol. The hand pose as *mudra* possesses esoteric virtues no less than the word as *mantra* and the pose as *āsana.* The *mudra* was meant to give a physical representation suggestive of the deep, inward consciousness of the devotee which the *mantra* or magic formula voiced. Its use as a religious symbol is discernible from Vedic times. With the emergence of

Tāntrism the *mudra* gained added spiritual significance and even magical potency. It is hardly possible to over-estimate its importance in the daily religious life of the Hindus or in their special rituals. These picturesque and symbolic hand poses act as a medium, in the hands of the devotee, for spiritual communion with the divine. Some of the *mudras* are said to have originated from the significant actions of the gods and came to be known as *"divya-kṛiya"* (divine actions). According to the *Abhinaya Darpana* (*The Mirror of Gesture*) the *Patāka* (flag-hand) originated from Brahma, when he hailed Para-Brahma "with the cry of victory", holding out his hand like a flag with the full palm outward. The *Ardha-candra* (half-moon) originated from Śiva's desire to add the half moon as an ornament to his *jaṭā-makuṭa* (coiffure). The *Muṣṭi* (fist) is traced to Viṣṇu who used it to fight the demon Madhu. The rich and warm imagination of the Hindu endowed these *mudras* with life and personality, as in the case of the *rāgas* and *rāginis* (melody modes), portrayed with exquisite lyrical charm in the Rajput miniatures. Each *mudra* or *hasta* has a patron deity and sage and belongs to a particular race and has a distinct colour [1].

This mystic language of the gods was soon adopted as the language of the learned. Even as early as the time of the Buddha [2], communication by sign-language or gestures had become an accepted practice and a hall-mark of the wise and the accomplished. It was included in the 64 *kalās* (arts). The really educated man in ancient India was the one who was accomplished in these arts. Gestures both natural and conventional were studied and elaborated with meticulous care and fashioned in complete obedience to rhythmic laws; they were an admirable artistic medium to suggest "the inexpressible in an unsurpassable way". "Never indeed has the spiritual value of the hands—these flowers of the flesh—which hold within their chalice the whole of human tenderness and thought, been comprehended with such

---

1 *Mudra.*	Colour.	Sage.	Caste or race.	Deity.
Ardha-candra	Smoky	Atri	Vaiśya	Mahādeva
Muṣṭi	Indigo	Indra	Śūdra	Moon
Sarpa-siras.	Turmeric	Vasava	Deva	Śiva.

2 *The Mirror of Gesture.* It is but reasonable to suppose that the art of gesture was practised as a deliberate art in days much earlier to Buddha's times.

mystical insight. The whole of the great peace of Buddhism is contained in the gesture known as *dhyāna-mudra.* The whole of the blessed One's power of gentleness is revealed in the *abhayamudra* in which for twenty four centuries past, half of humanity has found a refuge. On the other hand what calm assurance in the gesture by which he takes the earth as his witness; what supreme elegance—the finished grace of reason in the perfect sage—in the gesture of discussion and of the *dharma-cakra.* And as though to prove the universal value of the sacred gestures, are there not also the *añjali* and the *vara-mudra,* Christian symbols in which all pure hearts from Fra Angelico to the masters of Ajanta have joined in expressing their double ideal of faith and charity. These are, 'gestures of the soul', as Ruskin would say, transposing pure moral beauty into its direct aesthetic equivalent." [3]

A stranger visiting an Indian street or home will soon realise that eloquent gestures characterise every-day life in India. As in the frescoes of Ajanta so to this day "the supple wrists, palm and fingers of the Hindu, beseech, explain, deprecate and caress". As was pointed out in the opening chapter, in Malabar, the habit of gesture has remained a pronounced and persistent feature in the daily life of the people. Often communication is carried on solely by gestures. The orthodox Brahmins who are prohibited from conversing with lower castes while engaged in religious practices have recourse to sign-language. The gestures of the Nambutiri have gained a distinction and reputation even in Keraḷa. Perhaps it is not widely known that this is largely due to the fact that it is a long-inherited and cultivated tradition. They have a system of gestures (different from the *Nāṭya hastas*) to denote Vedic texts. It comprises a few key gestures of the hand based upon sound, somewhat like musical notation. When a Nambūtiri pupil learns the Veda he learns it to the accompaniment of *mudras.* Not only that: his proficiency is tested through *mudras.* When the examiner gestures, the pupil must recite the appropriate Vedic stanza; or, when one recites, another sits opposite to him gesturing, very often employing wrong *mudras* to mislead the pupil or the reciter. The one who falls into the "snare" is ridiculed and laughed at by the whole

---

[3] René Grousset.

gathering. From the finger-pose and hand movement the Vedas can thus spring into form or words.

Some of the gestures employed in daily life are also used on the stage, but they are naturally enough stylized, made more rhythmic and possess a wider range of significance. So it cannot be said that the entire gesture language is arbitrarily conventional or wholly technical. While the layman's knowledge of the gesture is limited, the initiate commands a wider range and is capable of enjoying the poetic subtleties of this conventional language much better. A simple villager watching a *Cākkyār* artist interpreting the passage "Rāvaṇa drank in the beauty of Sīta with his eyes" (the whole interpretation was done by eye-movements only), was thrilled and exclaimed to his equally thrilled companion, "See, see, how he drinks water with his eyes"! To him, this sign language was not unfamiliar, nor its general meaning unintelligible. What was beyond his comprehension was the significance of the conventional idiom which suggested the "beauty" of Sīta. This is no isolated instance. Plāçcery Nambūtiri, a great patron of Kathakaḷi, was also a highly accomplished actor and reputed for his role of the Brahmin in the drama *Rukmini-Svayaṃvara.* On one occasion two maid servants had come to see this play: one went to sleep in a retired corner asking her companion to wake her up when the Nambūtiri appeared in his famous role. At the time the maid was awakened, the Nambūtiri was interpreting the passage "Grieve not oh elephant-gaited one" and portraying "elephant-gaited one". She looked, rubbed her eyes looked again and exclaimed in undisguised merriment and much puzzled. "Why, why is it that the actor is walking like an elephant?" The elephant and its gait were well understood, but she had failed to grasp the poetic conception whereby it represented the gait of a proud and beautiful woman [4]. In some measure what contributes to this general intelligibility of gestures, is, that many of them are descriptive and illustrative. The Malayāḷi audience, inheriting and sharing as they do a common tradition with the actors, find no difficulty in following this conventional language. The process by which intelligibility is aided and the picture made impressive is dealt with elsewhere.

[4] Indian poets compare the gait of women to that of the *hamsa* (Brahmini goose), the elephant, etc.

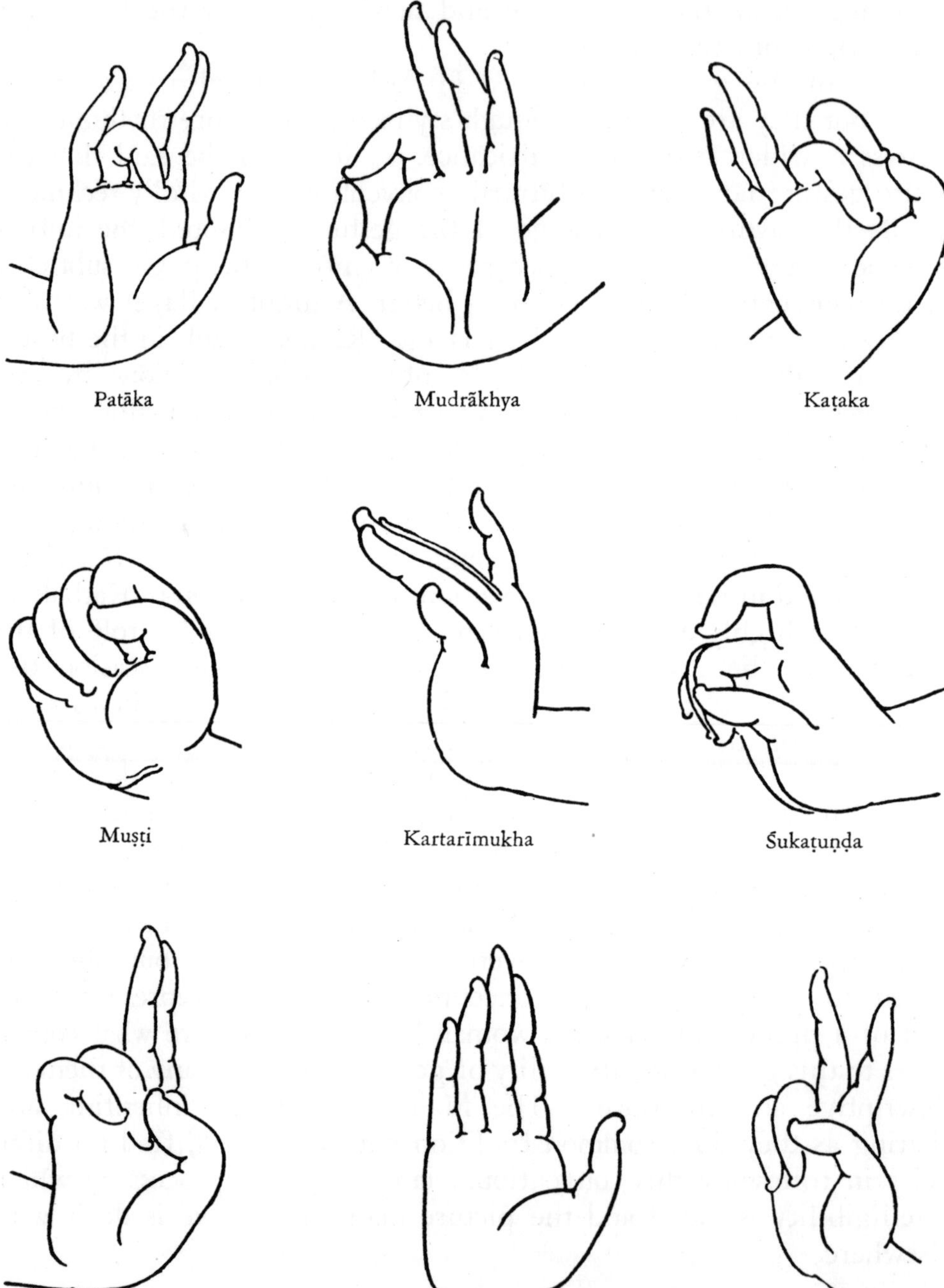

The twenty-four primary *Mudras*. Sketches by S. Rajam.

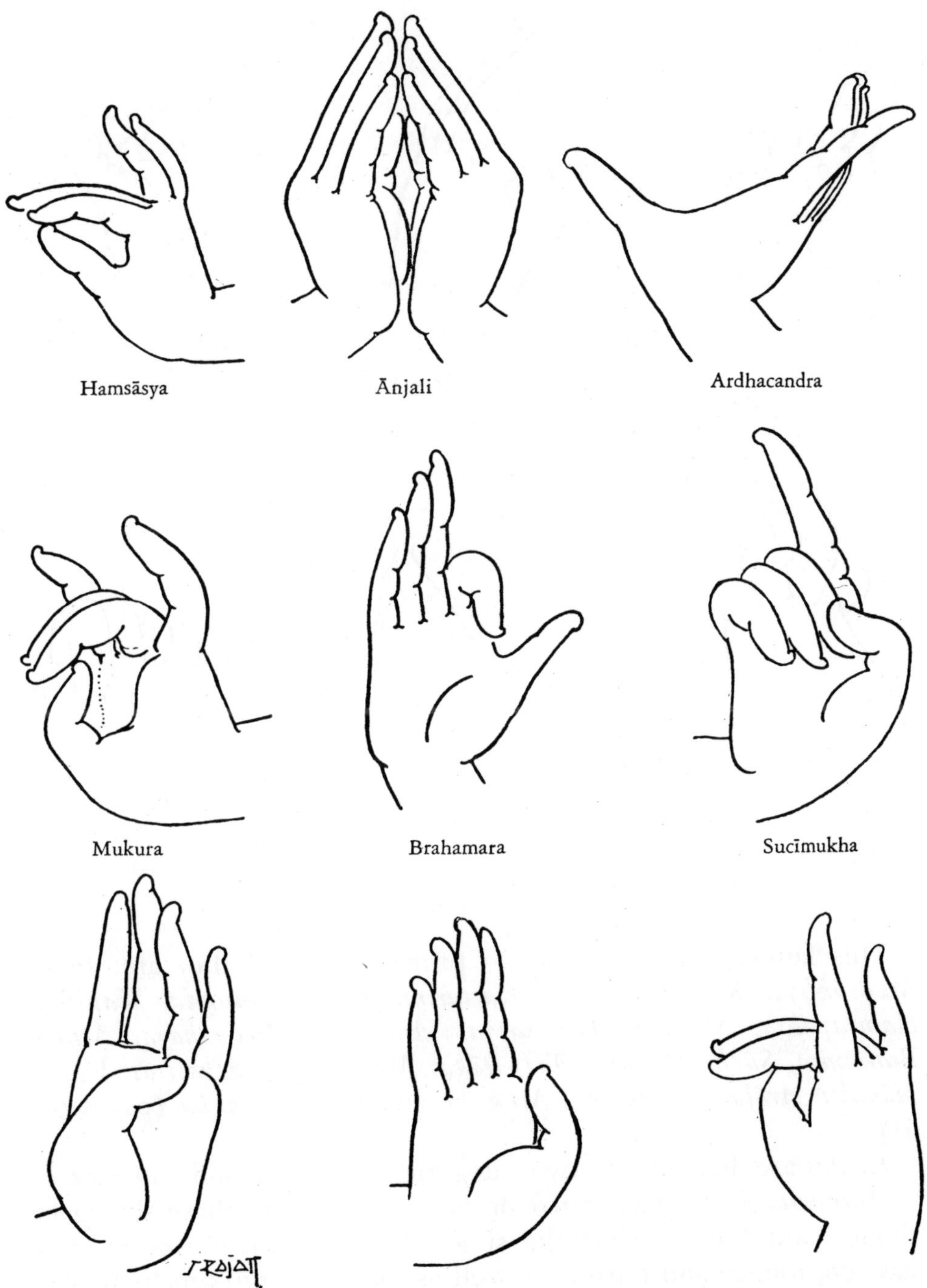

The twenty-four primary *Mudras*. Sketches by S. Rajam.

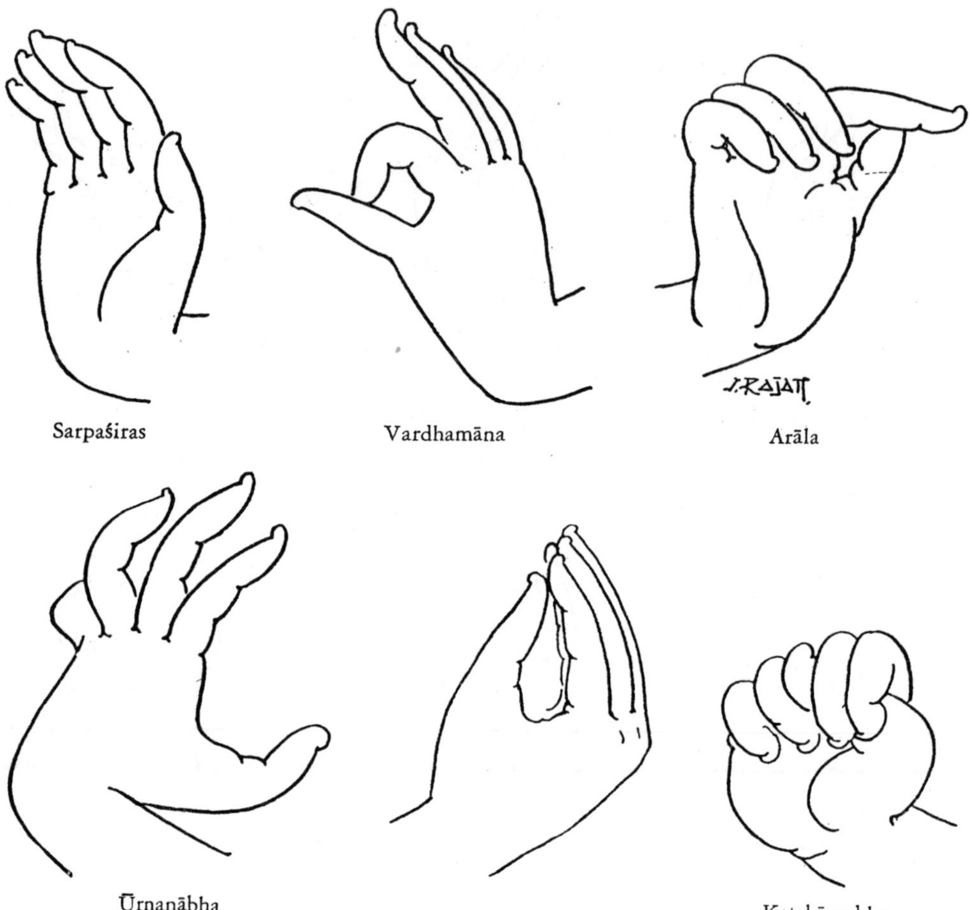

The twenty-four **primary** *Mudras*. Sketches by S. Rajam.

This language is based on 24 primary *mudras*: they are: *Patāka, Mudrākhya, Kaṭaka, Muṣṭi, Kartarimukha, Śuka-tuṇḍa, Kapithaka, Hamsapakṣa, Sikhara, Hamsāsya, Añjali, Ardha-oañdra, Mukura, Brahmara, Sūchi, Pallava, Tripatāka, Mṛigaśīrṣa, Sarpaśiras, Vardhamānaka, Arāḷa, Urnanābha, Mukuḷa,* and *Kaṭaka-mukha* (pages 62 to 64).

Hastas are divided into two categories, *Asaṃyuta* and *Saṃyuta*.

Asaṃyuta hastas (separated or single hands) are those shown by a single hand, e.g. as when the single *Patāka* hand is used to denote day, go, tongue and mirror, as well as those *mudras* which are shown by employing both the hands without their conjoint action; i.e. the hands remain separated and express a single idea, e.g. king, sun or flag, and enough (Fig. 27).

Saṃyuta hastas are combined hands where the *mudra,* as for lotus, fish, crocodile, conch, begging, mark etc., is formed by the conjoint action or union of the two hands (Fig. 7-11).

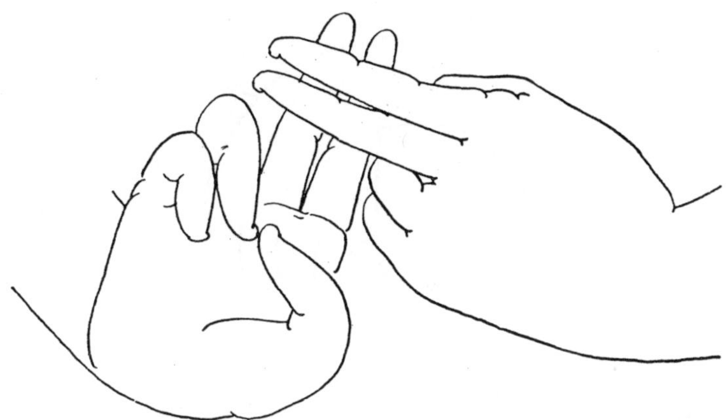

Fig. 7. *Angita* (mark, impression).

An idea is expressed either by a single hand or by both the hands by their conjoint or separate action. The significations of a *mudra* are many, some of which are expressed by double hands and some by the use of single hands. In some cases, like *Śukatuṇḍa, Kapithaka* and *Tripatāka,* single hands are rarely employed, as no specific significations are attached to such usage. The examples below are intended to show the vast range covered by the *mudras* both in single and double usage. *Patāka* in single usage signifies the following ten ideas: day, go or start, tongue, brow, body, similarly, sound, messenger, sand-bank and tender leaves. In double usage it expresses the following: sun, king, elephant, lion, bull, crocodile, festoons, creeper, flag, waves, nether-world (*pātāḷa*), earth, region of the navel, vessel, storeyed building, sun-set, noon-day, cloud, ant-hill, loins, servant, vehicle, tranquil or calm, crooked (villainous), door, pillow and ditch. In this way permutations and combinations of the primary *mudras* have resulted. In the *Hasta-lakṣana Dīpika*, the text book on hand gestures, which the Kathakaḷi generally follows, nearly 400 of such combinations are detailed. Apart from these it mentions a large number of mixed combinations called *Miśra mudras*. These are of course shown by two-hands, but then each hand is in a different *mudra,* their combined action indicating a single signification, *e.g.* Indra indicated by *Śikhara mudra* in one hand and *Muṣṭi mudra* in the other. Śiva is symbolised by *Mṛiga-*

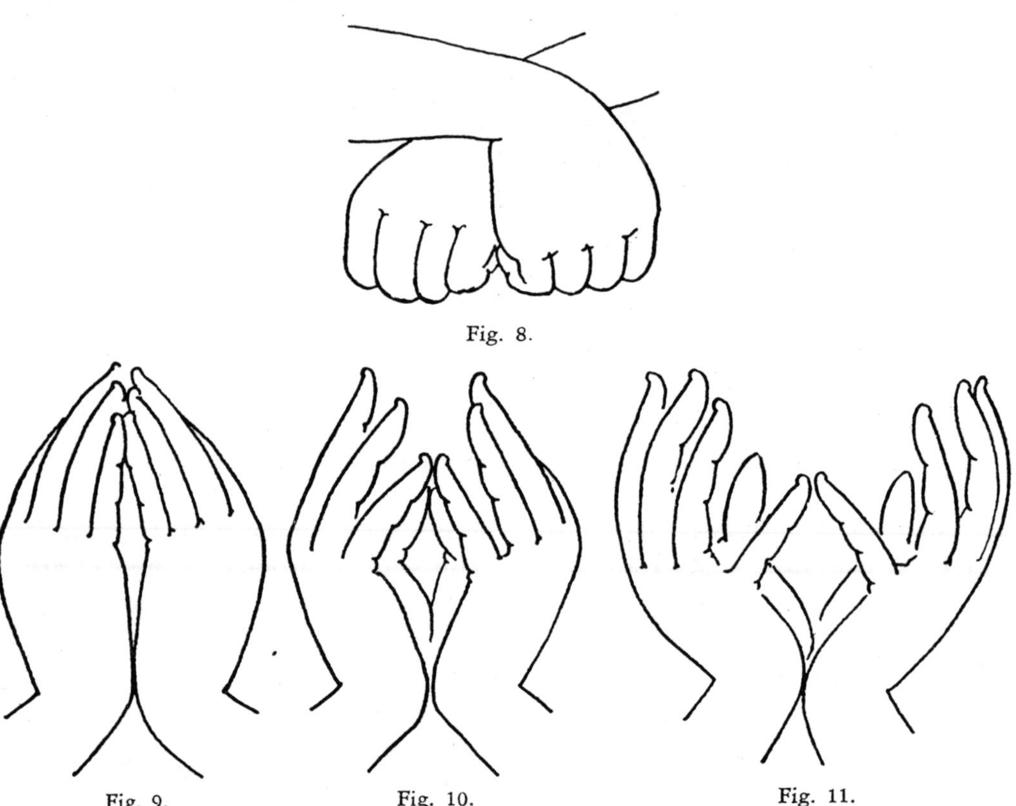

Fig. 8.

Fig. 9. Fig. 10. Fig. 11.

Figs. 8-11. A series of movements and gestures suggest an idea or thing. These sketches show the cardinal position of the hands depicting a lotus.

Sketches by S. Rajam.

ṣīrsha and *Hamsapakṣa mudras* (Fig. 12). Similarly, widowhood, sexual union, Sri Rāma, giving away (gift) of a woman and war are suggested by the varying combinations of the *Kataka* and *Muṣṭi.* It should be remembered that in this process of permutations and combinations, the *mudras* assume varying positions owing to the change in pose of the hands, palms and fingers. But when a *mudra* of the same shape or form indicates two things it is known as *Samāna,* similar or equivalent *mudra,* e.g. lake and water, Varuna (sea god) and sea, darkness and night, pride and youth, etc.

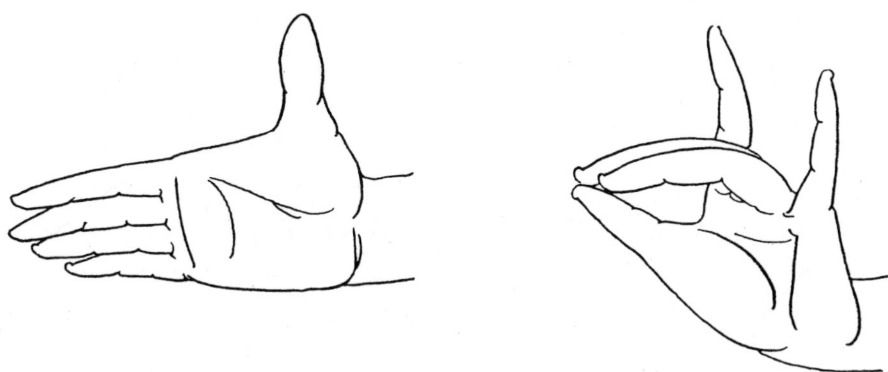

Fig. 12. Śiva.
Figs. 12-21 Hand poses by Kunju Kurup. Sketches by S. Rajam.

For personal names occurring in the text, for which no *mudras* are specified, the Kathakaḷi artists employ the *Kartarīmukha* which is held level to the mouth and then slightly moved forward. This is called *Nāma mudra* or nominal *mudra.* When a Kathakaḷi actor's vocabulary fails, which is rarely the case, he employs the *Nāma mudra* to cover it up and thus prevents a break in the continuity of the gesture sequences.

Hastas are also distinguished as *nṛtta* and *nṛtya* according to their function, meaning or signification. *Nṛtta* hastas are purely decorative and convey no specific meaning whereas *nṛtya hastas* narrate and interpret. Both these types of hands are employed; *nṛtta hastas* in the pure dances and *nṛtya hastas* in interpreting the text of the drama, in the conversational interludes and in the depiction of moods.

Mudras have a triple function, at least most of them have. When for example the *patāka* hands are held in a particular way, to symbolise an elephant, it pictures the *karta* (subject, doer). The subsequent movement of the hands descriptive of the elephant, its instinctive movements such as the swaying of the trunk and ear-lobes, etc., form the *karma*; the movements that follow illustrating the actions—its deliberate doings—form the *kriya.* It is on the amplification and extension of this *dharma* of the *mudras* that the Kathakaḷi style of *abhinaya* has taken a distinct turn, where every word comes to life with all its inner rhythms underlined. How this is done and how much it enhances *bhavābhinya* is dealt with elsewhere.

A great many of the *hastas* are imitative and descriptive signs; others

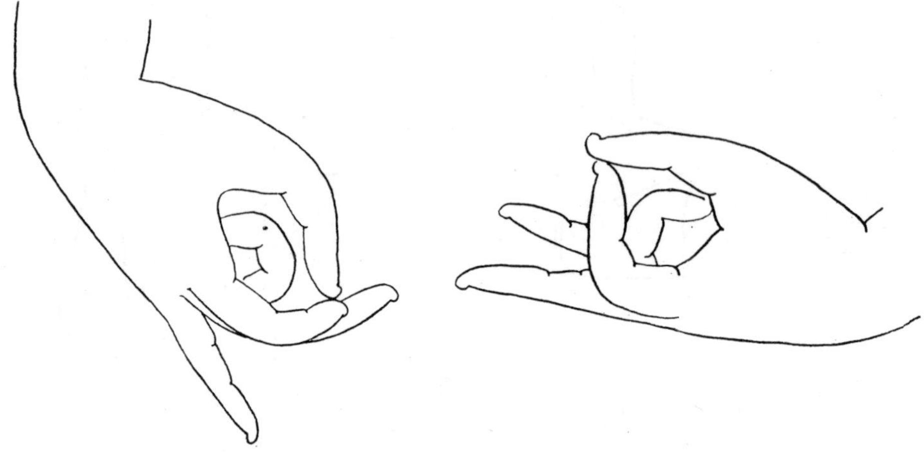

Fig. 13. *Rākṣasi* (ogress).

are symbolic. Each *hasta* stands for many concepts; their differing significance depends upon the position, movement and direction of the

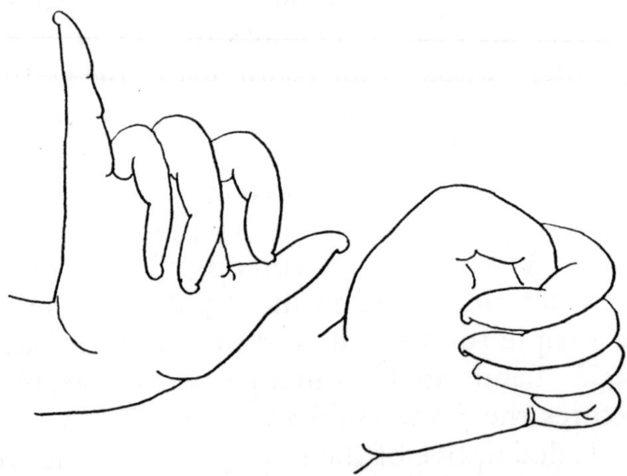

Fig. 14. Arrow and bow.

hand and palms, the disposition of the fingers, etc. The accompanying movements, bodily as well as facial, also vary and underline the meaning. An examination of the *hastas* would reveal, that even the conventional signs designed to express abstract concepts, like truth or beauty are, despite their conventionalised character, easily comprehensible, as may be seen from the explanations below.

Truth. This is rendered in gesture language as follows: The left hand in *Kaṭaka mudra* is held close to the heart, the right one in *Mudrākhya* is held over the former, then raised to the height of the forehead where the finger pose is released changing to *Hamsapakṣa*; a movement that calls to witness both the heart and the intellect, obviously suggesting truth (Fig. 15-16).

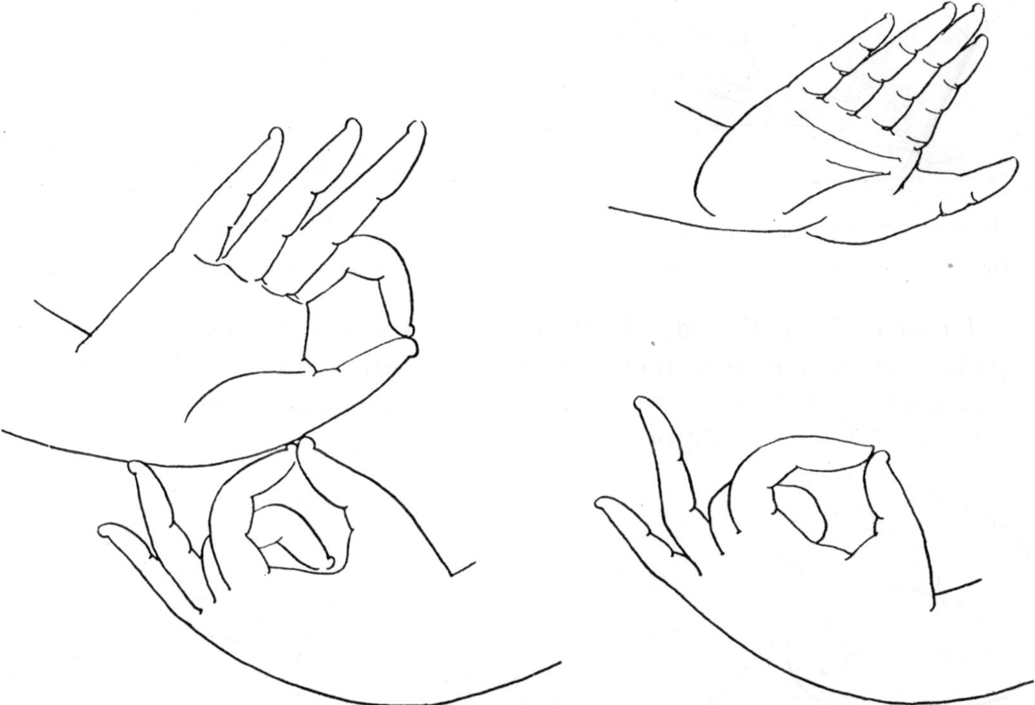

Fig. 15. *Satya* (truth). Initial hand pose. Fig. 16. *Satya* (truth). Final position of the hands.

Creation: The left hand in *Tripatāka* is held close to the navel or the solar plexus, symbolic of creative power, and the right one in *Mudrākhya* placed over the former. The *Mudrākhya* hand is then raised up with a wrist-turn; and as the hand travels up, the finger pose changes to *sūci,* suggesting rise, emanation or shooting up (Figs. 17-18). Probably it also recalls the nativity of Brahma the Creator who manifested himself on the cosmic lotus, that grew out of the navel of Viṣṇu.

In relation to Brahma the *Mudrākhya* can also signify contemplation associated with his creative function. These hand poses can also be explained as the representation of the sprouting of a seed (*Mudrākhya*) from the earth (*Tripataka* held below) and its growth (*sūci*).

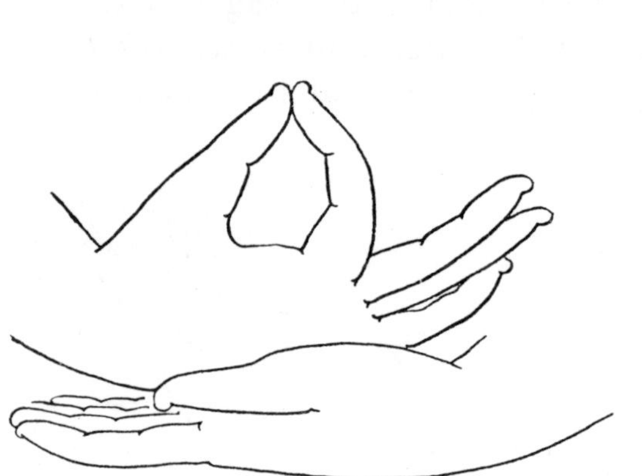

Fig. 17. *Śriṣti* (creation). Initial hand pose.

Fig. 18. Final position of hands in *Śriṣti*.

Heaven: *Tri-patāka* hands are held level to the forehead with the palms inward and then moved farther on either side, the finger pose changing to *Mudrākhya,* the face is slightly raised heavenward and the eyes suggest the feeling of bliss.

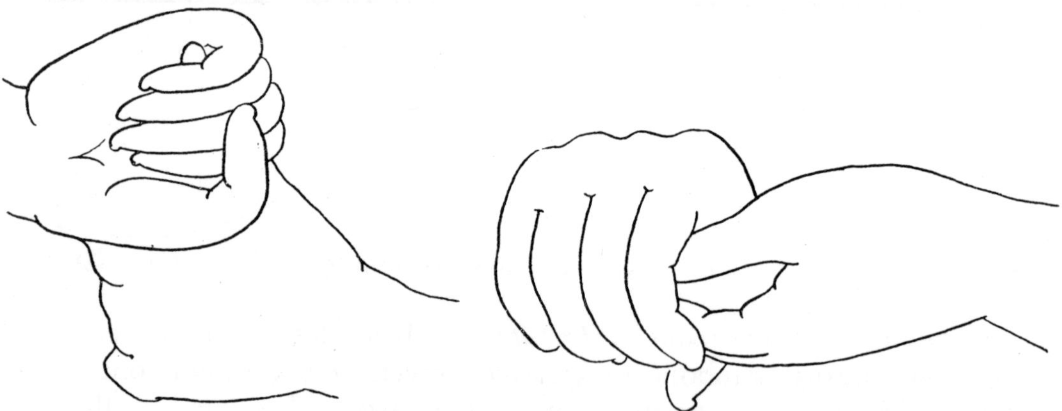

Fig. 19. *Vallabha* (husband).

Fig. 20. *Bhārya* (wife).

Gold: This is expressed by holding both hands in the *Kaṭaka* pose and then indicating or imitating the movement in the act of testing gold on the touchstone.

The *mudras* for *vallabha* (husband) and *bhārya* (wife) appear to have a sexual or erotic significance (Figs. 19-20). Deities like Siva, Brahma and Viṣṇu are suggested by indicating their associated attributes and are easily intelligible to the Hindu audience (Figs. 12 and 21).

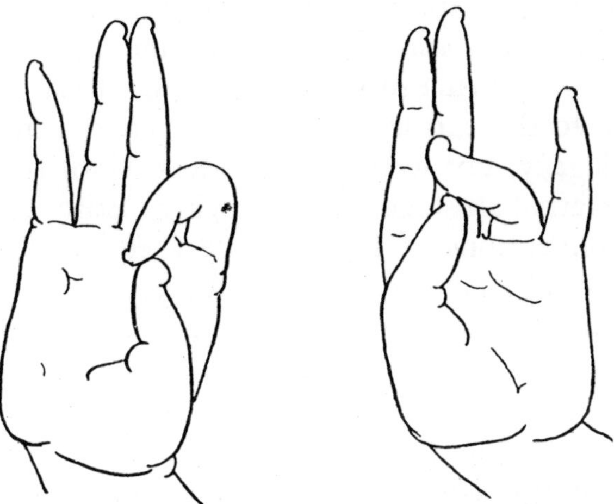

Fig. 21. Brahma.

In the scheme of *āngikâbhinaya* the hand movements (*kara-vartana*) are called *Śākha.* Like the branches of a tree the hands spread out into space, far and near, and in every direction. The fingers move like tender leaves or open out like petals. The *hastas* are easily the most conspicuous phase of *āngikâbhinaya.* In chapter II it was pointed out that a new artistic and theatrical problem arose out of the need to present the entire drama as a pantomime. This necessitated a more extensive as well as intensive use of hand gestures and greater efficacy in *rasa* delineation. The rich heritage of the past, in both these respects, was enriched further. In the process, permutations and combinations of the *hastas* were inevitable, which ultimately resulted in a vast vocabulary. The *Nātya Śāstra,* it should be noted, is no rigid text that concedes no freedom to any one who goes beyond it. It permits incorporation of new *hastas,* provided they are in popular use, indicative of *bhāva* (emotions) and *rasa* (sentiment) [5]. Katha-

[5] The author of the *Nāṭya-Śāstra* has stated that he has described only whatever is usually met with and things omitted by him should be gathered from the usage of the people. Cf. N.S. Chapter IX slokas 156-159 and Chapter XXVI slokas 117-118.

kaḷi, it is said, has now evolved about 800 *hastas*; the full extent of this can be known only when an authoritative and comprehensive code is prepared. To reconcile the Kathakaḷi *hastas* with those described in various texts like the *Nāṭya Śāstra, Abhinaya Darpana, Sangītaratnākara* and others, is rather a difficult task and of doubtful value, as all the above texts, in spite of a great deal of common ground differ in the number of *hastas,* their definition and application. The Kathakaḷi *Nāṭyāchāryas* (masters), like the true artists they were, were not afraid to add to the existing stock; they were not merely the custodians of a rich legacy, but were also builders. Until the beginning of this century the Kathakaḷi stage was a growing institution and naturally traditions and conventions of the past were enriched and new ones established [6]. That the Kathakaḷi has features foreign to, as well as some prohibited by the *Nātya-Śāstra,* is well known. Even on the question of *hastas* departures from the *Nātya Śāstra* have been noticed. But criticism on that score will not appeal to the Kathakaḷi actors or audience, for the reason, that the different *mudras* have by usage established their significance and associations; precisely the very basis on which a symbol or convention rests. Further the Kathakaḷi *hastas* and movements have acquired a distinct style, different from other schools—even from that of the *Cākkyārs.* The expanding need of a silent dance-drama, for a richer and more adequate vocabulary of gestures to suggest form and feeling more effectively and the persistent search to ensure grace and beauty of movement, were to a great extent responsible for this stylistic variation.

Now we will examine more closely and in greater detail how *hastas* communicate ideas, make vivid pictures and impart a lyrical charm.

While the hand gestures narrate through their plastic, flowing lines, facial expressions, movements of the body and appropriate poses aid the process of communication (Figs. 22-29, pp. 74-77). In this scheme, as has already been said, the eye movements discharge a vital function.

---

[6] 1934-40 was a brief but glorious period for Kathakaḷi, when almost a renaissance seemed to be in progress in Kerala Kala Mandalam under the distinguished leadership of the poet Vallathol. Master artists and brilliant pupils (well and carefully trained at the Kala Mandalam), in company with distinguished singers and drummers staged remarkable performances. During this period some experiments were made, specially in presentation. "Pūtana arriving at Ambadi", now a favourite piece, illustrates the masterly way in which improvements could be made in presentation.

"Wherever the hand moves, there the glances follow; where the glances go, the mind follows; where the mind goes, the mood follows; where the mood goes, there is flavour" [7]. This is but putting the matter is a nut-shell. How the meaning "springs into bodily shape" is best seen in the renderings of a Kathakaḷi artist. When he represents a lotus he is not merely content to show the conventional symbol for it. His method is more elaborate, suggestive of associated feelings and indicative of the vegetative urge that shapes the flower. First the actor takes a "look" at the lotus (*nokki-kāṇuka*). His eyes and face reflect the sense of marvel at the sight of the beauty unfolded before his gaze and that is an indication (*sūca*) of the impression he is about to convey. Another important point to be noted here is that invariably the starting point of all action is the eyes. As the actor takes his "look", his hands with closed palms in *Muṣṭi* or the fist pose, are crossed at the wrists, the right one over the left (Fig. 8 p. 66). By a pivotal movement the Muṣṭi hands are dipped. In the process, the fist is released and the hands rise up with conjoint palms resembling a lotus bud (*Kapota hastha*). This creates the impression of the upward urge of the lotus plant which rises up over the water. Slowly but gently and as subtle and imperceptible as nature's process, the conjoint hands grow and as we are looking on engrossed at this mystic rite—the eyes of the actor are responsive to every little movement of the enlarging life of the lotus—the growing bud opens ever so gently, petal by petal, as the fingers quiver, throb and expand. Here the drums almost simulate the unheard rustle of the opening petals (Figs. 8-11, p. 66).

At last, the hands picture the full blown lotus. The face of the actor lights up with the joy of the experience. His nostrils slightly dilate and the perfume of the flower is enjoyed with evident delight, as is seen from the gentle wave of exhileration that courses through the actor's frame [8]. The actor then withdraws the right hand; the left one, still in position, symbolises the flower. A bee comes to life with the quivering, fluttering fingers which move hither and thither; the lively

[7] *The Mirror of Gesture,* p. 35.

[8] This process resembles *Citrābhinaya* referred to in *Nātya śāstra,* Chapter XXVI. Spring is to be represented by acts of rejoicing and festivities characteristic of that season. A swing is indicated by the representation of its movement, agitation of the limbs and the holding of the string so that the moving swing is visualised. Cf. *ślōkas* 32, and 80-82.

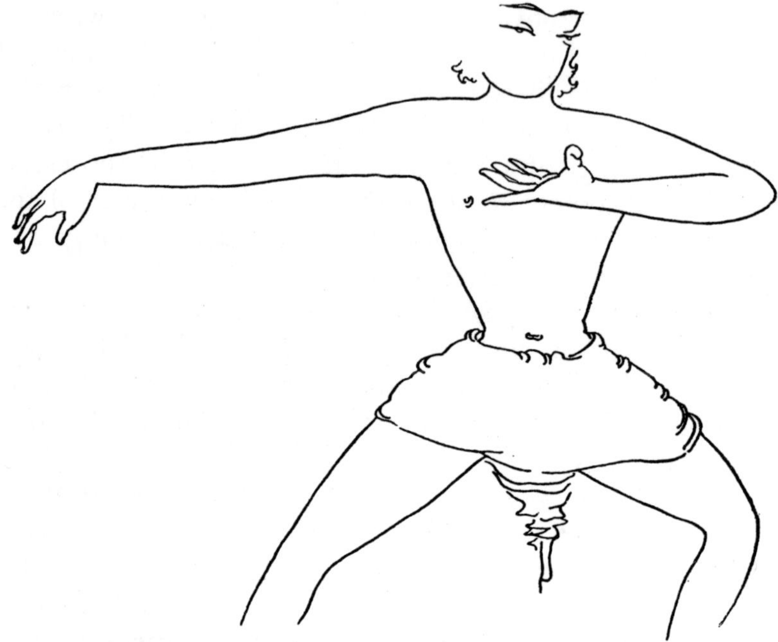

Fig. 22. *Nōkki-Kāṇuka*—gazing, studying, or looking at.

Figs. 22-29 poses by Kalamandalam Krishnan and Madhavan. Sketches by S. Rajam.

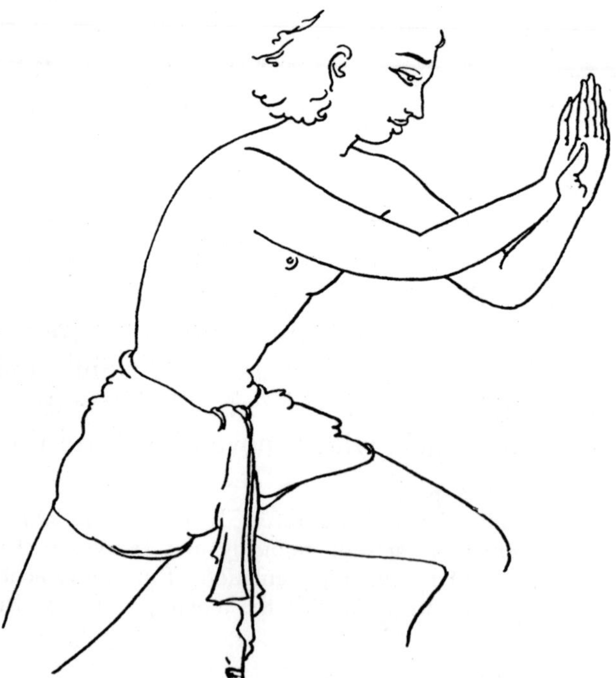

Fig. 23. Suggests hidden, covered, or obscured.

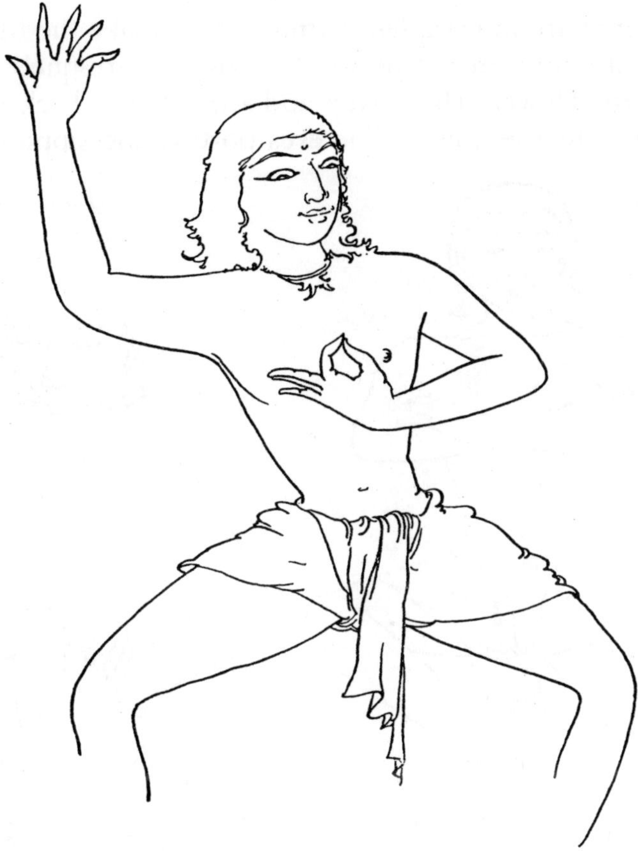

Fig. 24. *Sukriti* (blessed one).

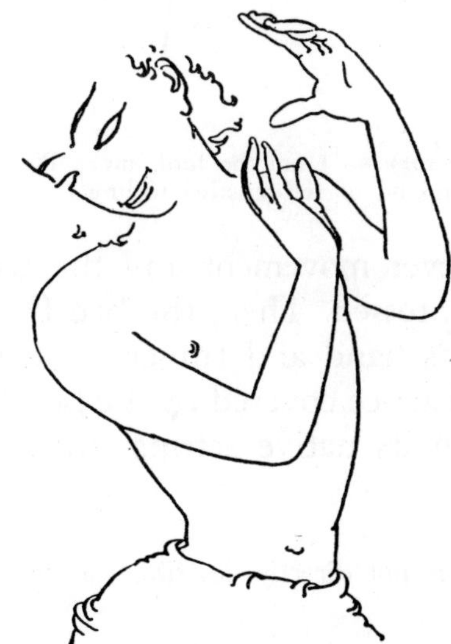

Fig. 25. *Karna-sudha* or nectar to the ears, meaning sweet-delight to the ears. The position of the hands suggest the holding of the pot containing the nectar.

eye-expressions are in complete harmony and make the illusion perfect. All the erratic movements of the bee are picturesquely suggested. It alights on the flower, flies away and then comes back and settles on it again and sips the honey. The eyes portray the sipping of honey by

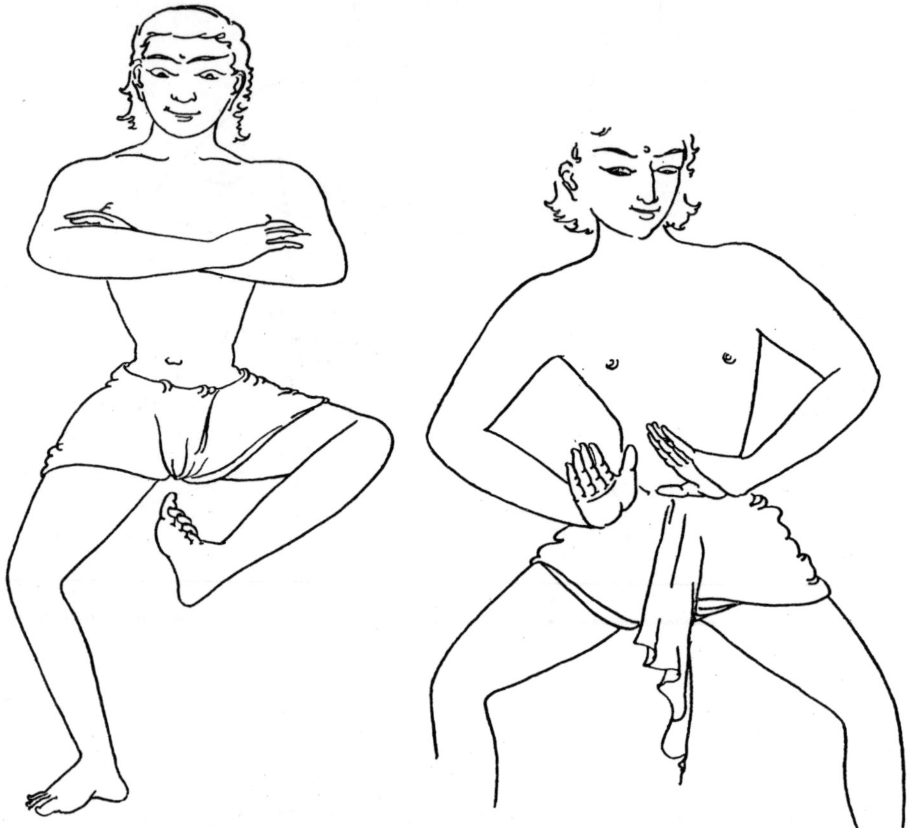

Fig. 26. *Sarvabhauma* (Emperor) — I am the lord, my right, there is none-to-question-kind of self-satisfied feeling.

Fig. 27. *Mati*—enough, fully satisfied.

an extraordinarily clever movement and the feeling of sweet delight and satisfaction is expressed. Then, the bee flies away leaving us still marvelling; the actor's hand and fingers, and much more than these the eyes, tell of the distance covered by the bee. The soul of an opening flower and its life in its native setting are pictured vividly and we are left enthralled [9].

---

9 Even when the lotus is not directly described, as when it has only to be alluded

Similarly when the actor translates into gesture vocabulary the word mountain by a descriptive process that recalls to mind its outline, movements of the eyes and other facial expressions generate space and envisage the immense proportions of the mountain (particularly the height) and register the feeling of wonder or awe of the spectator. In

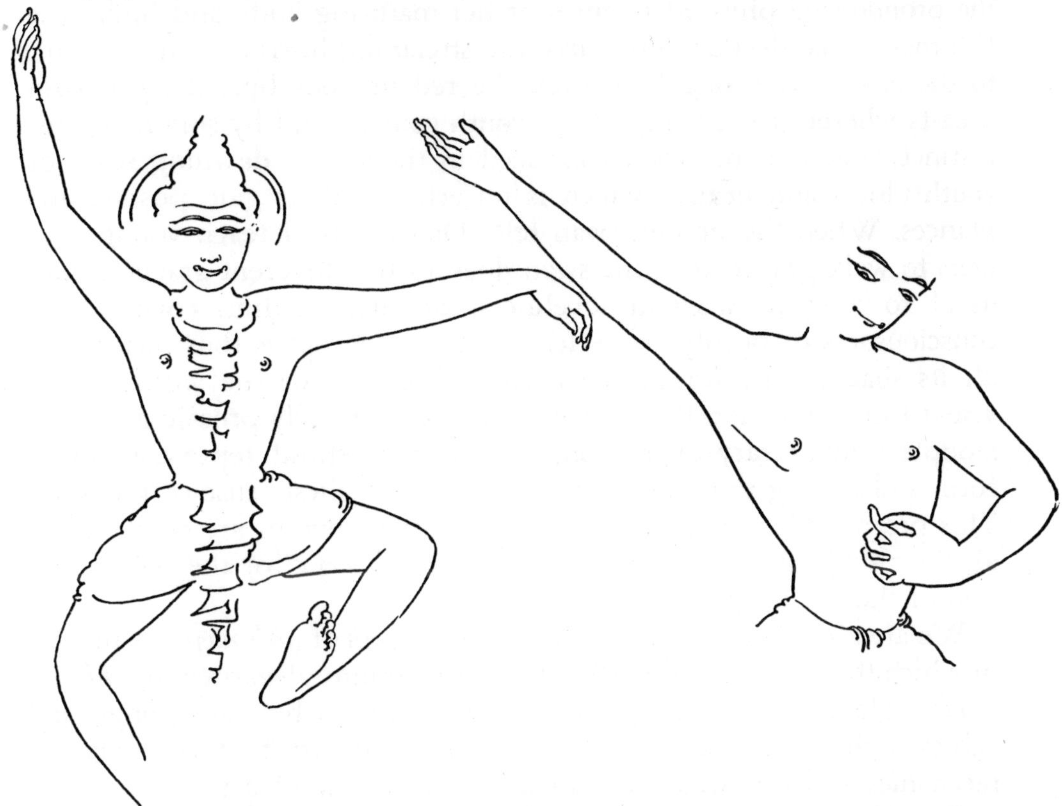

Fig. 28. A movement in expressing "I" in pride and egoism. Fig. 29. Conceit.

the case of an elephant its peculiar habit of frequently moving its ear-lobes and swaying the trunk are imitated, re-inforced by the elephant glances and gait. A lion or tiger is impressively visualised more by the facial expressions, the cold, steely look, the open mouth from which the projecting tongue quivers hungry for blood, the general distortion of the face suggestive of the animal and the pose of the beast of prey

to as in "lotus-eyes", "lotus-garland" etc., all the movements up to the introduction of the bee episode are done in full.

ready to spring on its victim. Here it is primarily an attitude that is employed. A slightly inward-bent palm indicates a snake but the movement of the snake with the raised hood (traced by the hand bent at the elbow) and the "snake-glance" suggest the reptilian form and characteristic (Pl. IX fig. 3). "Youthful maid" would be rendered by describing the pronounced physical features of her maturing body and limbs, the full-moon face decked with curls, the streaming lustrous hair that falls to the ankles, the long lotus eyes, the red luscious lips, the full firm breasts wherein the spring-tide of youth courses, and by simulating the instinctive actions of women induced in them by a dawning sense of youthfulness and beauty, which is reflected in their gait, posture and glances. When the golden swan tells Damayanti "I teach young maidens to walk gracefully", the swan does all the different graceful gaits usual to women, wherein loveliness, dignity, rhythm, coyness and consciousness of beauty are reflected. Every concept is thus pictured in all its shades. The implications and suggestions of the word assume visual forms. Further, things that would be extremely prosaic and commonplace in literary expression, assume, in gestural representation, a form and feeling that are truly poetic in the highest sense of the term. This process whereby form, feeling and inner rhythm are conveyed in all their suble shadings is called "*Padārthābhinaya*" or the representation of the meaning of words.

We are already anticipating the entire process of *abhinaya*—a process in which the actor co-ordinates different mediums of expression, *bhāva, mudra,* glances and other gestures with drum rhythms and song—and achieves this with skill and ease. That is an art that conceals the mechanics and the toils involved in the technique of art.

The Kathakaḷi language of hand gestures is comprehensive and complete; there is hardly anything that it cannot tell and the telling is always vivid and dramatic and soars to supreme heights of persuasive eloquence [10]. A language so austere, full of ceremonious beauty and

---

10 "...an art that transcends words, something that is silent, a silence that is punctuated only by gestures... is so delicate, so subtle, so intimate that it is in the heart and life of the people and cannot be commercialised. It is a beautiful pantomimic art that can portray every emotion and every gesture of human life in countless ways, by the raising of an eye-brow, turning of the knees, raising of the shoulders and

infinite suggestiveness as this, needs no aid, either of the spoken word or of painted curtains or scenes. More than anything else, this miraculous art of gestures befittingly appears as the language of the gods. Its vivid flashes transport us into that "land of dreams where the deepest essence of things instead of being blurred in twilight, flashes forth in vivid clarity".

This traditional and divine language, being a learned one, cannot easily be cheapened and vulgarised like common speech in daily chatter. Consequently it remains, like the gods themselves, ever fresh and vibrant.

---

movement of the hands and fingers." (Mrs. Sarojini Naidu on Kathakaḷi. *Advance*. Calcutta. Feb. 11, 1936).

"At any rate the *mudrās* of Kathakaḷi as an independent language do not require the support of the spoken word." Georgette Boner.

"How mighty is a gesture, convincing, exciting, lasting." Herder.

CHAPTER X

NAYANĀBHINAYA

The significant function of the eye movements in the communication of an idea or mood has already been noticed. The expressive qualities of the eyes were fully cultivated and exploited by the Keraḷa artists. The *Cākkyārs,* to whose marvellous histrionic talents reference has been made elsewhere, had specialised in this branch of *āṅgikâbhinaya.* In doing so, they raised *Nayanâbhinaya* to a new level by employing it as the dominant and sometimes the sole means of *abhinaya.* The traditions of the *Cākkyārs* and the standard of their achievement in this field are well reflected in the incident described below.

A *Cākkyār* artist was describing the occasion of Draupadi's [1] wedding. This princess was to wed from the assembled kings the one, who succeeded in shooting down by the neck, the fast revolving figure of a bird, that was fixed on top of a high post. This intriguing target eluded every marksman of repute, until at last, the greatest of all who ever wielded a bow, Arjuna, with one un-erring shot brought it down to the ground by severing its head. The *Cākkyār* artist was rendering this incident exclusively by eye-expressions. The fast revolving bird set on high, the well-aimed shot, the deadly hit and the movements of the collapsing bird, all these were told by the eyes. The exposition was masterly and superb; it thrilled everyone except the *Naṅgyār,* the lady musician, who was keeping time on the cymbals. The *Cākkyār* noticed her dissatisfaction. The puzzled artist later enquired of her the reason for this. She said that his acting was unconvincing. She then demonstrated it correctly. She went through every stage of the incident and did as well as the *Cākkyār.* But, when the wounded bird fell (the *Cākkyār* had closed the death incident of the bird at this stage) she proceeded a little further. The bird fell and then rolled over two or three times, flapping and fluttering its feeble wings in agony and then lay dead and motionless. This more than anything else emphasises how

[1] The heroine of the epic *Mahâbhārata.*

much tradition and convention rest on observation and experience and that mere virtuosity, however perfect, was never considered a sufficient artistic expedient.

How Rāvaṇa the demon king of Lanka, viewing Sīta for the first time was stupefied and ravished by her loveliness, how avidly he drank through his eyes her heavenly beauty, are depicted in one of the great pieces of the *Cākkyār's* repertoire [2]. The lighting of a fire, its leaping, rising, flames, the moths that are attracted to it, their erratic, frenzied, movements around the fire, and then each one falling and perishing in the flames [3], these form another effective scene acted by eye movements alone.

In this respect too, the Kathakaḷi artists have largely borrowed from and imitated the *Cākkyārs.* The following incident [4], associated with the remarkable artistic career of Kunju Pillai, tells how closely Kathakaḷi artists have kept pace with the *Cākkyārs* in the matter of *abhinaya* by eyes. He was on one occasion playing the role of Rāvana in "*Rāvaṇa Vijayám*" in which the demon king waylays the celestial maiden Rambha, pleads his love and when rejected, ravishes her by force. In this particular show the role of Rambha was taken by a woman actor [5]. Rāvaṇa urged his love repeatedly and ardently, only to be rejected. In the very act of urging his desire, the actor became as it were, a living flame of passion. In a final effort, his eyes, with all their artistry and seductiveness were turned on Rambha. They became the sole armoury of his passion. The eyes beseeched and implored; she resisted. Again his eyes called and caressed her; they looked too enchanting and ravishing. Rambha still resisted. A third time the eyes pleaded with animating passion, setting in motion a current of irresistable temptation; those looks were destructively seductive and inflaming. In a split second Rambha flew into Rāvaṇa's arms and embraced him in burning passion. The woman in her succumbed to the call; everything else was forgotten—the stage, the audience and the drama. Before the

---

2 *Pānadrūpa rasāyana.*

3 *Agni-śalabha.*

4 I am indebted to Kunju Kurup, the doyen of the Kathakaḷi stage, for this information.

5 Women actors are not welcomed on the Kathakaḷi stage. But there have been one or two exceptions.

gaping crowd could recover from its stupefaction, the woman actor regained her balance and like a stricken gazelle she disappeared through the sombre causeway of shadows into the darkness of the night, never again to return to the stage.

The degree of skill attained in eye-expressions was so high that one of the Kathakaḷi dramatists even went to the length of putting into the text of a play a situation where the hero had to reflect in one eye anger and in the other sorrow. Acting exclusively by eye-movements is no easy task; not all artists can do this. It is left to the skill and ingenuity of individual artists to incorporate such actions to enrich their presentation. Emotion and feeling are first reflected in the eyes, the feeling indicated by the eyes is then expressed by the *aṅgas*. This principle of *nāṭya* assigns to the eye-expressions a supreme role. Watching a Kathakaḷi performance we easily realise that the starting point of all *āṅgikâbhinaya* is the eye-expression and in many instances the actor first "looks" the *pada* or song—*nōkki-kaṇuka*; he takes the visual impression of the scene or object referred to, his eyes register his reactions or reflect the *bhāva* dominant in the stanza he renders. Then only he begins to interpret in gestures.

CHAPTER XI

RASĀBHINAYA OR DELINEATION OF MOODS AND SENTIMENTS

The primary "category" in the Sanskrit drama is *rasa,* translated as aesthetic flavour or sentiment, and a drama is judged by the skill with which the *rasa* or *rasas* are delineated. The function of the various modes of *abhinaya* such as make-up, costumes, hand gestures, movements and glances is to create the appropriate moods and sentiments [1].

Sanskrit rhetoricians and aesthetes have studied the emotions and their subtle shadings in detail and have catalogued them with meticulous care. The principal aesthetic emotions are nine. They are *Śṛingāra* (the erotic sentiment), *Vīra* (the heroic), *Karuṇa* (the pathetic), *Adbhuta* (the sentiment of wonder), *Raudra* (the furious), *Hāsya* (the comic), *Bhayānaka* (the fearful), *Bhībatsa* (the disgusting) and *Śānta* (peace or tranquillity). On the Kathakaḷi stage all these moods are delineated with great care and skill. Every mood or sentiment is handled like a jewel with cunning craftsmanship and care. Above all, the reverence, tenderness and dignity with which they are treated make the depiction of every mood a unique experience.

A picture of this process is attempted in the following close-up view of a love scene, though words can but poorly convey the subtle shades of an emotion. *Śṛingāra* (the sentiment of love) is referred to as the

---

[1] "Love is an emotion, *Śṛingāra* is the sentiment (*rasa*). The emotions believed to be existing in the actors develop into sentiment in the spectator. A sentiment is different from ordinary emotions, it is generic and disinterested while emotion is individual and immediately personal. An emotion is painful or pleasant, a sentiment is impersonal joy, characteristic of contemplation of the supreme being by the adept, a bliss which is absolutely without personal feeling."

A sentiment is produced by the union of determinants (*vibhāvas*), consequents (*anubhāvas*) and excitants (*uddīpanas*). The essential element in the production of sentiment is the dominant emotion (*sthāyī-bhāva*) like love in *Śṛingāra* and that should persist amidst transitory feelings (*vyabhicharis*). The transitory feelings are many, such as discouragement, weakness, anxiety, joy, shame, impatience, inconstancy, indignation, etc. *The Sanskrit Drama* by Keith.

Ādi or primary *rasa* and also as *Rāja-rasa,* king among the *rasas.* The sumptuousness, the delicacy and the refinement with which it is treated on the Kathakaḷi stage are an adequate recognition of the pre-eminence of this *rasa.* Love scenes are of sufficiently long duration; the text may consist of only 15 or 20 lines but the rendering might take an hour or more. Unlike *Raudra* where speed intensifies tension and dramatic effect, *Śṛingāra* acquires dramatic beauty by a more leisurely treatment. Seized by the erotic mood, the mind does not easily get detached; there is no hurry and the demands of love are imperious; it has to be caressed and coaxed to yield its pleasures. No weariness overtakes the devotee; his hunger only grows with what it feeds on. The Kathakaḷi stage accords full recognition to this essential nature of the love emotion. Love scenes are therefore *Patiñjāṭṭams* [2] (literally leisurely or slow-moving dance). The texts of these love scenes are highly poetic and romantic. The glances, postures, gait and facial expressions employed are so sweet, graceful and suggestive of the animating emotion that the actors look like embodiments of radiant love.

As the curtain is drawn aside we see the hero and the heroine in a very tender mood and in a lovely pose (Pl. X). The very pose conveys the feeling that they are melting into a state of "incoherent unconsciousness of their isolated selves". The left hand of the male is protectingly, caressingly, placed over the crown of the female and the right one enfolds her in tender embrace; the female clings to him with creeper-like intimacy and grace. The position they have taken is deeply related to their mood; they are slightly turned towards each other so as fully to attract each other's glances. They are gazing at each other and unsatiated, they continue to gaze. Their glances are activated by the deepest of passions and desires; they are the outpourings of the soul in its most exalted moments. The repeated raising of their arched eyebrows, moving like rhythmic waves, betoken repeated glances

---

2 The *Nāyaka* and *Nāyaki* (hero and heroine), *Upa-nāyaka* and *Upa-nayaki* (secondary characters, male and female), are introduced in love scenes, *Patiñjāttams,* which are fully utilised to develop *Śṛingāra bhāva* (love emotion). In certain plays these *patiñjāttams* occur more than once. What is important to remember in this connection is that the *patiñjāttam* is not merely a love scene—love scenes are found in almost every drama—but a significant convention on the Kathakaḷi stage just as much as the *Tira-nōkku* (curtain-look), *Niṇam* (blood scenes) etc.

—which as it were, are garlands of glances—with which they adorn each other.

These rhythmic movements seem indeed to symbolise the rising waves of the mood that possesses them. And those long, lingering, glances that tremble at the very suggestion of an interruption, the melting glances, the steady gaze of the hero, the timid, bashful, glances of the heroine that burn with suppressed passion, the ardour and even the subdued exuberance of the male contrasting vividly with the delicate restraint of the female, the many eloquent and lovely postures, the sweet and gentle movements that suggest the urge of youthful passion, all these embody a world of blissful intimacy and tenderness. One would love to float endlessly on the gently swelling and rocking waves of this ocean of happiness.

The situation may be one where king Naḷa and queen Damayanti, who had fallen deeply in love and had been pining for each other for long and in secret, meet in the royal garden for the first time, overcoming the many obstacles to their union. One can easily imagine the strength and sweep of the emotion surging within them. The king now finds that he has to overcome one more foe, the timid bashfulness of his beloved. He employs all the sweet and subtle strategy of love's game to overcome her shyness. At last, she begins to melt and beams on him (Pl. XI). He leads her gently to view the intoxicating beauties of the royal garden where spring runs riot. The flowering plants, the clinging creepers, the humming and honey-sucking bees, the pairing swans and the sweet singing *kokils* (Indian cuckoo) calling to their mates, inflame the lovers. Then they fall into a reminiscent mood. They begin to share those intimacies, the poignant hopes and fears of the days when they longed for each other, suffering in secret and not knowing the other's heart or how to reach it, until they found a god-sent friend in the Golden Swan [See App. III]. The scene lasts for nearly two hours during which love lives, thrives and thrills. Its varying shades are delicately and winsomely expressed. The subtle magic of the presentation leads us into the very heart of poesy and romance. The emotional delight remains unsullied by any "degradation into the sphere of individual willing" [3].

---

3 The learned technique of stylized gestures is in itself a guarantee against a too realistic effect and impression.

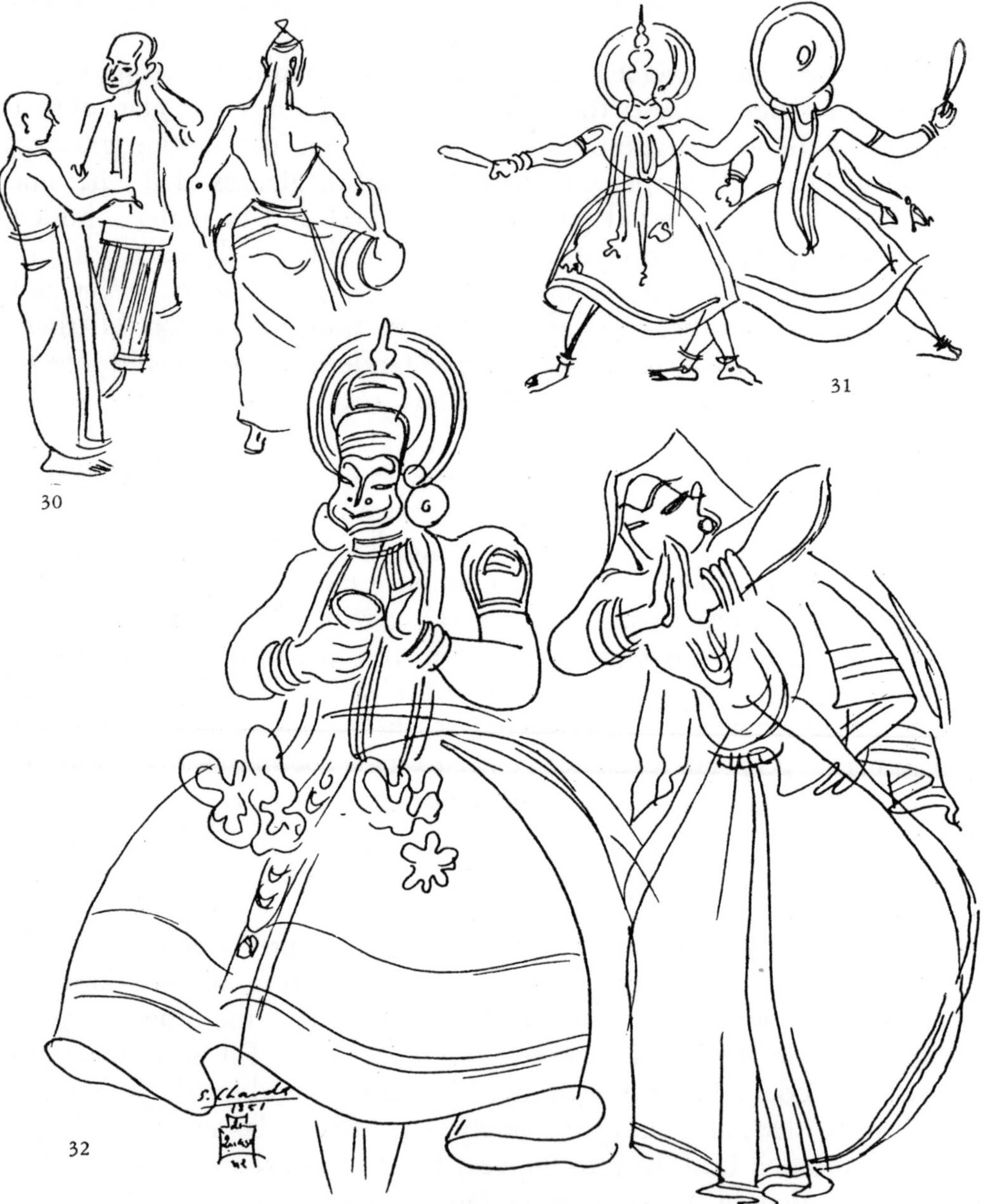

Fig. 30. Orchestra: drummers and singer.
Fig. 31. A fight.
Fig. 32. Naḷa and Damayanti.

If the drama be a different one like *Rāvaṇa Vijayam* or *Kīcaka Vadha,* depicting *Sṛingārābhāsa* (agressive and unrighteous love), we see this passion in its violent sweep reaching another climax. How skilfully and persuasively Rāvaṇa and Kīcaka express their ardent, burning passion for the unwilling and unyielding Rambha and Sairandhri! How infinitely seductive and tempting the male can become in an attempt to decoy and seduce the female! With what insistency the pursuit is kept up with varying tactics and how over-bearing and relentless he can be when the female rejects him and how distressingly desperate and embarrassing the situation can be for the female! The expression of *Śṛingāra Bhāva* varies with the age and type of the characters. The love emotion of heroes like Arjuna, Naḷa and Krisṇa, termed as *Vīra-Sṛingāra,* is in tone and texture different from that of *Śānta-śringāra* (calm and tranquil manifestation of love in *sātvic* types), as in the case of Dharmaputra [4], or from *Bhībatsa-śṛingāra* (coarse and vulgar love) of Śūrpanakha or Simhika.

In most of the plays, the philosophic and moral theme embedded in the story, is the eternal conflict that goes on between the powers of Good and Evil and the deserved triumph of the former against odds however heavy and formidable. This conflict is, as it were, the centre piece of most of the dramas and a good deal of dramatic craftsmanship is expended on it. The climax is reached in the elaborate scene of challenge and fight, the tense struggle and the annihilation of the wicked. It is in this context that *Vīra* (the heroic) and more particularly *Raudra* (fury) are developed fully and delineated with such superb mastery on the Kathakaḷi stage.

The very entry of a fierce character is in itself capable of creating the impression of a world reeking with uncontrollable forces, a world of hatred, revenge, fury and blood hunger. This ceremonious entry called *Tira-nōkku* (literally curtain-look) which seems to be a peculiar but impressive stage device, deserves special treatment and is therefore dealt with elsewhere. In this section an attempt is made to describe a scene of conflict in which the climax is reached and is intended to indicate how the sentiment of fury is built up to its peak.

As a preliminary to the actual scene of conflict, *Paḍa-purappaḍal* is

[4] The eldest of the Pandava brothers of the *Mahabharata* and a saintly character.

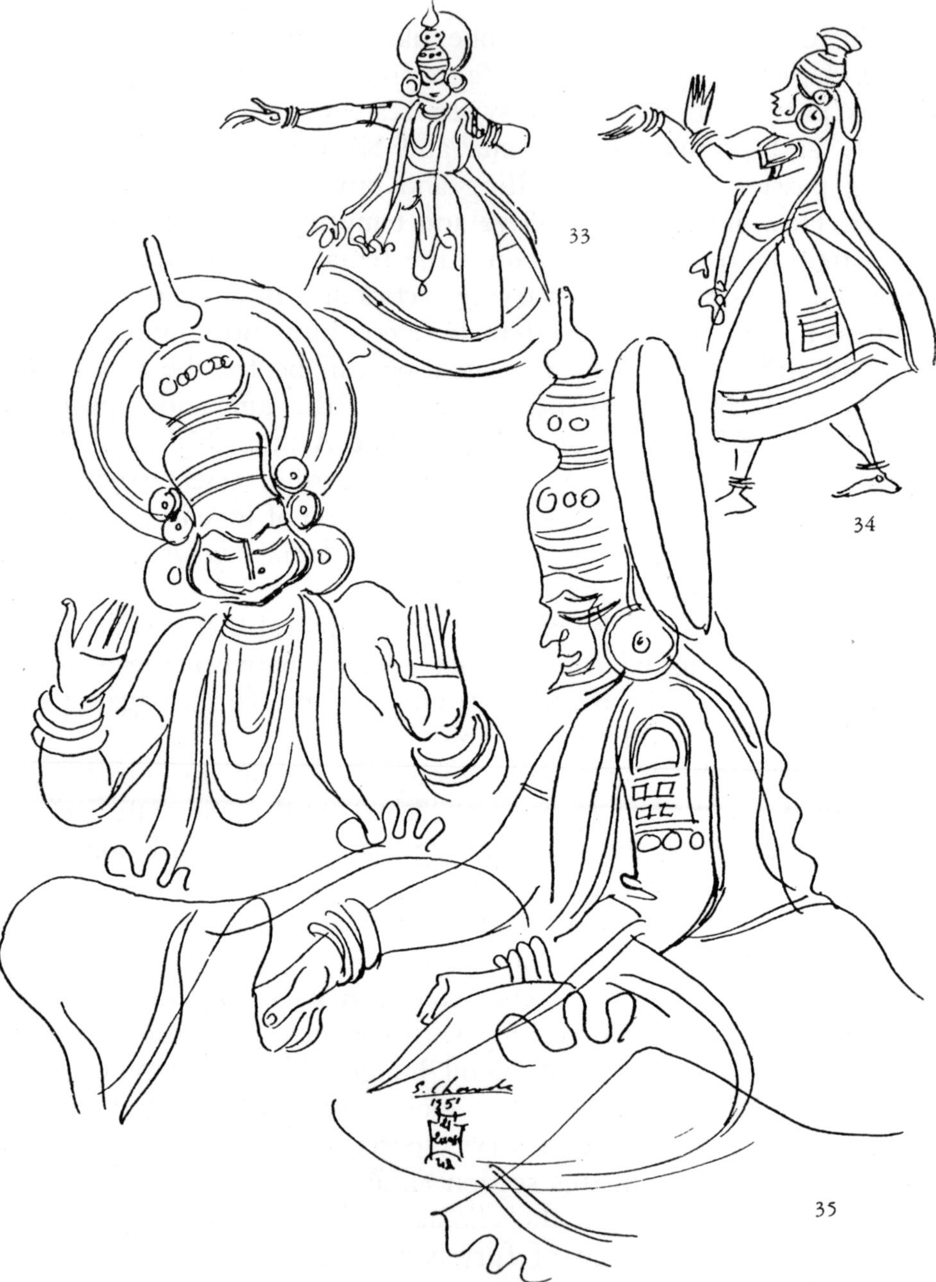

Fig. 33. Nala.
Fig. 34. Kriṣṇa.
Fig. 35. Naḷa and Pushkara playing dice, at which Nala loses and forfeits his kingdom.
Sketches of Figs. 30-35 by S. Chavda, Bombay.

staged; it means military preparations, such as inspection of various weapons in the armoury, testing their efficiency, formation of the forces of attack, etc. This is done with such ingenuity that the sharpened sword gleams and seemingly cuts the fingers, delicately caressing its edge. The great bow is so well-strung (no factual stringing takes place) that the impression of the tension created abides with the spectator. The prancing steeds are harnessed to the chariot with all the loving care of the master for his fine steeds and then they are driven with great breath-taking speed. Sometimes the troops (consisting only of two or three attendants) are put into a formation march in which they show off their physical prowess and mime encounters.

Another preliminary is the *Pōṛ-viḷi* or the challenge which takes an important place in the depiction of some memorable fights, such as that between Bhīma and Duśśāsana, a very spectacular and stirring incident. Bhīma is in a frenzy of anger which is mounting every minute. He stands on the stage on a wooden mortar towering over the squatting audience, brandishing his club and challenging his formidable foe Duśśāsana, who approaches from the opposite end of the auditorium (generally the open ground). The latter emerges from darkness preceded by flaming torches, uttering deafening war cries and counter challenges: the very embodiment of Fury (Pl. XIII). A verbal exchange follows (of course all gestured) wherein each one belittles the other, heaps insults and describes in very menacing terms the dire fate awaiting his opponent. How much more biting and provocative contempt and slight can be when gestured, can easily be realised during these encounters. By reason of such bitter provocations they become possessed by greater fury. The drumming is spirited and rises to a transport of passion, but the war cries rise over it like the rumblings of a monsoon thunder-storm. Thus the scene mounts to the climax with cumulative force.

The battles are fought out as combats between the principal characters, as perhaps was the practice in olden days, when, despite the armies, the leaders came to close grips and the outcome decided the fate of the battle (Pl. XIV and fig. 31, p. 86). This is also in accordance with the texts which describe the two principals as engaging themselves in combat in the midst of a general battle. These two, aided by the tremendous din of the drums, the quick and massive steppings, the provocative gestures, the pursuits and the retreats, create the illusion of a whole war in the savage heat of their conflict. On the narrow span of the stage they seem to cover a vast space in the course of the fight, so intense and dynamic are their movements. The combatants go through the various stages of the fight. Weapons like the club, sword, bow and arrow are used, but when the fight grows in intensity and fury they discard them and engage themselves in hand to hand fights and with mighty blows try to destroy each other. The pounding drums release a tempest of sound waves; the leaping, blazing fire, the whirls and sweeps, the wild sway of the skirts and scarves, the cries and mockings, the massive movements and giant strides, all these set in motion a hurricane of frenzy and we are swept off into the very vortex of this maelstrom. We shudder and yet remain captivated and thrilled.

A fight between a *Pacca* character and a *Katti* or a Red-beard is clearly indicative of the contrast in the expression of violence and fury on the part of these types. The heroism of the former has an austerity of passion, a dignity and an inherent sense of invincibility, while that of the latter, however great and impressive, is flamboyant and boisterous, like a totally undisciplined mountain torrent. When two demons meet in conflict it is hell-fire let loose. The spectacular and emotional value of the fights on the Kathakaḷi stage is very considerable; they are cast in so massive a mould as to excite the sense of the marvellous.

From such savage, monstrous, fights to bloody scenes (where a blood-like liquid is used) is only a logical step to reach the very height of an emotional crescendo. Such scenes are staged to illustrate graphically the mythological incident of the slaying of the demon Hiranya-Kasipu by Nara Simha— the Man-lion incarnation of Vishnu—and the slaying of Duśśāsana by Bhīma. Wrongs and crimes too deep for words to express are avenged by this gruesome, awful rite. In the slaying of Duśśāsana, Bhīma the victor rips open the abdomen of the fallen foe. His face is contorted by demoniac fury, his hands and mouth are dyed in the warm blood of the slain enemy. The reckless frenzy and the consuming wrath then cool by degrees. Consider the villany and the treachery involved in being dispossessed of a kingdom by deceit practised at a game of dice; Draupadi, the queen, dragged by Duśśāsana by her hair from her seclusion, driven, insulted and then disrobed in public (Pl. XII); the king and brother princes disarmed, derided, enslaved and driven out into the wilds to perish of hunger and thirst. What wonder, if Draupadi, in the very depth of her misery, should take a vow, that her unbound tresses shall so remain, until oiled and dressed in the blood of that black villain Duśśāsana, who was responsible for her misery and dishonour? For thirteen long years the sight of the unbound tresses and the utter miseries of exile, kept alive in Bhīma, a monstrous rage and thirst for revenge till he became vengeance incarnate. For such colossal tensions blood alone is the solvent as we soon realise when we watch this drama. Similarly it would be dramatically disastrous to stage the story of Prahlāda without depicting the scene where the Man-lion slays the demon Hiranya by ripping open his abdomen and laps up the gushing blood. The terrific fury of the avenging Man-lion and the shrinking horror of death that seizes the demon as he is clawed and torn [5], is an intensely terrifying scene and one vital to the drama. The texts have described in detail all these incidents. The omission of this scene, on which alone depends the climax of passion in this play, would leave it a very tame and undramatic affair. The Kathakaḷi stage does not pass over such situations; it has developed an adequate technique to express convincingly the most violent sweep of passion. A representation of the horrid and the ghastly [6], in an artistic way, gives to the drama a completeness which otherwise it would miss.

Much more eerie and gruesome to behold is the scene of Śūrpanakha's tragedy. This ogress, in the guise of a charming damsel, makes love to Lakṣmaṇa and having failed to impress the prince, she tries to abduct him, whereupon, instead of killing the ogress (for slaying a woman is unrighteous), he chops off her nose and ears. The

5 Medieval Indian sculpture has several striking examples representing this scene, notably at Elura, Candpur (Jhansi) and Devāngaṇa (Sirohi). See appendix II for the story of Prahlada.

6 "The savage and the product of civilization can easily become one under the impulse of a sufficiently powerful agent." *Nijinsky* by C. W. Beaumont.

This was proved by Nijinsky in the ballet *Le Sacre du Printemps* which attempted to show the birth of human emotion in a primitive age and successfully created an extraordinary and savage atmosphere.

"The contemplation of the horrid or sordid or disgusting by an artist, is the necessary negative aspect of the impulse toward the pursuit of beauty... The negative is the more importunate." *The Sacred Wood* by T. S. Eliot.

"The devil is the other face of God"—Havelock Ellis.

succeeding scene (her flight back to Lanka) is *Niṇaṃ* (blood display). We see a loathsome *rākṣasi,* all black, streaming with blood, howling in pain and rage, emerging from the darkness of night (she approaches from the opposite end of the auditorium, making her way through the audience) like the very spirit of evil let loose, and preceded by the lurid glow of torches which, fed with resin powder, shoot out angry tongues of flame. The effect is accentuated by the monstrous, insistent, drumming. We are terror struck to the marrow of our bones and disgust, utter disgust, for the weird spectacle seizes us. But then a strange unearthly power keeps us riveted to our seat and our mind and eyes remain glued to the scene. *Bhayānaka* (utter fear) and *Bhībatsa* (utter disgust) are graphically depicted and produce an abiding impression. Such blood-displays are announced beforehand and children, the craven-hearted and pregnant women are dissuaded from witnessing such frightful scenes.

In this connection it is relevant to remember that these blood scenes are described in the legends themselves and are not an invention of the Keraḷa stage. Their enactment is necessitated by an artistic and dramatic need. It is not the outcome of a morbid mentality, or merely the memory of the blood feuds of the Keraḷa chieftains [7], as some argue. It would be as well to recall here that the builders of the Keraḷa stage are the Nambūtiri Brahmins, a highly refined and sensitive class whose life even in these days of general decadence, reminds one of the great peace and spiritual atmosphere of the Vedic age. Steeped as they are in Aryan traditions and Sanskrit learning it is not easy to believe that they connived at what may appear an anti-social spectacle of barbarism

---

7 This slaying and drinking the blood of the Titan is not cannibalism. The meaning of the symbol is explained by Dr. Coomaraswamy in his great book *Hinduism and Buddhism,* lest we forget its meaning altogether. "He in whom we were imprisoned is now our prisoner; as our Inner Man he is submerged in and hidden by our Outer Man. It is now his turn to become the Dragon-slayer; and in this war of God with Titan, now fought within us where we are 'at war with ourselves', his victory and resurrection will be also ours, *if* we know Who we are. It is now for him to drink us dry, for us to be his wine." Again: "You and I are the psycho-physical prison and Constrictor in whom the First has been swallowed up that "we" might be at all. For as we are repeatedly told, the Dragon-slayer devours his victim, swallows him up and drinks him dry, and by this Eucharistic meal he takes possession of the first-born Dragon's treasure and powers and becomes what he was." *Hinduism and Buddhism*—Philosophical Library. New York.

and morbidity, held to be opposed to the practices of the classical Sanskrit stage with which they were only too well acquainted. In all probability they followed an older stage tradition, daring to convert such scenes into powerful artistic entities vital to the emotional or *rasa* aspect of the drama. The *Nāṭyasāstra* states that the sentiment of fury (*Raudra*) is aroused by deeds terrible and fearful such as cutting,

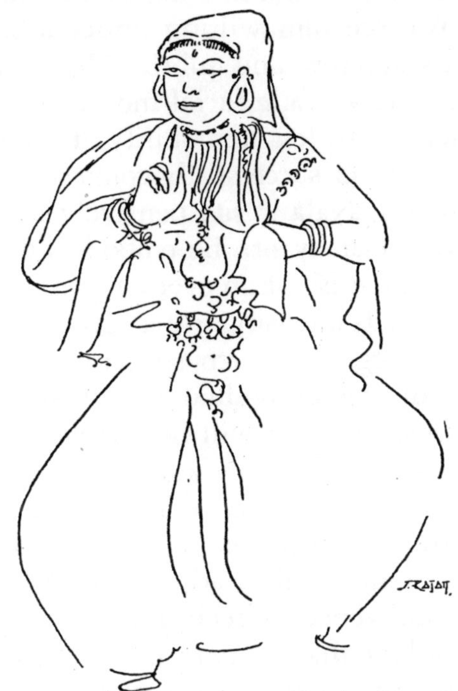

Fig. 36. Pūtana arriving on the sly to poison Kriṣṇa.

mutilation, piercing and cutting off the head. Therefore it is difficult to believe that the *Nāṭyasāstra* prohibits display of blood on the stage. The climax of the passion built up with such cumulative force, as in the slaying of Duśśāsana or the destruction of Hiranya, can alone be reached by actually staging this vital situation in all its grim reality. This is an instance where convention and realism meet, but realism here is but a magic wand that serves to complete the hypnotic spell.

A feeling or mood finds expression in a tense or relaxed flexion of the body, which in turn is transformed into the equivalent of the mood or feeling. When the ogress Pūtana in the guise of a charming damsel enters the royal nursery at Gōkul to poison the divine child Krișṇa [8], the suspicious glances, the halting, light, foot-steps and the cautious bodily attitudes make her the very embodiment of sly deception (Fig. 36, p. 93). When king Rugmāṅgada [9], after all his pleadings had failed, is faced with the inescapable demand of his mistress Mōhini to slay his son, we find him seated in a state of extreme dejection under the weight of an unutterable grief. We see him wilting under a severe mental strain. Here the movements are few and subtle. Here pose or posture is of primary importance; a few subtle facial movements of eyes and lips, an inclination of the head, a listless immobility of the hands, these express an anguish and despair never successfully conveyed by speech. Similarly, when the love-lorn king Naḷa [10] sits pensively in the seclusion of his garden, brooding over Damayanti, he embodies the very pain of frustrated passion. All the anguish of an ever-deepening but unfulfilled love almost self-destroying in its intensity, and a feeling of absolute loneliness and helplessness are suggested. Such supreme moments of the drama are the focal point of the individual actor's skill in *sātvikābhinaya.* Mere technical proficiency alone will not create the desired effect.

The great drama is here and now and all around us; so the actor is enjoined to observe the movements of the world. The life of a lotus, its blossoming and the closing of its petals at night-fall, as depicted by the actor, are not mere mechanical adjustments of palms and fingers. All these have to be enlivened by feeling or flavour. Kunju Kurup, the well-known actor, told me that his *guru* made him live the life of a lotus; from dawn till sun-set he was required to watch the lotus pond carefully to absorb the "atmosphere". This was not intended to imitate nature in the manner of a realist. The great masters were never content with mere technical perfection in their disciples. They strove to generate in them *svānubhava* (self-experience). This is an instance from the life of a well known actor which will help to repudiate the idea that the canons of this great art are taught and transmitted to disciples merely as a rigid hieratic code, confining them to a highly perfected mechanical

8 Salvation of Pūtana. See appendix I for the incident.

9 *Rugmāṅgada Carita.*

10 *Naḷa Carita.*

drill. Kathakaḷi, though a traditional art, is—or was until recently—a living, growing, art form. Hence the insistence on self-experience.

In the drama *Rāvaṇa Vijayam* there is a remarkable love scene in which Rāvaṇa makes love to his spouse Mandodari. The scene is known as *"Kamala-daḷa"* after the first word of the relevant song. Generally this is considered as a test piece for an actor's ability to delineate the love emotion. Impassioned, Rāvaṇa takes Mandōdari on his lap and feels her charms with intoxicating effects; a very difficult and delicate situation for an actor who is expected to warm up but not to burn, to get intoxicated without going into a frenzy. In the very swing and sweep of passion there should be inherent a delicate sense of restraint that will engender poignancy of feeling: it should not allow itself to be shattered by its very force. No amount of instructional training could achieve this supremely austere standard in the pupil. The great master who loved his art and his gifted pupil decided to go the whole hog [11]. This master had a youthful and charming daughter and she was asked to play the part of Mandōdari. The young pupil was at that period of life when every youth is highly romantic, and more particularly so in this instance where both were in love with each other, unknown to the teacher. The pupil was asked to take the young lady on his lap and then interpret the song. What could be more intriguing and intensely alive? The youth afire with love and burning with passion at the physical proximity of his beloved and the young lady finding herself in such close intimacy with her lover; while the formidable teacher and father demanded all attention for the instruction and interpretation. Their limbs ached with passion, yet they had to hold themselves in restraint. The restraint accentuated the tension and made every movement and gesture surcharged and more eloquent. The whole body became a living flame, glowing with love and by the very restraint imposed, the artist attained a freedom from himself. As Dr. Coomaraswamy observes, "It is the re-collected man and not the excited man who can either make or do well". An art so perfected is passed on to successive generations and not a mere convention or tradition that has lost touch with life. Not every teacher and pupil go through such direct experience.

---

11 I am indebted to Kuñju Kurup for the information.

Apart from the love scene, which occurs in almost every play, as one of its vital phases, in dramas like *Naḷa-carita* and *Rukmini Swayamvara, Śṛingāra* appears as the chief sentiment which is delineated. In *Kucela-carita* and *Rugmāṅgada, bhakti* (piety) and *karuṇa* (pathos) are the chief moods depicted, while in *Kirātārjuniya* we have an impressive picture of the heroic mood.

Humour finds expression in almost every play. This happens especially during the conversational interludes which entertain and excite laughter. But the comic as such is delineated in certain dramas: by the carpenter in *Baka-vadha,* the *Vaṇṇān* (washerman) in *Lavaṇāsura-vadha* and by the *mohut* in *Kaṃsa-vadha.*

Kathakaḷi artists have an astonishing command over the entire range of emotions and the facility with which they change from one mood to another reveals that extraordinary mastery. In *Prahlāda carita* the smouldering fury of the Man-lion, dripping with the blood of the slain demon, changes to loving kindness towards the boy devotee Prahlāda: this is a very touching scene. So too Bhīma after killing Duśśāsana and drinking his blood, glides down to a mood of tenderness at the sight of his long-suffering wife, whose wrongs he had just avenged.

Moods like love, delight, anger, displeasure, pity, pathos, pain, contempt, hatred and the like are universal and their expressions are fundamentally and unmistakably the same everywhere. As every thought, idea or feeling expressed in the drama is related to some mood, it is but natural that the depiction of a mood or sentiment will not fail to evoke the impression desired to be communicated to the audience. *Bhāvābhinaya* or *rasābhinaya* is therefore a basic language that is capable of being understood by all. In a limited way its expressions are well understood even by the animals. It is the vividness and eloquence with which feelings and moods are expressed that contribute so very largely to the intelligibility and impressiveness of Kathakaḷi *abhinaya.* The passages quoted in appendix I and II record the visual impressions received by two European spectators, totally unacquainted with the language of the songs or the complex technique of gestures. Their testimony shows to what extent the highly developed *bhāvābhinaya* of Kathakaḷi raises it to the level of a universal art notwithstanding its conventional language of gestures.

CHAPTER XII

ABHINAYA: A GENERAL SURVEY

An actor is judged not by his extensive knowledge of the various *mudras* and movements alone; "the mere excellence of his drill" is not in itself considered a distinction. Many a reputation has been wrecked by the fatal verdict of "lacks in *bhañgi*"; *bhañgi* is grace or beauty. It is "the sheen of order"; it makes us forget the mechanics, the toil and the effort involved in the technique and makes it appear spontaneous. Mere technique without *bhañgi* is not only ineffective and artistically sterile, but is also a monstrosity. When the movements lack grace, they look abnormal, affected and exaggerated. In the absence of grace, that happy state of visual dreaming which the drama should induce in the spectator, is either not engendered or, if existent, is shattered. The bad artist (non-adept) is a sinner [1] and his art is tainted. Every dramatic element in Kathakaḷi has been rigorously subjected to this major test of *bhañgi*. The many changes brought about by the various schools of reform known as *Veṭṭam, Kallatikōṭan, Kapliṅgaṭan* and *Koṭṭa* were efforts to ensure the pre-eminence of *bhañgi*.

Another feature welcomed in an actor and considered a distinction, nay, even a necessary quality, is *manōdharma* (imaginative faculty and its appropriate application). The actor who does not possess *manōdharma,* which is a reflection or measure of his intellectual refinement, has not attained maturity. On the Kathakaḷi stage the actor is given ample opportunities to display his skill and imaginative faculties. By subtle and pleasing variations, the accomplished actor makes the presentation of the same thing ever fresh. The actor with *manōdharma* adds

1 Sage Narada had a feeling that his mastery over music was incomparable. Legend says that Krisṇa once took Narada to Naraka (purgatory) where they found innumerable deformed and maimed beings howling in pain. Krisṇa enquired of them what sin they had committed to deserve this misery. They replied "we have done no wrong, we are *ragās* (melody modes) subjected to the unskilled handling of Narada and so we are maimed and deformed. Narada's pride was humbled and he had to apply himself to a far more serious study to get the poor *ragās* out of their misery.

to the common stock which is transmitted to his students in pupillary succession. He is expected to enrich his presentation by supplementing the text. Opportunities for this present themselves during the interludes, when the *dramatis personae* are expected to engage themselves in dialogues that are a natural sequence of the action, but are not incorporated in the text of the drama. Such impromptu dialogues, of very frequent occurrence [2], enhance the human appeal of the drama and create in the audience an added relish. But they demand a healthy sense of imagination on the part of the actors. Sometimes the text may indicate the line to be pursued, as when it contains an allusion. Similarly, when the text refers to a situation or a scene such as a festival, assembly of *devas,* royal wedding, forest, the celestial city of Indra, a lake, an ocean, the Himalayas, etc., the actor would describe these according to his own imaginative capacity, or by an appropriate use of descriptions by gifted poets, which is again, a measure of his refinement or cultivated tastes. Such occasions are also utilised to employ the actor's sense of humour and wit to the utmost effect, provided the context permits. During these interludes, known as *Eḷakiāttam,* acting is done to the accompaniment of slight drumming only; the singers retire as there is no text to be sung.

The following is a favourite episode from jungle life, which the Kathakaḷi artists depict, the text of which is a single verse of four lines in Sanskrit.

A lordly elephant in a deep jungle puts out its trunk, breaks the branch of a spreading tree and proceeds to make a leisurely meal of it. From the rear, a hungry python slowly crawls forward and seizes a hind leg of the elephant in its cavernous mouth. The startled elephant turns back and seeing the python at its leg, tries to free itself from the deadly grip. But the python pulls with renewed force. While this conflict is at its height a lion (the traditional enemy of the elephant) appears on the scene, in search of prey. This new threat increases the fury of the elephant. With a sudden spring the lion lands on the head of the elephant, who, in a great rage, violently tosses its head and puts out its trunk to seize and hurl down the lion, at the same time it

---

2 These occur in every scene, liberating the drama from the limitations of the text and making it more spontaneous.

violently kicks and tries to free itself from the python's grip. The lion grips the head of the elephant and drives deep into it its cruel claws. The struggle and the strain cause despair to the elephant but the will to survive grows a hundred-fold. It fights ferociously, but unable to withstand this unequal fight, weakens and finally drops down dead. This episode is utilised to delineate, moods and conditions admirably. *Vīra* or the heroic mood is well brought out in presenting the elephant at the commencement of the story. This changes to *Adbhuta* (wonder) when the python seizes the leg and then to fury when it realises the threat. The python exhibits gluttonous appetite. The lion illustrates the mood of fury. The raging wrath of the fighting elephant gives way to sorrow and despair and then to a feeling of frustration and weakness. The graphic illustration of all these moods makes the jungle incident an intensely dramatic one and full of human appeal. The presentation is very much more than what the verse chronicles. Such descriptions are like enrapturing lyrics within a great epic, each one as perfect as a masterpiece.

A very noticeable feature of the Kathakaḷi drama is its almost complete freedom from scenic settings and other mechanical aids. Yet the actor—that is too narrow a term for him—is required to conjure up every scene relevant to the situation by the suggestive and persuasive quality of his *abhinaya.* He creates scenes that have an extraordinary living quality; he puts us into intimate touch with the vital principle of the object, its pulsating life or dominant trait, so that its physical features are recalled to our mind. Far more than factual reality is obtained and it becomes a subject of intimate experience. If a particular situation is laid against a mountain back-ground, the mountain comes into being, not only by the descriptive hands of the actor but also by his moods, which picture his mental reactions and his eyes which measure distance and height and envisage the massive proportions of the mountain. He will then depict the peaks that rise in serried ranks and the clouds that remain intercepted. From the heights he will take us, perhaps, to the deep gorges below, through winding and perilous paths. Tall trees festooned with creepers, some glowing with sweet scented flowers and others heavy with fruits, come into view. Suddenly, you stand before wild life in all its glory or savage fury. If the latter, we see nature red in tooth and claw as revealed by the murderous avocations of the beasts and birds of prey. Otherwise, we get an enchanting picture of a majestic mountain scenery; the details depending upon the situation of the drama or the reference it contains.

Similarly, a musical scene comes into being, as instruments such as the *vīṇa,* drums and cymbals take shape in the hands of the actor. Feeling the strings, tuning the keys, posturing the *vīṇa* in the characteristic way, the delicate suggestive movements of the fingers simulating playing, the reactions of the player evident in his gesture and facial expression, all this create the immediacy of experience. An imperial court scene is effectively suggested by attitudes and behaviours, not by the splendour of rich ornate effects or royal pomp. The majesty and distinction of a king are seen in his posture and glances, which are set against the servility of the attendants and the respectful and anxious attention of the minister. The very wooden mortar on which the king sits, partakes of the regal majesty that he radiates; it looks transformed into a befitting throne. If the actor is describing a garden and has to depict a peacock in that setting he becomes the very thing. The bird becomes an artistic reality not through the conventional *mudra* but by the glances, postures and gait that are unmistakably of the peacock (Figs. 37-39). The rumble of thunder is heard in the drumming and in the actor's steps; the lightning flashes forth from the dark massive clouds, conjured up by the actor. The peacock spreads its wings (suggested by the hands only) and there comes into view, the proud bird, spectacularly displaying its outspread plumes and dancing in rapture. Not the trifling and transitory features of the peacock, but its essential form, qualities and animating passions are vividly portrayed. What magic of colours or dexterity of the brush can ever hope to achieve such effect? Are not the cleverest scenic contraptions of the most finished stage, awkward and halting, before this vividness and eloquence? [3] How poor are they as aids to the spectators' imagination! In this way, a palace, a street,

---

3 "No elaborate stage arrangements, no revolving scene, no complex mechanism can give a more convincing illusion. Such mythological subjects, dealing with a supernatural world which would cause despair to any Western stage producer are their familiar atmosphere; and their simple suggestions create the marvellous without ever falling into the ludicrous. The visions they conjure will always be exactly suited to every spectator's imagination, and avoiding the crude materiality of even the best stage arrangements, will satisfy all from the roughest to the subtlest conception." *Kathakaḷi* by Alice Boner. *Journal of the Indian Society of Oriental Art,* June 1935.

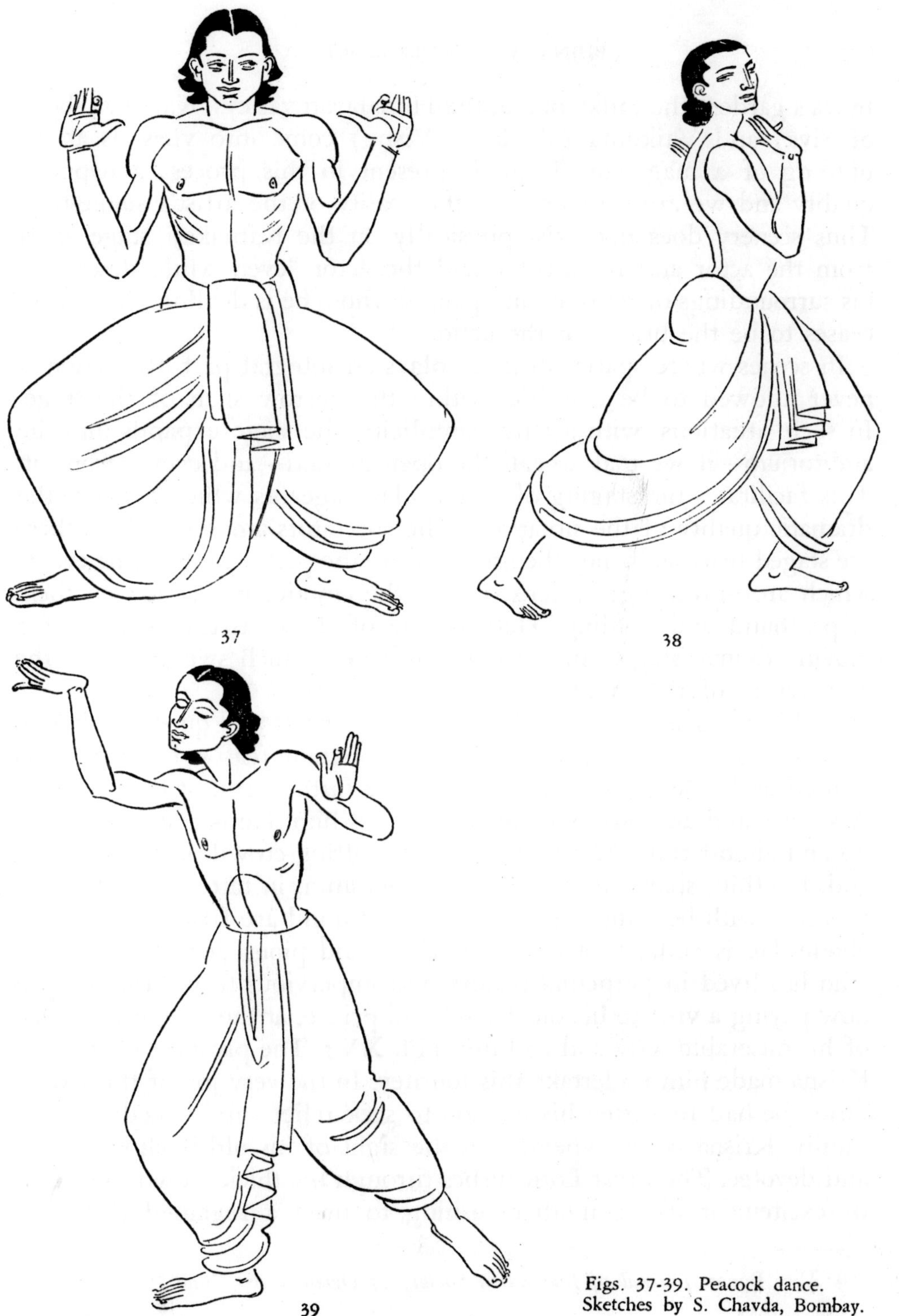

Figs. 37-39. Peacock dance.
Sketches by S. Chavda, Bombay.

Indra's garden, the milky ocean, the Himalayan valleys, Kailāsa (abode of Siva) and Vaikunṭa (abode of Viṣṇu) come into view as at the bidding of a magician. There is present in this process a hypnotic quality and we are convinced of the reality of the artist's suggestion. Thus scenery does not exist physically on the Kathakaḷi stage apart from the actor and his artistry and the actor "even while describing his surroundings or representing people whom he is dealing with, never ceases to be the bearer of the action" [4].

In scenes where spatial distance plays an integral part, the action is never allowed to be cramped within the narrow span of the stage. In such situations, with a naive simplicity, the stage expands into the auditorium—if we may so call the open ground—and even beyond it. This facilitates the staging of spectacular pageants which enhance the dramatic quality of the situations. The spectators amongst whom these are staged react as if they themselves were the participants in the events which are unfolding; in consequence the emotional reaction on them is profound and abiding. Here is one of those stirring events of a moving drama, staged amongst the audience, which sweeps it into the very centre of the event.

Śri Kriṣṇa is seen in his palace with his consort and queen, Rukmini, in a love scene. Suddenly and for no apparent reason he withdraws himself and is seen looking intently at the farthest end of the highway. A serious and anxious expectancy animates him. He is restless; he gets up and almost runs through the thick squatting crowd. From the other end, the thin, spare figure of a poor Brahmin, in tattered clothes, approaches with hesitant steps. His eyes and mind are fixed on the royal abode. He is Sudāma, a boyhood friend and pious devotee of Kriṣṇa who has lived in perpetual penury and impervious to its stings. He is now paying a visit to his old friend and prince, at the urgent entreaties of his miserable wife and children (Pl. XV). The prospect of meeting Kriṣṇa made him undertake this journey. In the very joy of this expectation he had forgotten his mission to seek relief sorely needed by his family. Kriṣṇa is overwhelmed at the sight of his old boyhood friend and devotee. The great Lord rushes through the thick crowd in a fever of excitement like a mother rushing to meet a regained child. He

---

4 Alice Boner. *Journal of the Indian Society of Oriental Art,* June 1935.

prostrates himself at the feet of the poor Brahmin, gets up and then repeatedly hugs him in a fervour of joy, relieves him of his little burdens like the tattered umbrella and then gently leads him on with loving kindness and many sweet intimacies, very much to the bewilderment and embarrassment of the Brahmin (Pl. I). At the palace, he is given royal honours and the queen herself waits on him. The great Lord is the servant of his humblest devotee. Thus a mythological event so well known to the spectators comes to life and becomes their experience. The audience reacts in the way the texts describe the reaction of the crowds that lined the streets of Dwāraka on that memorable occasion. The incident has now taken place in their very midst. What a privilege and what an experience! What can equal this intense spiritual exaltation of the audience, so steeped in the legends of Krisṇa? Small wonder then, that a drama that could generate in the spectators such pure emotional exaltation, should be regarded as sacred in the true sense of the term. Judged even by purely aesthetic standards, the scene enacted achieves the highest purpose of the drama [5].

Transformation scenes in the drama are handled with a simplicity that is only equalled by the astounding effects achieved. It is the inherent vitality of a never-failing technique that helps to achieve this triumph. In the drama *Pūtana Mōksha* [5a] (Salvation of Pūtana the ogress), Putana is commissioned by the wicked king Kaṃsa to poison the divine child Krisṇa, for he has heard it said that he would meet his doom at the hands of Krisṇa, who is the son of Devaki his own sister. Pūtana transforms herself into a beautiful woman. Stealthily she enters the royal nursery at Ambadi (Gokul) and feeds the child at her poison-besmeared breasts; but the strange child, in feeding, drains her very life. In her agony the beautiful damsel assumes her own ugly and fearful form. Slowly but surely the transformation takes place in the same person while the spectators are looking on. This striking change which thrills and creates in the audience a sense of creeping terror as

---

5 Duśśāsana dragging and driving Draupadi from the royal chamber to the assembly hall, where she is disrobed in public; the challenge and fight between Bhīma and Duśśāsana; the wailing Śūrpanakha, streaming with blood (after her nose and ears were cut off by Lakṣhamaṇa), returning to Lanka, are some of the scenes staged amongst the audience.

5a See appendix I.

the situation develops to its fateful end, is achieved by deftly smearing on the face a black twisted patch (by the nimble fingers of the artist), the baring of a pair of *dhamṣtrās,* the horrible contortion of the mouth from which the tongue is thrust out when seized by writhing pain and the general facial expression that changes into the hideous features of an ogress furiously fighting against her doom. The illustrations (Pl. XXIII and Pl. XXIV) will convey some idea of this remarkable transformation.

Another striking feature of Kathakaḷi *abhinaya* is the practice of emitting cries, usual to *Kātti, Tāṭi* and *Kari* types. This, of course, belongs to the sphere of *sātvikābhinaya.* The *Pacca* and *Minukku* do not utter any cries, even under the gravest of provocations, in keeping with their restraint and poise. The cries emitted are of various kinds and are indicative of psychological states, such as anger, revenge, contempt, hatred, slight, pity, sorrow, pride, arrogance, love and passion. By modulation of the voice it is possible to express these feelings or moods and this contributes considerably to enrich the total effect of the drama.

The actors are not to conduct themselves as mere impersonators; their behaviour should, therefore, conform to that of the mythological characters they represent. Through convention, use of symbols and discipline much has been done, as already explained earlier, to enable the actors to reach the standard. The actor is a *yogi* [6]. The actions on the stage

[6] In speaking of the deep interconnections between *Yoga* and the hieratic art of India, Dr. Jung makes the following observations on Kathakaḷi, which are of special significance to the point of view expressed in this enquiry. The passage occurs in his "Remarks Upon the Psychology of Eastern Meditation" his contribution to the Coomaraswamy homage volume, *"Art & Thought",* edited by the author, (Luzac, 1948). "It is not the world of the senses, the body, color and sound, or human passions, which are born anew in transfigured form, through the creative power of the Indian soul; but it seems as if there were an "underworld" or an "overworld" of a metaphysical nature, out of which strange forms emerge into the familiar earthly world. If one observes closely the tremendously impressive impersonation of the gods, performed by the Southern Indian Kathakaḷi dancers, there is not a single natural gesture to be seen. Everything is bizarre, both subhuman and superhuman. The dancer-gods do not walk like people—they glide; they do not seem to think with their heads—but with their hands. Even the human faces disappear behind enamelled masks. Our own world offers nothing which can be compared to such grotesque grandeur. When watching one of these spectacles one is transported into the world of dreams, for that is the only place where we might conceivably meet anything similar. The representations of the Kathakaḷi dancers, or those depicted in the temple pictures, are however no nocturnal phan-

should appear spontaneous; they should transcend the artificialty and limitations of the text. The conversational interludes that occur in every scene create that air of spontaneity. In the actual process of *abhinaya* itself, even while interpreting the text, spontaneity is secured by *ankura*[7] (sprout). An actor while acting is expected to watch carefully the reactions aroused in his companion or opposite characters whom he is addressing. His subsequent actions should show an awareness of those reactions; that is, his actions gain their strength, emphasis or intensity from this psychological reaction in him. Like a subtle and mysterious force *ankurabhinaya* spreads a glow of spontaneity over text, technique and actor.

The *Tira-nōkku*[8] (literally curtain-look), as was said before, seems to be a distinct and peculiar stage device to create an impressive and highly dramatic atmosphere. This ceremonious and spectacular function is reserved to usher in the *Katti, Tāṭi* and *Kari* types of characters, generally the aggressive, fierce ones and those possessed of enormous physical strength such as Rāvaṇa, Śiśupāla, Bāli, Hanuman, etc. This manner of introduction vividly portrays the physical prowess, the mental qualities and the violent emotional urges of the characters. The accentuated pounding of the drums drives out of us every trace of lethargy and indifference; we are galvanised into an acute sense of expectancy. Engulfed in ceaseless stirring rhythms which penetrate our inmost being, we are awakened in a dream-world where every moment is pregnant with the strangest of possibilities. What is unfolding before us is a drama within the drama. Rapid and heavy steps behind the curtain, in keeping with the tempo of the drums, announce the intricate

---

tasms. They are tensely dynamic figures, logically constructed with the finest details, or as if they had grown organically. These are no shadows or likenesses of a former reality, they are more like realities which have *not yet been,* potential realities, which can step at any moment over the threshold of existence."

7 *Sūca* and *Aṅkura* are described as follows in the *Nāṭyaśāstra.* "When the meaning of a sentence or the sentence (itself) is indicated first by Temperament and Gestures, and then the Verbal Representation is made, it is called *Sūca.* When one skilfully represents by Gestures in the manner of the *Sūca* the words which one has in one's heart it is called the Representation of *Aṅkura.*" *Nāṭyaśāstra* Chapter XXIV slokas 43 and 44. (M. M. Ghose). With reference to Kathakaḷi, "words" of course mean the text of the play sung by the singers. Indications of mental reactions of feelings aroused are made by facial expressions, other gestures and by *sātvikābhinaya.*

8 An extract of this was published in *Art And Thought* (Luzac 1948).

movements of a spirited, earth-shaking dance. The impression of a giant energy gathering momentum and struggling to overwhelm opposing forces is created. An occasional weird cry, an angry growl, a thunder-like rumbling or an intermittent shriek rises over the tremendous din. The curtain held up by two men is ruffled violently, like the surface of a wind-lashed sea. All that is seen are fleeting glimpses of the shining top of the head-gear of the whirling figure within. After a few minutes of this seismic activity a beautifully coloured canopy is held over-head, close to the rim of the curtain, to form a picturesque pavilion. We are soon to witness the appearance of Rāvaṇa, the august demon king (according to legend possessed of ten heads and twenty arms), of invincible might, destroyer of the pride of the *devas,* now on a spectacular march to subjugate Kubera, the Lord of Wealth. The generously oil-fed lamp raises its twin tongues of flame; they are now riotous, now fitful and positively in a raging temper. Two palms suddenly grip the top of the curtain; the long, silver nails of the fingers gleam, quiver and fly over its rim. The gripping, clutching hands lower it a little by degrees. The hands appear over the curtain holding the picturesque lotus-ends of the scarves. Now, the enormous and scintillating head-dress slowly comes into view; when almost half of it emerges over the curtain a rumbling growl is emitted by the demon king and the flourish of the drums intensifies the tension. The grip on the curtain is then suddenly released, it resumes its former position, completely screening off the figure. The animated steps and movements continue behind the curtain in greater vehemence; the very ground underneath is shaken with tremors. After a few minutes, the silver-nailed fingers grip the curtain again and then lower it, while the drums pound faster and the curtain quivers as if in extreme excitement. It is lowered, lowered still more this time, but only to give another graduated view: perhaps a fuller view of the head. This touch-and-go, reachme and reach-me-not attempts, repeated three or four times, raise expectancy to an acute pitch. The gripping palms appear once again over the curtain, holding the trembling, quivering lotus-ends. Slowly, very slowly, it is lowered again with the drums in a final outpouring releasing a tempest of sound. The curtain is convulsed with extreme agitation, the flames of the lamp leap and burn with greater violence and the two torches held close to the lamp, fed with resin powder, rage with ever-growing fury. The glare of

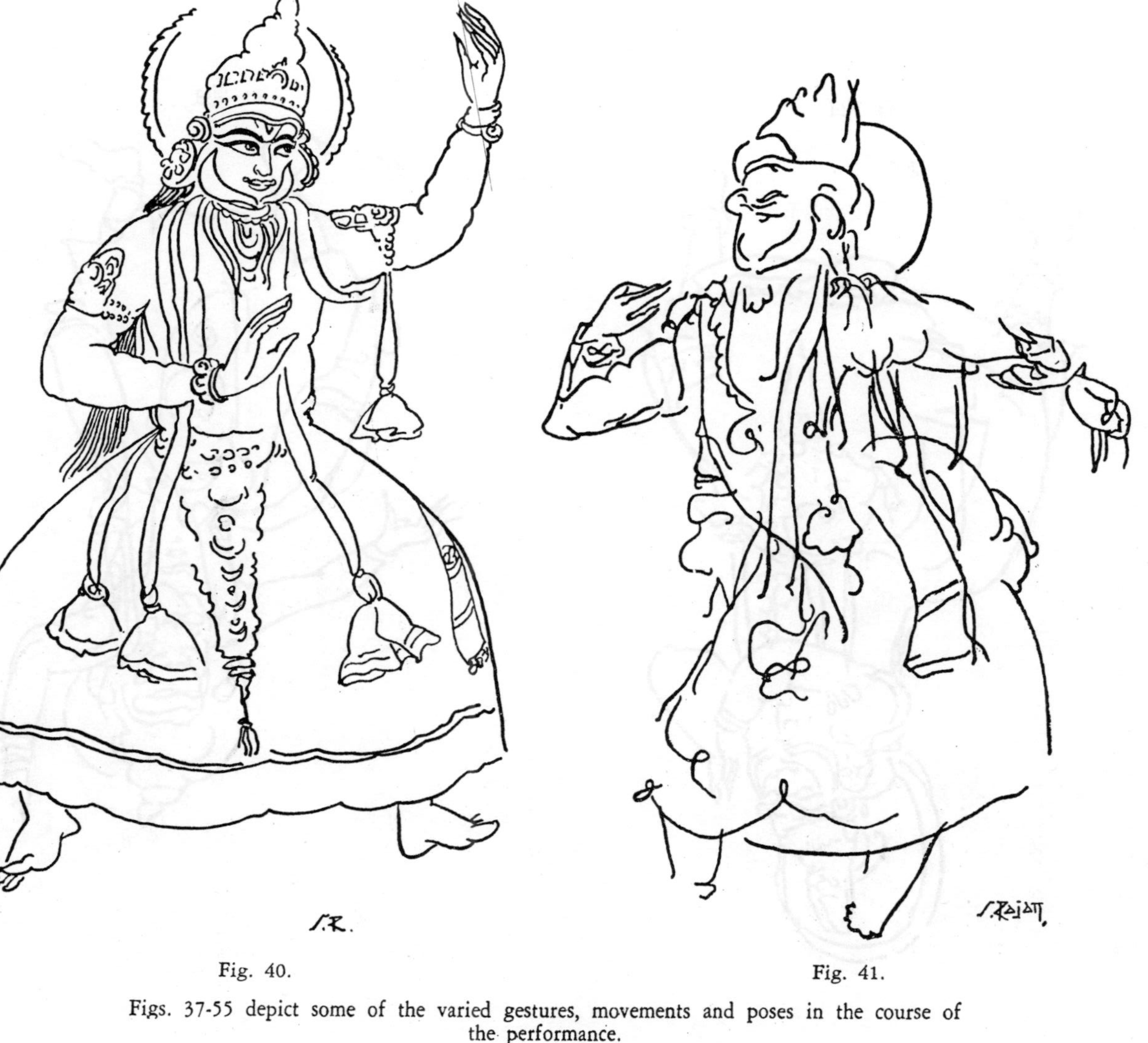

Fig. 40.

Fig. 41.

Figs. 37-55 depict some of the varied gestures, movements and poses in the course of the performance.

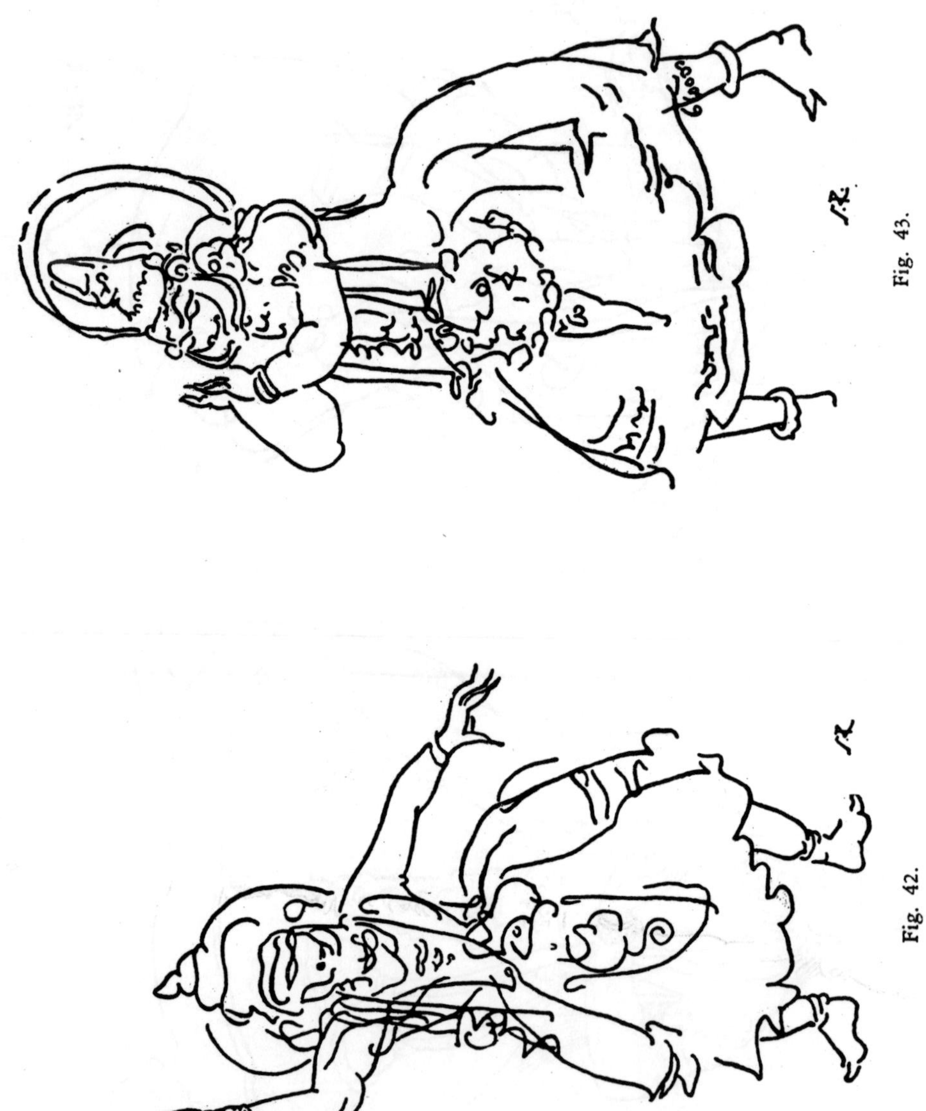

Fig. 42.

Fig. 43.

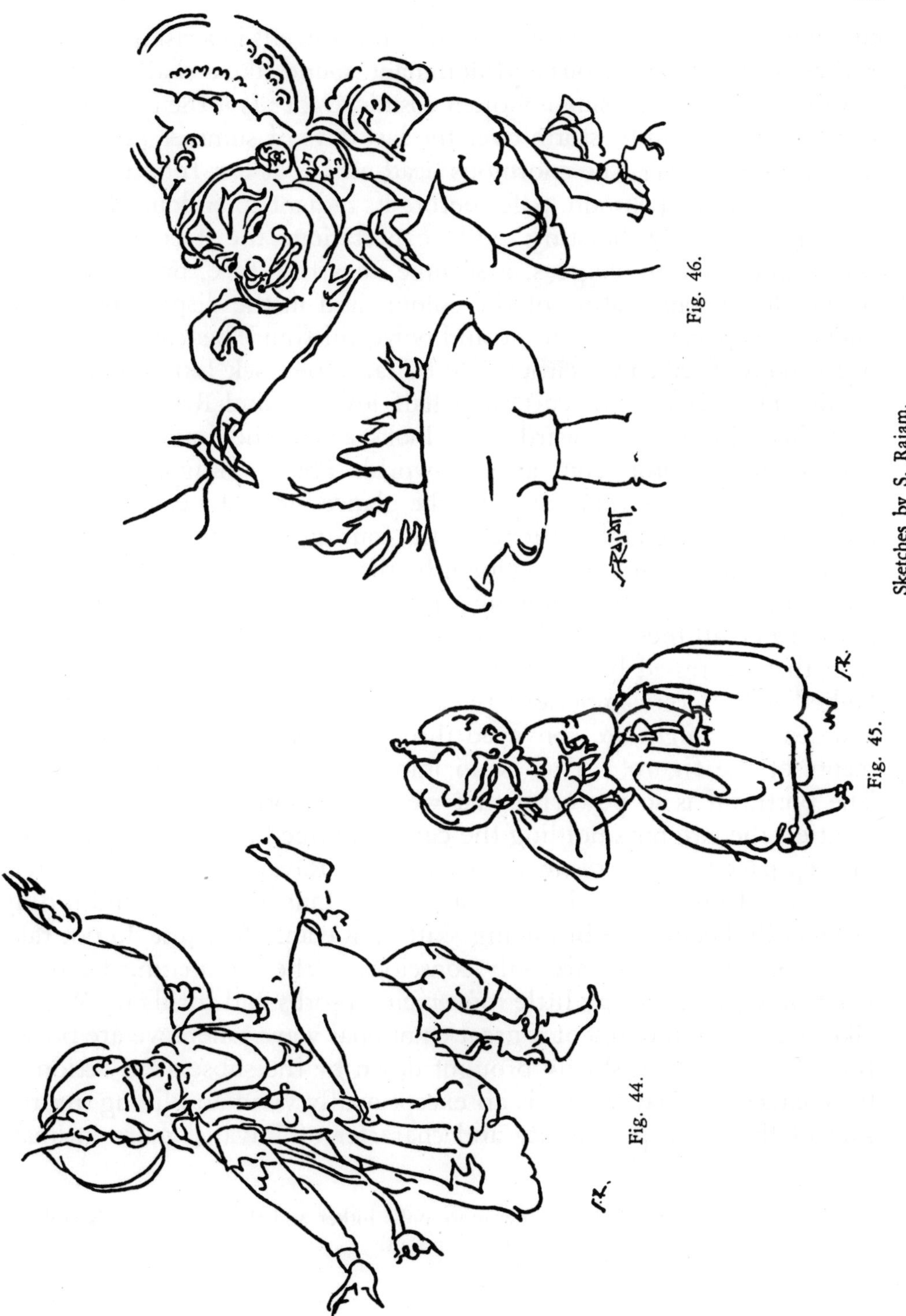

Fig. 44.

Fig. 45.

Fig. 46.

Sketches by S. Rajam.

the light is intense. The blowing of the conch swells in a rising crescendo and cries, weird, imperious and dominant, sound like a challenge to the worlds. Are we witnessing a violent cosmic event? Is it the first outburst of a monsoon thunder-storm over the last days of summer (so familiar a scene in Keraḷa)? The enormous head-gear is at last fully revealed—even the colourful curtain, pales before its radiant splendour. When the audience is fairly bursting with expectation, the face of Rāvaṇa comes into view by degrees, a strange unearthly face, but fascinating in the clever combination of the colours and in the disposition of the knobs. He appears as a majestic and powerful figure beneath a picturesque canopy, flanked on either side by large peacock fans, emblems of royalty (Pl. XIX). The curtain is half lowered and Rāvaṇa is visible only from his waist upwards. He looks across the flames, a strange apparition, a visitor from a super-world. The flaming red eyes, the snouty nose, the intermittant cries, the glances at first steady and steely and then sweeping and challenging the four quarters, the repeated pulls at the curtain which agitates violently, then the cold and intent stare at the flames, the violent blowings at them, the imperious and stately movements, all these put us into a strange, tense mood. A fury greater than that expressed by the flames of the lamp and the torches is embodied in this very imperious person. What majesty, heroic grandeur and sense of might are conveyed through the stately poses and movements of the figure! [9] This is no impersonation but an embodiment. The portrayal is so powerful that we fail to notice some little incongruities; the two boys holding the curtain obliged to adjust themselves, to keep pace with the restless movements of Rāvaṇa and the two torch-bearers in front and the bearers of peacock fans, crouching and hiding awkwardly behind the billowing skirt of Rāvaṇa. We just do not take notice of all these; we are only conscious of the dominating figure in front of us, whose every little movement absorbs and thrills us. We are taken steadily to the crest of a great emotional wave where we are poised for a time and then slowly brought down by the subsequent action of the character. What we get is an exceptionally vivid and living impression of the form, personality and character of Rāvaṇa, more intimate

[9] The curtain is let off after a few more pulls hither and thither as if he is fighting against some heavy odds and emerges victoriously.

in certain respects than literary descriptions of him. Qualities and passions that form the very warp and woof of the story are thus woven into a fabric of unforgettable, haunting visions.

The *tira-nōkku* requires special adjustment to suit particular characters and specific situations. Thus the *tira-nōkku* of Rāvaṇa in another play *Rāvaṇōdbhava* (nativity of Rāvaṇa), differs from the one described above or from that in *Baḷi Vijaya* in which also he figures. The *tira-nōkku* of Śisúpāla, a highly proud and aggressive monarch, who was singled out and insulted by not being invited to the *Rājasūya* ceremony held at the court of the Pandavas (where every crowned head was present), while Śri Kriṣṇa his bitter foe, was offered the seat of great honour, a place which he himself very much aspired for, is a grand spectacle of power and fury. Here we are in a world of giant forces and passions and we are inescapably whirled in their currents. Time and space vanish from our perception and we live intensely in a dream-world. Here is primitive strength,.passionately impelled and seeking expression of the spirit, in an idiom alien to the Sanskrit stage.

NOTES

Some characters mount a wooden mortar and then perform the *tira-nōkku* towering over the squatting audience, successfully creating an even more awe-inspiring impression through so simple a device. In the *tira-nōkku* of Hanuman, in *Kalyāṇa saugandhika,* an impression of his reputed *bhakti* (piety) is effectively conveyed in the *yogic* pose of devotion and tranquillity, skilfully blended with the more stirring activities designed to suggest his wild elemental strength and heroic qualities.

CHAPTER XIII

DANCING IN KATHAKALI

"Life on the Kathakaḷi stage is a dance." Kathakaḷi is a dance-drama; the drama and the dance are so blended that they exist throughout as inseparable, as a word and its meaning. There is hardly a moment when the dance ceases; there is no lapse into prose from the lyrical movements. Even when the *naṭa* (actor-dancer) sits down and carries on the dialogue, the rhythmic movements of his arms, wrists, fingers, eyes and eye-brows continue the dance. Here dancing exists with its highest possibilities fully developed and employed, to express moods, to communicate thoughts, to heighten the effect of the dramatic, to enrich the lyrical tone and to build up and sustain the entire fabric of the drama on rhythm (Pls. XXV and XXVI, and figs. 33-55).

Kathakaḷi dancing is chiefly *Nṛtya*[1] (interpretative dancing). But that does not relegate *Nṛtta* (pure dancing and non-interpretative in character) to an inferior role. *Nṛtya* and *Nṛtta* exist side by side: the one lending distinction to the other. After every *Khaṇda* or *Caraṇa* (four lines of a song) is rendered in *Nṛtya* (acting-dancing) technique, the actor breaks out into a pure dance called *Kalāśa* (dance-conclusion). These dance-conclusions set the mimed stanzas in a frame-work

---

1 The term "dancing" can hardly convey the Hindu conception of *Nātya.* Its implications have been brought out in the course of this survey. The attempt of a well-known American artist La Meri to explain the term is of interest. "We are accumstomed to think of dancing as a rhythmic movement of the legs, accompanied by the body and arms which express the basic emotions of joy, sorrow, love, peace etc. and of a dancer as a beautiful young thing with a sense of rhythm and an expressive face. But *Nātya,* touching all the shadings of the human heart through mental and physical experience, is as far removed from dancing as Beethoven from John Strauss."

Terence Gray also writes to the same effect "Dancing ... in its fullest meaning —to include all forms of studied movements not the least of them studied immobility— including what is known as mime rendered rhythmically, is as verse to which mime is as prose, it is in fact every form of emotional expression by which the human being can express himself, using his physical body as his medium."

as it were, much like the *hasiya*—the rich and colourful designs that grace Persian and Mughal miniatures. There are many *Kalāśas,* each one in a different *Tāḷa* or timing. The tempo of each *Kalāśa* must accord with the prevailing mood or sentiment expressed in the *Caraṇa.* This is again an instance of *Nṛtta, Gīta, Vādya* and *Bhāva* or *Rasa* synthesising and seeking their underlying unity. At the conclusion of certain important *Caraṇas,* the *Kalāśas* are doubled or done twice. When done a second time *mudras* are shown for the key words in the *Caraṇa* which indicate the *Bhāva.* The various flexions of the body, the quick turns, the weightless easy leaps, the rapid intricate steppings, the sweeping angular movements of the arms, the quick facile turns of the wrists, the picturesque finger poses that alternate with the wrist turns, the rhythmic co-ordination established and the succession of exquisite patterns, one fast melting into the other, these make the *Kalāśas* supreme examples of pure dancing. The *Aṣta Kalāśa,* which is done to eight different timings, is the most intricate of these and is the acid test of the terpsichorean abilities of the actor.

Kathakaḷi dancing belongs mostly to the *Tāndava* (masculine and vigorous) type and this is in accord with the general character of the drama, for Kathakaḷi is pre-eminently a male art. *Tāndava* movements are characterised by strength and majesty, speed and expansiveness. Their curves have a broad sweep and every movement is urged on by an imperious elemental force. There are many conspicuously angular movements in Kathakaḷi *Tāndava.* Even the position that the Kathakaḷi actor takes is angular; he scarcely stands erect, certainly not when he is acting: that would be a lapse into prose and a fall from the rhythmic tension in which he is held all the time. When he stands with slightly spread out knees, the legs form a sort of rhomboid; the hands bent at the elbow, with the palms placed on the hips, echo the angular position of the legs. The very stance or pose from which the actor commences his other movements, is dynamic and nothing can upset his balance. The actor's feet are never in flat contact with the floor. In maintaining perfect balance, the weight is thrown on the outer edges of the feet which remain slightly bent and curved. What may seem unnatural, is really the stance of an adept or a *yōgi,* whose activity is dictated by a conscious inner force. The angular movements, tense and virile, impart to the fabric of rhythms he weaves, a sustaining strength. In the great

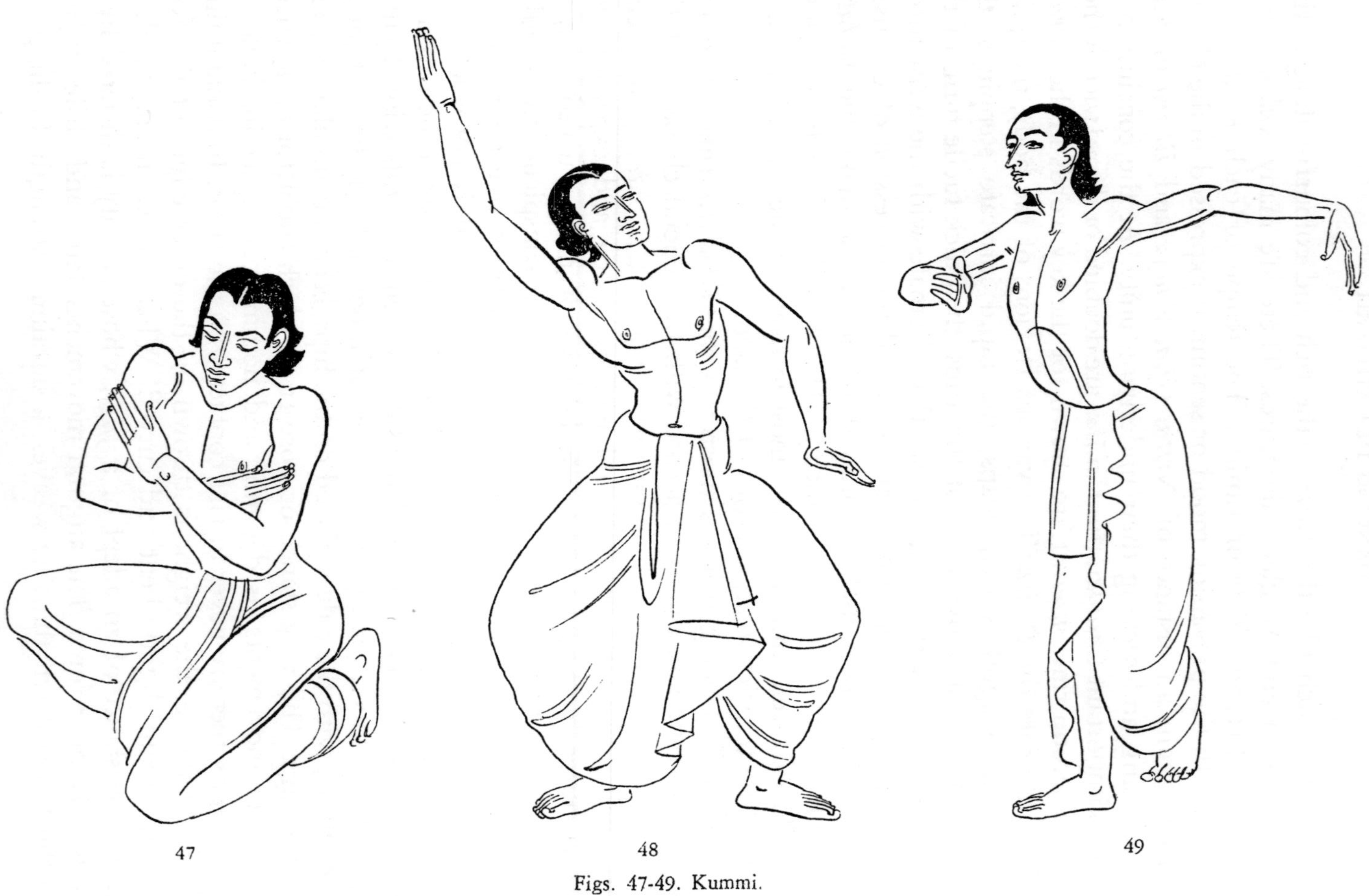

47 48 49

Figs. 47-49. Kummi.

sweeping movements and gestures of Kathakaḷi *Tāndava* one feels, as it were, the pulsations of cosmic energy.

This vigorous *Tāndava* moves against a delicate background of *Lāsya* (the gentle and feminine aspect of dancing). In *Lāsya,* lightness, gentility and grace are much in evidence and a sense of restraint guides the flow of lines. These qualities are well brought out in the acting and dancing of the women characters of the drama and particularly in the

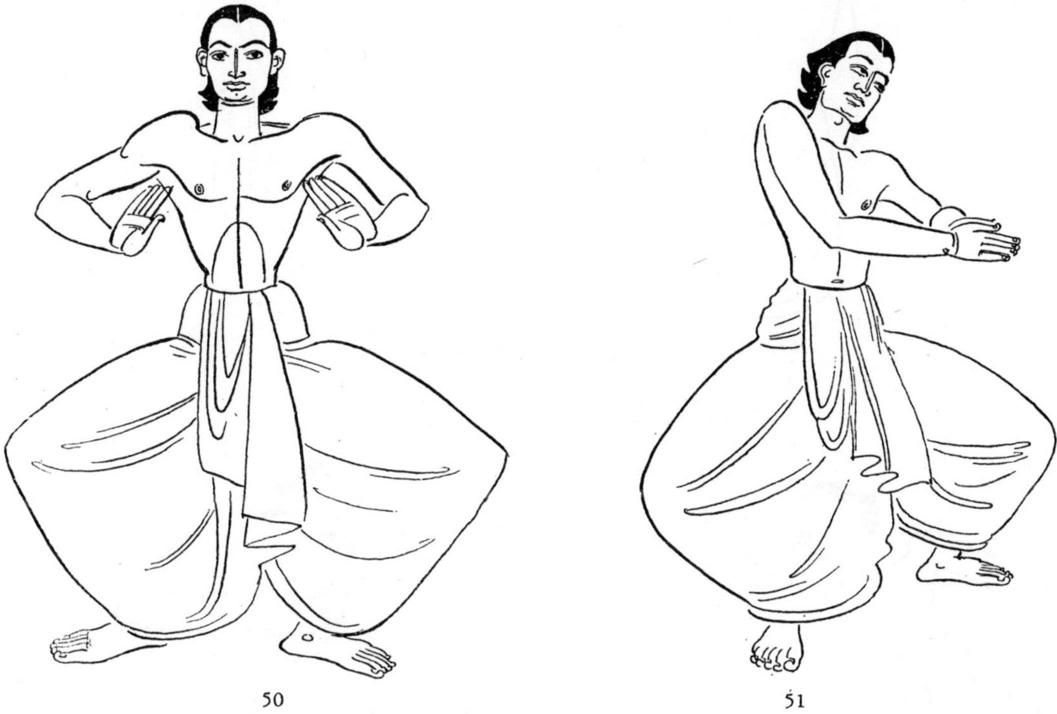

50 51

Figs. 50-51. Sāri dance.

love scenes (*patiñjāttaṃ*), where even the movements of the male are mostly in the *Lāsya* mode. But that is a *Lasya* which the Kathakaḷi stage has developed as specially suitable for the male dancer. The *Kummi* and *Sāri* are the best examples of the Kathakaḷi *Lāsya* which are in the nature of pure dance (Figs. 47-55).

In this mimetic art, the disciplined and intelligent movements of the body remain always "poetic in that highest sense, in which poetry is a perception of the specific significance and beauty that informs an idea or theme and renders it alive and valid" [2].

[2] Mc Collum—*The Dance of Siva* (Kegan Paul).

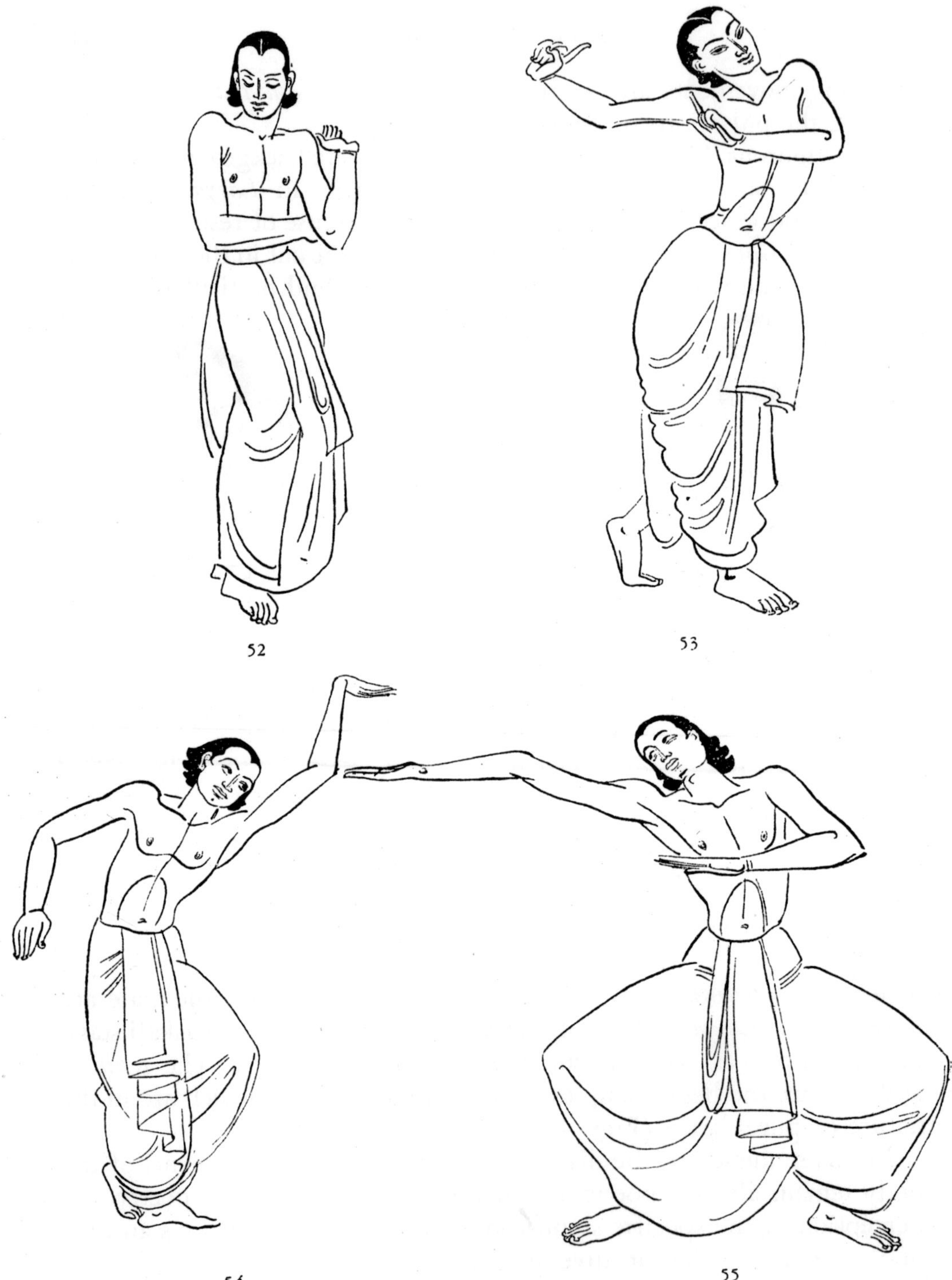

Figs. 50-55. Sari.

Figs. 47-55 Poses by Kṛishnan Kutty, (Bombay).
Sketches by S. Chavda, Bombay.

CHAPTER XIV

KATHAKALI AND THE BALLET

Critics have often compared Kathakaḷi to the ballet, a term widely known after the spectacular success of the Russian Ballet. I am not certain that the popular conception of the term "ballet" is identical with the ideal ballet, the search for which was the subject of serious experiments on the part of Jean Jacques Noverre, Blasis, Massine and Nijinsky. The stand taken by Noverre, known as the Shakespeare of the dance, approaches in certain respects the ideals of the Kathakaḷi stage, at least outwardly. Mr. Arnold Haskell has summarised Noverre's ideas [1] and I am indebted to him for the following. "The well-composed ballet should be a living painting of the drama, character and customs of mankind, it must be as moving in its effect as a declamation, so that it can speak through the soul." Again "...the rules of the drama apply to the ballet which must have an introduction, a development and a climax... dancing in ballet is the means of expressing a dramatic idea." It is of particular interest to this survey that Noverre in his search for the fully developed dramatic ballet disapproved of the mask altogether (a feature of the earlier ballets) and wanted the development of the pantomimic art. The ballet remained an exclusively male art till the early part of the 17th century. Thereafter it gradually changed into a preponderantly female art, where grace, roundness and softness were the leading characteristics. So predominant were these qualities that other necessary virtues were over-looked. Nijinsky after the success he achieved in *Prélude à l'Après-Midi d'un Faun,* disapproved of these qualities and "insisted that the ballet must be angular, tense and virile, while for lightness, he proposed to substitute heaviness". And the ballet too is a convention as Haskell reminds his readers. Readers can judge for themselves how far the much sought after 'ideal qualities' are to be found in Kathakaḷi as fully developed and comple-

---

[1] *Ballet*—Pelican Series.

mentary elements. But the differences of Kathakali from the European ballet are fundamental and vital and should not be over-looked in our enthusiasm for a term.

The European ballet is of comparatively recent origin; it is still in the experimental stage. Its notable achievements remain mostly as the personal triumphs of individual dancers who are regarded as unusual persons and isolated by that formidable term "genius". The distinctions of a Nijinsky, Karsavina or Pavlova are personal rather than integral to the ballet. The mental climate of the European ballet is far removed from that of the Indian or Eastern ballets. As a mimetic art utilising the body as a means of expression of every thought, feeling or idea Kathakaḷi has travelled far beyond the ballet; in scope and range it is epical. The elaborate scenic background of the ballet which is a great example of the painter's art and of mechanical ingenuity, is entirely absent from the Kathakaḷi stage. The Kathakaḷi actor's art which is a "living painting" needs no such extraneous aid. Kathakaḷi possesses in a rich measure the great virtues sought after by Noverre and others and which the European ballet has not yet fully acquired. Further, Kathakaḷi is the great heritage of a race, true and inspired in the deepest sense of these terms, and is embedded in and nourished by the living traditions and piety of the people. Unlike the European ballet it is religious and sacred.

Parallel features and developments are to be found [2] in the dramas of

---

2 "The Greek stage is grouped round a sacrificial place, an altar. Kathakaḷi is lit by the flickering light of a big brass oil lamp, which also serves the actor as pole of concentration. Can we venture to draw an analogy of origin between this lighting system and the central Altar of the Attic tragedy? Both, Greek tragic performance and Kathakaḷi, are built up on rhythmic sequences. Both theatrical schools have adopted a peculiar way of walking, thus creating an unusual contact with the earth, the one by means of the cothurnus, the other by the rule that the actors have to step on the outer edge of their feet. Most Kathakaḷi characters appear in a make-up which one can describe as a flexible mask. This mask-like make-up is probably derived from the former use of real masks. This links up with the Greek mask... The Greek tragedies, however, were the expression of timeless grandeur brought into visible and audible form, a vision and reassimilation of the world beyond, a metaphysical complement of the pulse of nature. They attested the continuity of bygone life. They interpreted the values of the past as present rhythm. They reflected the unconscious soul and transformed dread and fear into word and shape. Thus, great tragic fates, Prometheus, Oedipus and Iphigenia, fatal and silent heroism, greatness and destruction became expressible and conciliated to human life."

other countries which undoubtedly help to bring into clearer perspec-

---

The Liturgical and mystery plays are religious plays . . . . "their texts were derived from the Bible and the holy legends." Vernacular was introduced in the Liturgical plays later on leading to its prevalence. "Thus all modifications tended towards a relaxation of the bonds between liturgy and performance. The Kerala story play undergoes a similiar transformation... Finally, there is in both, in the liturgical plays as well as in Kathakaḷi, a mixture of symbolic and realistic elements. The persons represented stand not only for themselves, but reveal secrets of human destiny, grace, salvation, redemption, saintliness... This brings in a strong ethical note. But in spite of the highly symbolical character, everyday circumstances are liberally portrayed. In the midst of the serious we get a glimpse of the comic. Life is seen in its entirety. And this entirety we find to be a mirror of the transcendental". (Extracts from *Story Plays in Living Tradition*—Lecture delivered by Georgette Boner.)

No less striking is the similarity to the Chinese theatre, a reference to which has already been made elsewhere. Apart from the symbolism of the colour scheme of facial painting this is well reflected in the technique of acting. The stylized gestures of the Chinese actor though not so well developed and elaborate as that of the Hindu actor are no less precise and subtle and owe allegiance to analogous principles. In the present state of our knowledge it is not possible to say what exactly has been the influence of the Hindu stage tradition on the Chinese theatre and the gesture art. But the probability cannot be excluded in view of the early Indian influences traceable in Chinese culture. Further we read in an article by Hiroo Omichi in "Present Day Nippon" No. 11 (1935)—on *Bugaku—Ancient Oriental Dancing and its Music*—that BUGAKU has two parts, *Sabu* and *Ubu. Sabu* represents Indian and Chinese music, literally it means "left dancing", so called because at the end of the 8th century the musicians who practised Chinese and Indian music resided at the left side of the capital. The *Sabu* dance was introduced from India. The *Bugaku* which flourished in ancient China and India survives only in Japan. What this exactly means and whether the original prototype is traceable to India is a matter for further investigation. However that may be, this establishes and lends weight to the theory of Indian influences affecting the Chinese theatre.

The following interesting observations from *Famous Chinese Plays* by Arlington and Acton reveal the fundamental unity in certain features of the traditions governing Kathakaḷi and Chinese theatre. "The Chinese theatre is essentially an art of actors and regisseurs; the Chinese dramatic literature is a mere facet of the diamond; the scenarios merely contribute the raw material, the canvas for the actors to embroider on. It is for the splendid synthesis of gestures, movement, facial expressions, as well as the singing and dancing and ensembles of the actors that the Chinese theatre is unique..." Again the actor, "is scenery, singer, dancer, acrobat and mime at once. By holding a whip he can indicate that he is riding a horse, by standing on a chair he can conjure a mountain... And with consummate art the actor can conjure a complete visual impression out of the air. Nothing so material as a needle and thread is introduced for sewing: the actor's movements suffice and we can count the stitches under his nimble fingers... the actor peeps from side to side and the whole fabric of the door is conjured before our eyes. The actor must follow definite rules and conventions... It is by the quality of his light and shade under an almost Prussian discipline that the fine actor can be distinguished; not by the mere excellence of his drill." Reference has

tive the fundamental unity of all traditional forms of art. The extracts in the note below may prove of interest in this context.

Kathakaḷi is no doubt influenced by the great traditions of the classical Sanskrit stage; in fact for a right understanding or reconstruction of the latter, a study of the Kathakaḷi stage is absolutely necessary and much of the material that eludes us elsewhere is only found here. Its *abhinaya* technique is fully developed and is encyclopaedic. However that be, it should not be overlooked that in tone and temper the non-classical and non-aryan strains are also insistent [3]. Kathakaḷi art, it will be noticed, maintains that vital contact with the primordial which alone permits a complete expression of the spirit. It has the integrity characteristic of all great and anonymous art. Free from all sophistry it remains one of the most sincere art forms. Its very exuberance is a storehouse of inexhaustible beauty disclosing unexpected felicities. The product of a rare synthesis, it remains the complete expression of the original unity of *Nṛtta* (dance), *Vādya* (instrumental music), *Gita* (song) and *bhava* (mood). As Emily Gilchrist reminds us it is "more than pantomime, more than dance, more than acting: this art combines

---

already been made to the symbolic character of the make-up. We are also told that the Chinese audience is highly critical. The female roles are played by men only, but every finger of the female impersonator, we are told, must contribute to the effect of fragile femininity and if a woman points at any person or object she must do so in a way that must distinguish her from a man. This distinction is observed on the Kathakaḷi stage and is recognized by the *Natyasāstra* too. Attention has already been drawn earlier to the similarity between the Chinese drum and the drum of the *Kuttu* (fig. 2). The make-up of Ma I, the heroic servant in the play Chiu Keng T'ien (picture facing page 125 of *Famous Chinese Plays*), looks like the *minukku* make-up of a *ṛishi* (Pl. XVII).

3 The Sanskrit drama (also the *Kūttu*) is staged in well constructed theatres. The Kathakaḷi is staged in the open. It has not adopted such features of the Sanskrit drama as *Prasthāvana, Nirvacana Sūtradhāra, Vidūṣaka,* etc. The theme of the Sanskrit drama may be epic or historical. The Kathakaḷi story can only be from the epics, i.e. mythological. No scenery or other mechanical aid is admitted on the Kathakaḷi stage where the actor is expected to create scenic effects by his art. While the *Todayam* and *Vandana* of Kathakali may be parallelled with the *Poorva-ranga* and *Nāndi* of the Sanskrit drama, the Keḷi, Arangu-keḷi (Suddhamaddaḷam) and Purappād are not met with in the preliminaries of the Sanskrit stage practices. The *patinjattām* (this it should be particularly noted is not a mere love scene which any drama anywhere may have, but a definite convention on the Kathakaḷi stage), *Tira-nōkku, Por-viḷi,* the elaborate battle scenes and *Niṇam* (blood display), etc., are other significant departures from the Sanskrit drama.

all these into a perfect whole making each an integral part. Nothing can be taken from the Kathakaḷi; there is nothing to add to it, it is complete" [4].

Kathakaḷi presents many strange features; it is, as has been said at the beginning, a form of dramatic art remote from what many are familiar with, either in the East or in the West or in the rest of India, outside Kerala. And yet, to see it is to be impressed unforgettably, to understand it, is to love it and to be enraptured and conquered by it. Why is it so? Another European observer answers the question. "Kathakaḷi attracts us because of its traditional qualities, because it is a bearer of lost wisdom. It reflects a perception of universal relations which has boundless significance. It appears to us like the realisation of a long searched-for dream" [5].

---

4 *Age Old Drama*—Emily Gilchrist, Asia Magazine, December 1937.
5 *Story Plays in Living Tradition.*—Georgette Boner.

APPENDIX I

THE SALVATION OF PŪTANA

The wicked King Kamsa, having been foretold of his death at the hands of his nephew who was secreted at Gōkul, commissions the ogress Putana to kill the child by poisoning him with her milk. She transforms herself into a beautiful damsel and enters the nursery at Gokul on the sly to accomplish her evil intention. The following is the impression of Miss Alice Boner on witnessing the play *Pūtana Mōkṣa.*

"The boy who played Pūtana was an extremely gifted pupil of the Kalamandalam. In his female attire he incorporated, whether consciously or unconsciously, one of those experienced, cunning kind of women, always out for intrigue and mischief, dreaded and propitiated by all. A female who might be twisting a man's will for evil or good on to destruction, enchanting, bewitching and extremely clever. She enters the stage with innocently wondering eyes, as if searching the way to the village where Krisṇa lives (Fig. 36, page 93). Approaching the village she complacently describes people who play and gossip, and mimes their dances and games of ball with an entrancing grace. On finding out Krisṇa's abode, she depicts ecstatically the beauties of the seven-storied mansions, the shining courtyards, the cool water running through flower groves, the enraptured peacocks dancing on mount Govardhana, the lovely cowherds and Nanda's house, from which arises the fragrance of curd drops and sweet butter. After having admired her fill, she swiftly slips into the house. To suggest this a small bench is introduced, on which lies a primitive wooden doll representing the child Kṛisṇa. Pūtana carefully looks round to see whether anybody has noticed her intrusion and being reassured slowly approaches the child. On horizontally spread knees she stealthily advances, gliding like a snake without lifting her feet from the ground. All her evil intentions are expressed in this gait. But she contrives the sweetest and most loving smile on her face and starts playing with the child (Pl. XXIII fig. 1). To amuse him she delicately snaps her fingers in his face and surreptitiously caresses him. Then turning back to Krişņa with tender glances, she describes his dark blue colour, the envy of the clouds and how he is sitting on the leaf swimming on the water, raising his toe to his mouth. Enrapturing herself by his sight, strange scruples assail her heart (which is a woman's after all) and with compassion almost weeping she contemplates the infant she is sent to kill. Suddenly she shakes herself to proceed with her task. Seeing the baby weep, she affectionately asks him whether he is hungry and offers to feed him, describing voluptuously the roundness and plenty of her breasts. Cheering the child she takes him in her arms, quickly smears poison on her breast, and sets him to drink. Rocking the child on one arm and resting her head on the other hand, she looks absorbed and forlorn as women often do when they nurse. She takes the child from one breast to another, shakes him when the milk runs into his nose and smiles at him, till all of a sudden a flash of pain runs over her face. She looks alarmed, as if apprehending a menacing danger, but swallowing down her fear goes on feeding, rocking, smiling. But the pain increases. She rubs her bosom with a contracted face. No use, the pain becomes ever more violent, till she writhes scratching her neck, her breasts, her legs and tries to remove the child. As she does not succeed in this by force, she tries to persuade him by an engaging, and—how artificial—smile to take the other breast. Nor is this of any avail. She becomes mad with suffering, she pulls and pinches the child while pain distorts her face, she hammers wildly on his head, she tears her own feet, but the godly child is not to be shaken off the breast and slowly sucks the life out of her (Pl. XXIII fig. 2 and Pl. XXIV fig. 1). She jumps to her feet in wild despair running up and down (Pl. XXIV fig. 2), alternately beating her head and chest and the child hanging from her breast. Her features in agony are disfigured to a horrible grimace, the grimace in which her real devilish nature is revealed. When finally she drops dying on the floor, no trace remains of the lovely woman she was before. She is a ghastly Rakşasi killed by her own wicked deed". (*Journal of the Indian Society of Oriental Art,* Calcutta, June 1935).

APPENDIX II

THE STORY OF PRĀHLADA

The following is the record of the visual impressions gained by Mr. M. H. Brown (formerly editor of the *Illustrated Weekly of India*) on witnessing the story of the boy devotee of Viṣṇu, Prahlāda, and his father the demon king Hiranya Kasipu.

"The King is so powerful that he has come to believe in his own divinity. But one thing annoys him. His son is a great devotee of Viṣṇu. In fact, with an expression of devotion in his eyes, Prahlada continually counts on his fingers the names of tne great god.

Hiranya Kasipu becomes enraged ... The demon king is angry. In stately fashion he takes counsel with his Dewan, a series of infuriated roars supplementing the real thread of the story told by hands, face and eyes.

Even to the unfamiliar with any dance technique it is clear that this King is angry. He positively exudes rage. Though on account of the chutti his face is almost immovable from the nose downward, his eyes tell of frenzy and his hands are gesturing threats, torture, death.

The music is reaching a transport of passion. And in spite of this storm Prahlada continues to worship Viṣṇu.

The Dewan gives his advise in equally harsh terms; of course the son must worship his father.

Finally a guru is called in ... The Great King exhorts him "Take my son; remove him from this foolish devotion for Viṣṇu. Teach him to honour me".

The son departs, and the King rages on against Viṣṇu; for Hiranya Kasipu is an Asura and the sworn enemy of the Devas among whom Viṣṇu is one of the greatest.

The son returns after his years of exile and instruction. His father welcomes him and then examines him. Again Prahlada's devotion to Viṣṇu is apparent; again the father rages. Previously it would seem that he had reached the limit of anger but now the storm is really unleashed. At this point the scene on the stage seems to detach itself from the range of ordinary human emotions. It seems impossible that any human being could represent wrath so terrible.

The huge Kathakaḷi drum thunders out the frenzy. The singer reeling, keeps time with his gong. Hiranya Kasipu seems to be swelling, growing even more terrible every second. Brandishing a sword he threatens his son. The latter remains inhumanly resigned to fate.

With flying fingers the King describes the tortures which await Prahlada: clubbing, trampling under an elephant, to be pitched from a mountain, mutiliation with the sword. Still the boy is immovable.

Two hunters are called. They stand with veiled faces before the frenzied King to hear his commands. Prahlada shall die; die a hundred times. He who dares to worship Viṣṇu shall suffer the extremes of the demon's ire.

Mere speech would be useless to express such horrible fury... So comprehensive is the Kathakaḷi technique that these people are able to represent anger, the basest of the passions, in a series of gestures, horrible, yet exquisite in their subtle expression.

Prahlada's trials begin—and so too the miracles. His hands are cut off—they grow again. He is unscathed by the elephant—uninjured by the mountain....

Like the comparatively calm centre of a cyclone comes the next episode.

"Where is your Viṣṇu?" enquires the King, wondering at the miracles.

"He is everywhere" replies Prahlada.

"What even in this rotten stump" Hiranya Kasipu asks kicking the tree.

An ear-splitting crash of cymbals and out of the despised log rises, Viṣṇu, Viṣṇu the destroyer in his Narasingha, man-lion incarnation.

No other theatre in the world can show such an appalling apparition. He has a lion's head beneath his crown. His face is covered with fur and bristles, his eyes are huge, his teeth like knives, his arms are furried, his hands carry huge claws.

At last Deva and Asura have met.

Narasingha threatens the raging Hiranya Kasipu with upraised talons. The din is terrific, both are roaring to the full capacity of their lungs. The singer's voice is strained to cracking point.

The hurricane of sound from drum and gong hits the listener with a violence that is physical.

A fight far above the human plane is going on on the stage. The struggle, bereft by the laws of drama of actual physical violence, is even more awe-inspiring on that account. The demon is being destroyed by the god's anger. Gradually he weakens and falls, just as it seems that the drum can grow no louder.

The climax has been reached. The God tears up the Asura; and in a victory dance which displays his marvellous power, Narasingha rips yards and yards of entrails from the body of the fallen king.

... Human ears and eyes seem to be giving up the unequal struggle. One's mind is numbed by the impact of noise and drama ... But the drama is reaching its end. The demon king lies in tatters and it is time for Prahlada to be rewarded with the blessing of Viṣṇu. This is one of the points at which the actor's wonderful control over their expressions are displayed. Though he has been raving for half an hour, Narasingha changes from wrath to benevolence and Prahlada from resignation to adoration.

In a final ecstatic burst the story ends and the stream of epic poetry, expressed in some of the world's most beautiful gestures, comes to an end". (The Gods Walk Again—*Illustrated Weekly of India,* 19th Jan. 1936.)

APPENDIX III

NALA-CARITA

The following is a transliteration of a few songs from Naḷa-carita. A free translation is also given below.

IST DAY'S STORY: NALA AND THE GOLDEN SWAN

RĀGA-KANTARA, TĀḶA AṬANTHA

Pallavi (Burden)

Śiva Śiva! entu ceyvū ñān ennē
caticcu kollunnitu rājendran.

Anu-pallavi

Vivaśaṃ niravalambam mama kuṭumabvumini,
janakan mariccu pōyi, tanyan ñānoruttanāyi;
janani tantē daśayiṅṅinē.
apica ma ma dayitā kaḷiya
llanaticirasūta prāṇan
kaḷayumatividhurā ennāl
kulamitakhilavum aṛuti vannitu
ceṛutum pizha ceyyātorennekkonnāl bahu
duritamuṇḍu tava bhūpate!
manasi ruci jenakam ente
ciraku manikanakam ituko-
Nḍāka nī dhanikan ayyo
guṇavumanavadhi doṣamāyitu.

Saveri— atantha

Aṛika hamsame arutu paridevitam
virasabhavamilla ninnil mē
dehamanupamitam kāṇmān
mohabharamuditam, niṅkal
snehamevihitam. na maya

drohamitupozhut amrakhagavara guna nidhe.
khedamarute, parannicchaykottavazhi gaccha ni.

Kamodari- cempata Pallavi

Ūrjitāsaya pārthiva tava ñān
upakaram kuryam.

anupallavi

oṛtu kaṇdoḷam uttāmanām nī
upamā nahi, tava mūnnulakilum.
bhūtalamkhilam bhrūlatikā pari-
pāti nṛipādhipa! tē
nūtana suṣumam vapurakhilekṣaṇa-
kautukamātanute,
ādaranīyamaśeṣamho tava
bhūtadayāvasate.
cūtaśarābhā, gunairucitā dayitā tava jātu na miḷita sulaḷita.
darpita ṛipunṛpakalpakṛśānuvi-
darbhamahīramaṇan,
kelpuḷḷa Bhīnmanu colppērumoru maka-
ḷapratimā bhuvanē.
tval priyayakil analpa guṇatvam
niṣphalamallayi tē
tal ghatanāya pragalbhata ma mate
yām taravenamatinnāyanumati
Kāmini rūpini śīlavatīmani
hemāmōdasamā.
Bhimanarendrasutā Damayantī
nāmaramā navamā.
sāmaradhāma vadhūmadabhūmavi-
rāmāda komaḷimā.
tvāmnurāginiyam atinikkubharam
amrādhipatim apahāyarāgiṇam.

Toṭi- campaṭa (Pallavi)

Priyamānasa, nī poy varēṇam
priyayōṭenté vārttakal colvān

anupallavi

53 Priyamennōrttu parakayo mama?
54 kriyakoṇḍevamirunniṭumō nī?
55 palarum coḷḷikeṭṭu nalinamukhitān katha
56 balavadaṅgajārti peruttitu hṛdi mē.
57 oruvan sahāyamillennurutaravedanayā
58 maruvunneram ninṭé paricayam vannu daivāl.
59 akhilavum keṭṭu dhariccazhakotu colluvānum
60 sukhamāyañumiñum natannettuvānum,
61 nakhalu sandeham vidhimikaverum niṅṅe mama
62 sakhiyayittaḷḷa nidhiyāyittaḷḷōtaṅṅu.
63 vacanakauśalena kāminimārmaniyé
64 vaśagayakki mama tarika sakhe nī.
65 itinu pṛatikriya vidhitannē tavạ ceyyum,
66 catiyaḷḷa niyaḷḷatorugatiyiḷḷinikkārum.

The author of this three-night play is Unnayi Varier, a gifted poet and dramatist. The following translation is by no means a literal one. It is only intended to give the readers a general idea of Kathakaḷi dramatic literature.

The story of Nala and Damayanti is one of the greatest love stories in Hindu mythology and literature. King Nala fell deeply in love with Damayanti, daughter of Bhīma, king of Vidarbha, having heard of her incomparable charms and high accomplishments. But not knowing her heart, he hourly brooded over her and his love steadily flared into a burning, consuming passion. He lost all interest in the affairs of state and in other normal avocations and pleasures of life. One day he sought refuge in the loneliness of his garden; while listlessly wandering there he chanced to come across a golden swan quietly sleeping on the bank of the lotus pond. The sight of this marvellous bird, so rare and unusual, excited the king's wonder and curiosity. He desired to possess it; tiptoeing gently, he approached and caught the sleeping bird. Rudely awakened and finding itself a captive, the bird, screaming in terror, piteously wails and begs for the mercy of the king.

1 *Swan*—Śiva, Śiva (O God) what am I to do, I am
2 Deceived and being killed by the king.
3 Without support my family (hereafter).

4 (My) father dead, I his only son left behind,
5 (My) mother's plight thus.
6 Then, my wife in truth
7 Not long since confined.
8 She will kill herself grief-stricken; if so,
9 My line will be extinct for ever.
10 I who haven't done the smallest wrong. If thou kill,
11 Great sin will befall you, Oh! king.
12 Mind-captivating (indeed) my
13 Golden wings, with these
14 You will never become rich.
15 Alas! this excellence is all a great fault (curse).
16 *Nala*—Know you swan, no need for lament,
17 Unfriendly intentions none have I towards you.
18 Body incomparable (so lovely) to see
19 Desire great arose. To you
20 Love only have I. From me
21 No harm now will befall, great and celestial bird, abode of virtues!
22 Grieve not, fly away where thou wilt.

The bird set free, flew back to its nest in feverish haste. Having joined its kith and kin and having tasted its new found freedom, the composed and assured bird comes back fearlessly to the king and addresses him thus.

23 *Swan*—Magnanimous one, ruler of the world! To you I
24 Shall do a service.
25 To my mind noblest one art thou.
26 There is none comparable to you in all the three worlds.
27 All the worlds, by your eye-brow twitch,
28 Oh king, you control.
29 Your fresh lovely form to all eyes
30 Delight yields.
31 Everything in you indeed is admirable (worthy of respect),
32 Seat of Compassion;
33 Radiant as God of Love. One with excellences
34 Befitting you there is. She, that lovely one un-united remains.
35 To the proud hosts of enemy kings,

36 A consuming fire is he, the king of Vidarbha.
37 To this mighty Bhima, a reputed daughter there is.
38 Without a peer is she, in all the worlds.
39 Thy beloved if she becomes,
40 Great excellences thine, will not fruitless be.
41 To unite her to thee I have skill enough.
42 Pray, permit me, to do that.
43 Desire-generating, of beauteous form, crest jewel of the virtuous,
44 Delighting as gold, is she the
45 Daughter of king Bhima. Damayanti
46 Is her name. A new born Rama (Lakshmi) indeed!
47 Humbled is the pride of celestial ladies
48 By her excelling graces.
49 Mine the duty to lead her heart to thee.
50 From Indra's love even will I wean her (for thee).
51 *Nala*—Dear one, go and come back (quick)
52 To tell my beloved of me (of my state).
53 Do you say all this because it is pleasing to me?
54 By deeds wilt thou be like that?
55 Hearing many speak of the lotus-faced one,
56 Mighty passion in my heart grew.
57 Helpless and in utter misery I remained,
58 When by God's grace I chanced to make your acquaintance.
59 To hear and grasp everything told and to say it winsomely,
60 To go and come back with speed and ease,
61 You have skill enough. Providence gave thee to me
62 Not merely as a friend but as a veritable treasure.
63 By the skill of your words, O! friend, for me
64 Win her, who is the crest-jewel of lovely maids.
65 Recompense for this Providence will (give);
66 In truth, I have none but thee to help.

The Golden Swan then took to its wings after many endearing intimacies between the two. The king anxiously watches till it becomes a tiny speck on the horizon and disappears altogether.

Having heard repeatedly of the great excellences and virtues of Nala, Damayanti too had fallen deeply in love with him. Her secret desire was consuming her and made her ever restless. So she sought shelter and diversion in her garden where she came with her confidantes. But the garden only fanned her passion and made her more miserable.

DAMAYANTI AND THE GOLDEN SWAN

Damayanti to her companions

The humming of the bees and the song of the kokils
To my ears intensely painful.
The perfume of flowers smarts my nostrils.
Great pain-causing this garden visit—.
(*seeing the Golden Swan*)
Is it lightning that comes descending?
Is the moon coming down to earth?
Is this an ambrosial stream for the eyes (meaning a sweet delight to the eyes)!

How delightful to look at this. Ere this
I have never seen nor heard of the like.
Gold-coloured swan, sweet voiced too.
Methinks, I can surely befriend it.
Oh, I just touched it with my hands. Friends
If I can secure it how delightful to sport with.
He is no wild one but gentle this lovely one.
Go you all far away, let none be near me.

The bird having alighted near to excite their interest cleverly eludes them. Damayanti sportingly chases and the bird skilfully leads her away from her companions while she thinks that with the next forward step she will secure the bird. When it had decoyed her to a safe distance it addressed her thus.

Swan

Oh Jewel amongst beauties, tender one, what may your desire be?
How can you catch me, who roams the high skies?
Even with the advent of youthfulness your childish ways are not on the wane.

Indiscretion this, if seen, you will be laughed at.

Some will blame thee and you will miss your way.
No need to capture me, I am thy friend.
Trust me more than your confidantes.
One who is the envy of Indra and the God of Love
Will become thy beloved.
In the city of Nala I dwell. At the behest of the Lotus-born (Brahma)
I teach the lotus-eyed damsels their gait.
Tender and graceful, reflecting pride of youth.
Believe me, this is no jest.

Damayanti

I have seen you at close quarters and heard too your pretty jesting prattle.
Vehicle of the Lotus-born, Golden one, charming are your words.
Art thou the emissary of the Lotus-born?
Is Nala's city your sweet home?
O, thou of sweet form, ocean of excellences,
Emperor of birds, I bow to thee.
Vehicle of the Lotus-born, do tell of the great qualities of Nala.
Your words will end my misery,
Make my ears blessed.
All my thoughts I will confide in thee
If thou art friend, noble and kind hearted one.
To me helpless and miserable, you are adorable.

The clever bird messenger knowing half her mind makes another strategic move to know it in full.

Swan

Be pleased to tell me your thoughts, daughter of king Bhima.
Shedding all your doubts and fears, regard me as one of your confidantes.
Lighten the burden of bashfulness, have no anxiety.
First amongst the lovely-eyed ones, sister of Dama, tender one,
Tell me, who among men claims your heart.
Most blessed indeed is he.
Gazelle-eyed one, tarry not to tell,
Nor seek to hide it in bashfulness.
I am here to aid you, fair one.

I won't betray nor cause disgrace.
Your secret desire will soon be fulfilled.
What I say now is all true.

Damayanti

Oh Swan king, to you what shall I tell?
Gentle maidens' secrets hidden in their hearts, can they be ever told?
Hearing people singing much of Nala's glories,
Enraptured, I dwelt on his beauteous form.
Riven by love's cruel darts I am burning,
I have grown (by this consuming passion) utterly miserable.

Swan

Since you have spoken the truth, without doubt,
Tender-limbed one, you will attain your heart's desire.
Good must unite with the good.
To be your lord none is the equal of Nala.
He is mightier than Indra.
His form enchanting, he is the abode of excellences,
Fair one, yours is the union of diamond with gold.
As Viṣṇu to Lakṣmi, Moon to Night, Śiva to Uma.
so is Nala to you (meaning thereby so ideal a union).

BIBLIOGRAPHY

Kerala Theatre—K. Rama Pisharoti—Annamalai University Journal. Vol. No. 1 and Vol. III No. 2.

Kathakali: A Unique Dramatic Art—M. Mukunda Raja—Bulletin of the Rama Varma Research Institute Vol. V Part I.

Kathakali Souvenir: Rangoon Kathakali Committee.

Kathakali—Alice Boner—Journal of the Indian Society of Oriental Art. June 1935.

Kathakali—Story Plays in Living Tradition—Georgette Boner (lecture delivered at Ernakulam on 28th June 1938).

Kathakali—The Classical Dance-Drama of Malabar—K. B. Iyer—Indian Art & Letters. Vol. XII No. 1 and No. 2 (1938).

Kathakali—K. B. Iyer—The Illustrated London News—March 20, 1937.

The Gods Walk Again—M. H. B. The Illustrated Weekly of India. 19th January 1936.

Is the Hindu Dance worth Reviving? L. Lightfoot—Hindu (Madras).

The Mirror of Gesture—Ananda Coomaraswamy and G. K. Duggirala (E. Weyhe, New York).

Nandikeswara's Abhinaya Darpaṇam—Edited by Manomohan Ghosh Kavytirtha—Calcutta Sanskrit Series No. V (Metropolitan Printing & Publishing House Ltd., Calcutta, 1934).

Nrityanjali—Hindu Dancing—Sri Ragini (Hari G. Govil Inc. Oriental Publishers, New York).

Hand-Symbols in Kathakali—Kuttikrishna Marar—Modern Review (June 1937).

Kathakali—R. Vasudeva Poduval. Archaeological Dept. of the Govt. of Travancore.

Dance Traditions of South India—K. V. Ramachandran. Triveni Vol. VII No. 4.

Kathakali and Other forms of Bharata Natya outside Kerala by V. Raghavan. Triveni, Vol. IV No. 2.

Sanskrit Drama and Dramatists—K. P. Kulkarni (Satara Dist).

The types of Sanskrit Drama—Prof. D. R. Mankad.

Dance-Drama Experiments in the art of the Theatre—Terence Gray (W. Heffer & Sons Ltd., Cambridge 1926).

The Dance of Siva—Mc Collum (Kegan Paul).

The Dance of Siva—14 Indian Essays—Ananda Coomaraswamy.

Mudras—Tyra De Kleen.

Ballet—Arnold Haskell (Pelican Special).

Ballet Panorama—Arnold Haskell.

Cochin Tribes & Caṣtes. Vols. 1 & 2. L. K. Ananthakrishna Iyer.

Cochin State Manual—C. Achyuta Menon.

The Sanskrit Drama—Keith.

Famous Chinese Plays—Arlington & Acton (Published by Henry Vetch).

The World History of the Dance—Curt Sachs (George Allen & Unwin).

Age Old Drama—Emily Gilchrist—Asia Magazine. December 1937.

Dancing in India—La Meri—Indian Art and Letters. Vol. XIII No. 1.
The Naṭya Śāstra—Translated by Manomohan Ghose (The Royal Asiatic Society of Bengal. 1950).

MALAYALAM

Keraliya Nrithya Kala or Kathakali—G. Krishna Pillai. Travancore.
Āṭṭakatha—P. Krishnan Nayar (Madras University Malayalam Series 5. 1939).
Hasta-Lakshana Dīpika (Publishers K. R. Bros. Calicut, 1926).

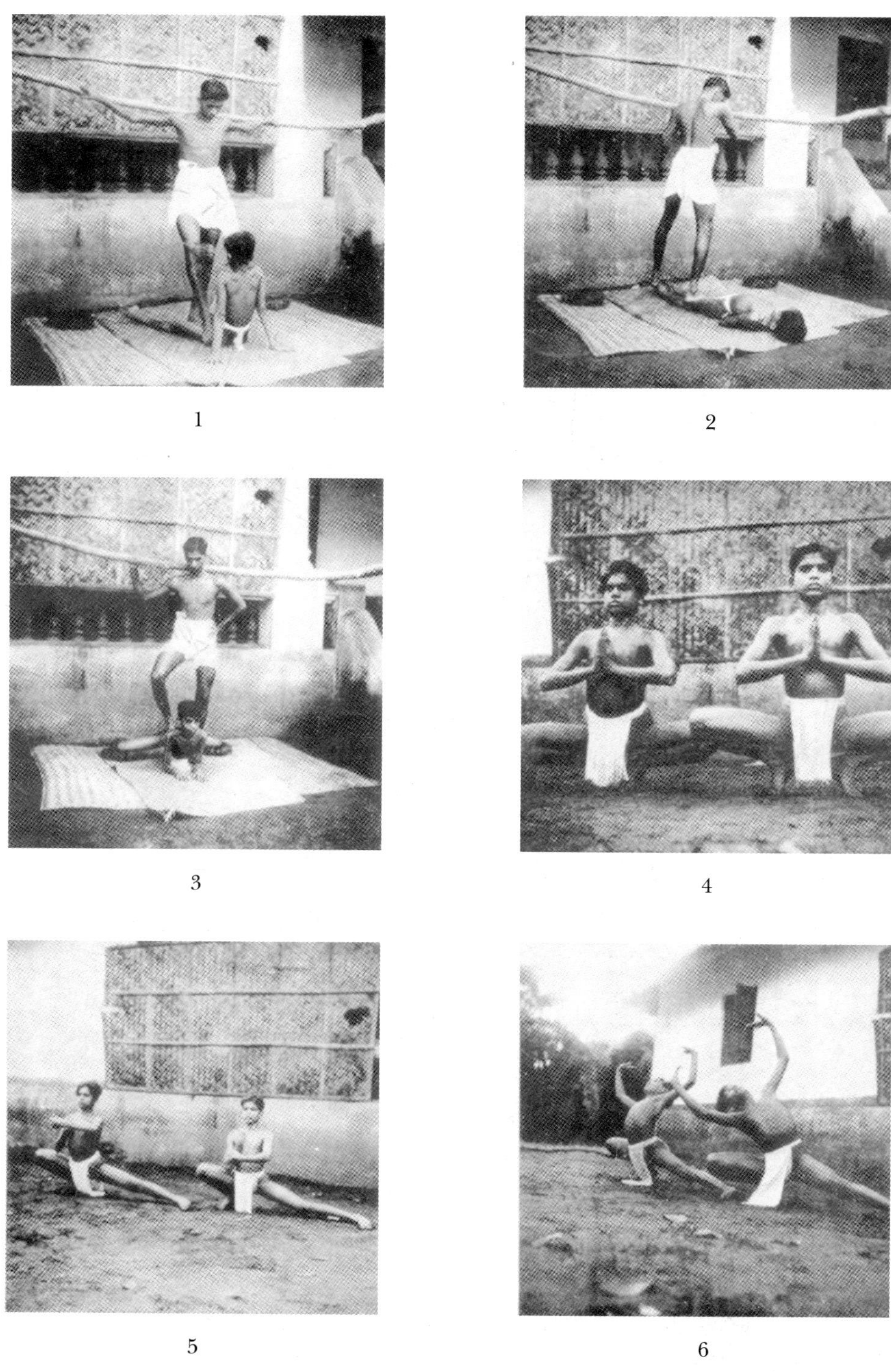

1

2

3

4

5

6

Fig. 1-3. Massaging the body of the young actor.
Fig. 4-6. Some of the many Kathakali exercises (p. 29).

Photos by the author.

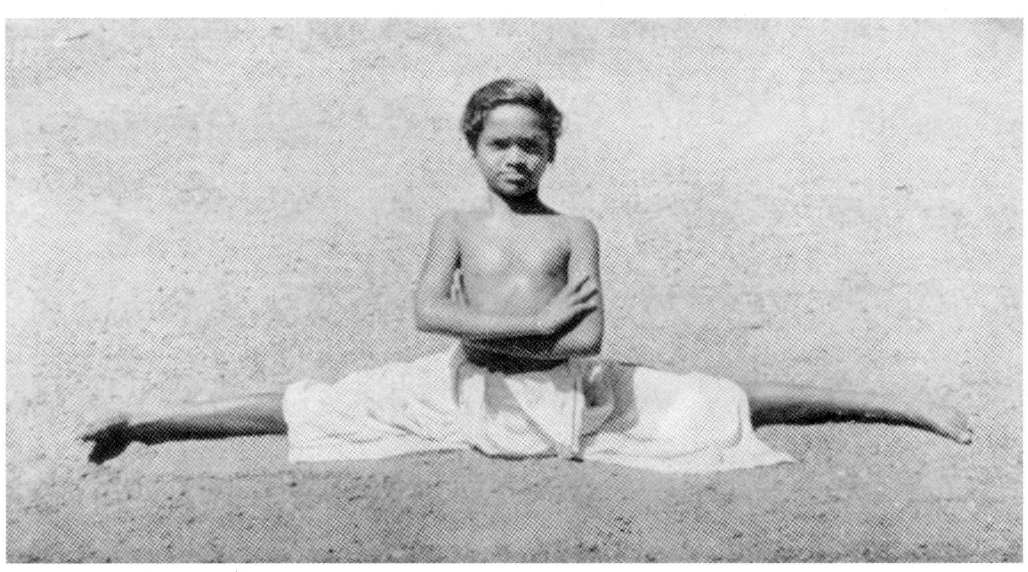

Fig. 1. *Sama-cūci*—needle points (p. 29).
Photo courtesy of A. Janta.

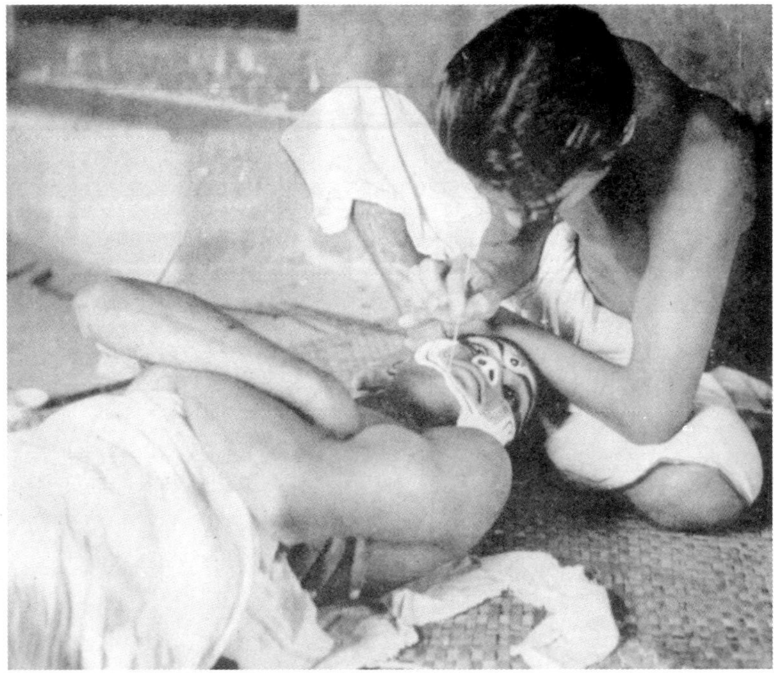

Fig. 2. Painting the face (p. 25 and 45).
Photo courtesy of S. Jepson.

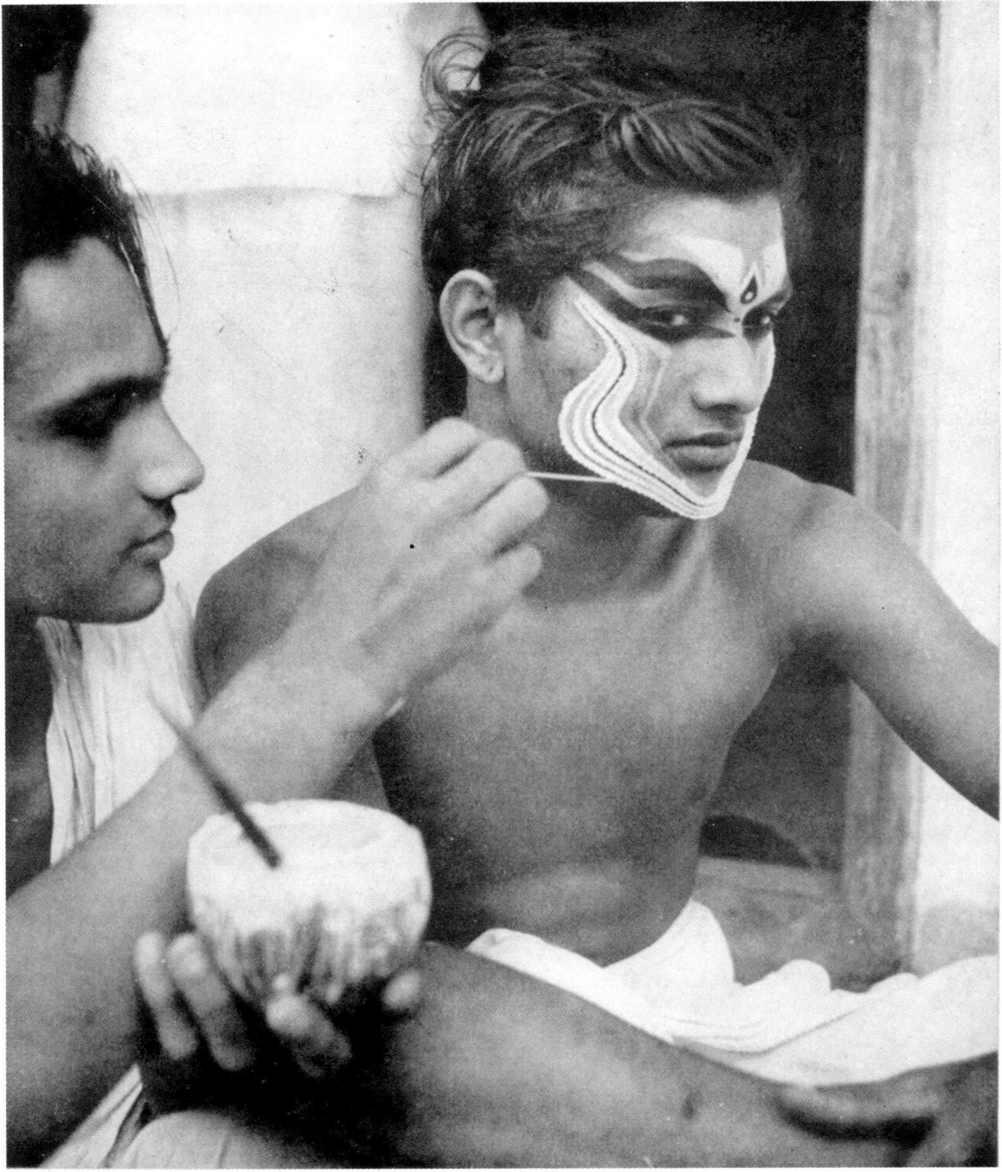

Building up the *cutti.* The elongated eyes and the *vaiṣṇava* mark may be noticed. The face is not yet coloured (p. 45).

Photo: Paul Popper, London.

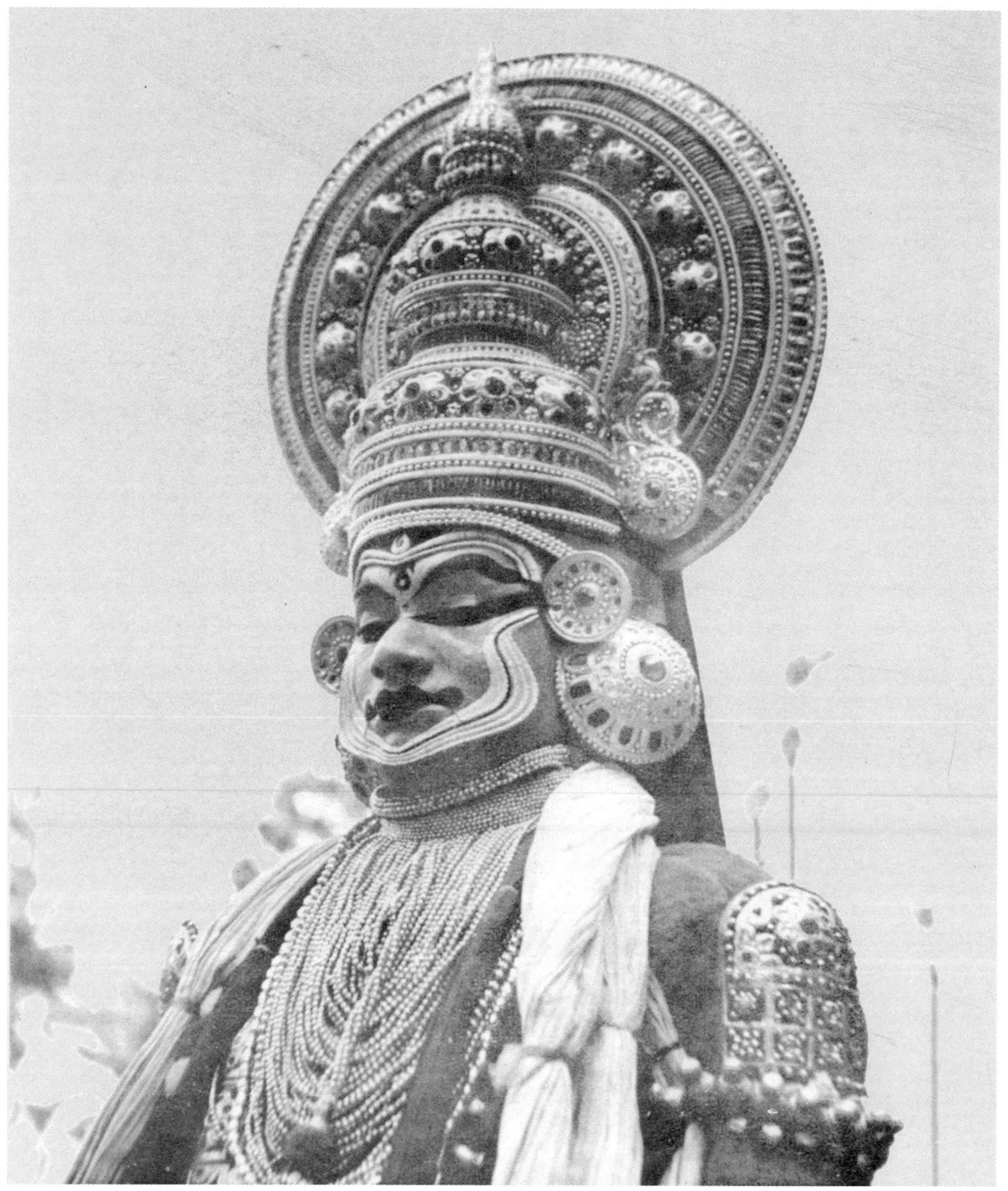

This stately but pensive figure is of King Rugmāngada (*Pacca* type) who is being urged by his mistress Mohini to slay his son the young prince (p. 39 and 44).

Photo: Paul Popper, London.

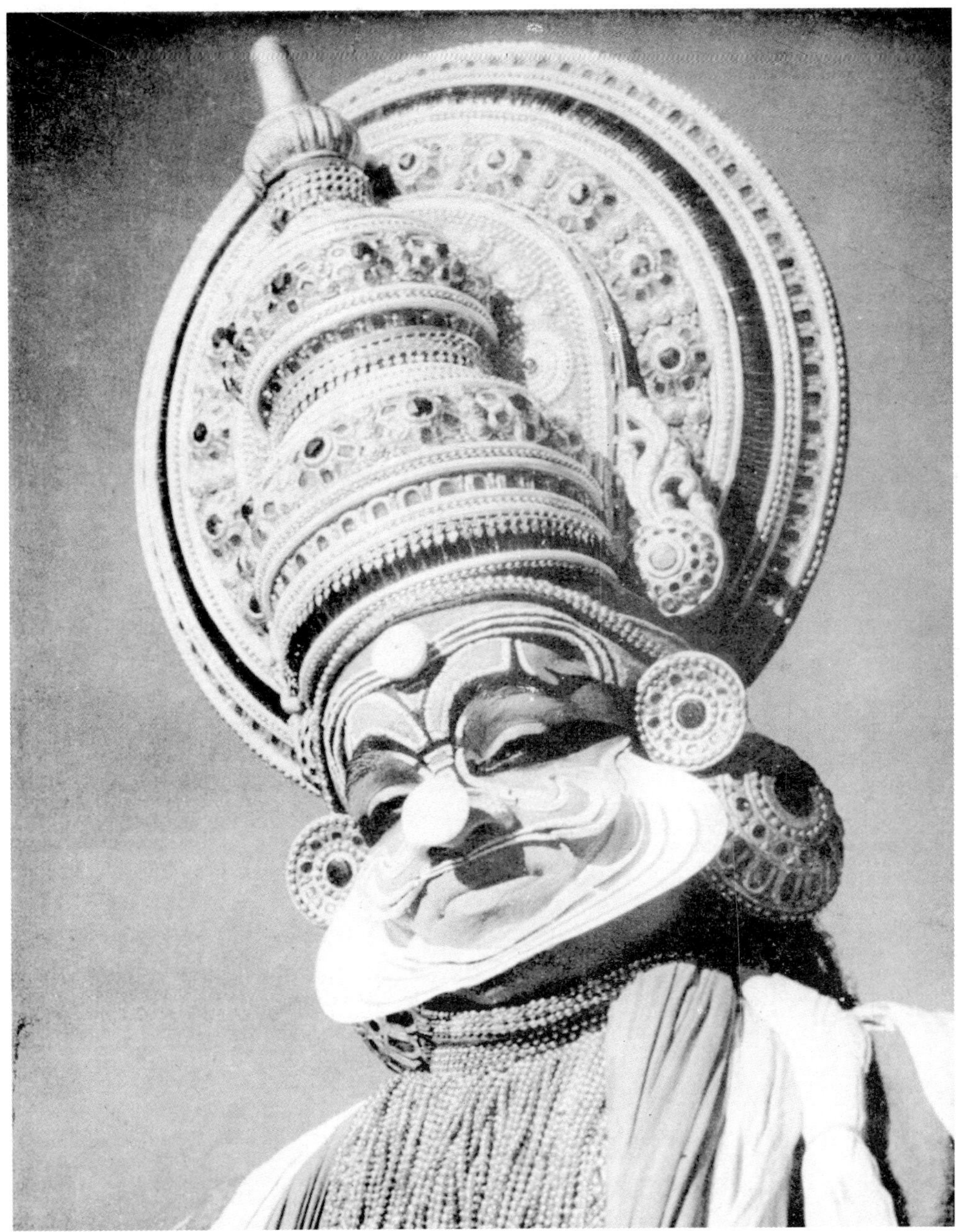

Rāvaṇa, *Katti* type (p. 46).
Photo: R. R. Prabhu, Bombay.

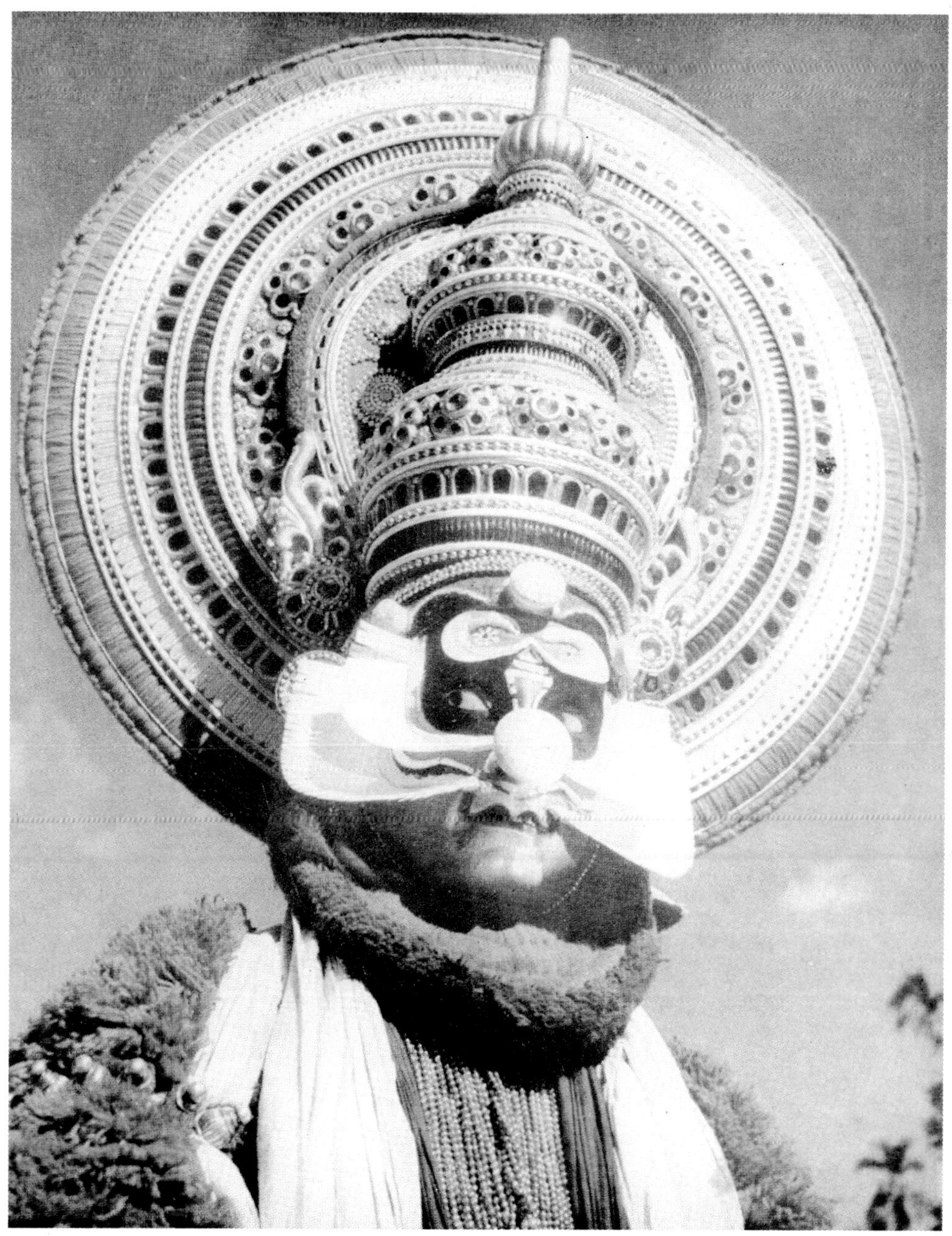

Duśśāsana, the Red Beard type (p. 47).
Photo: R. R. Prabhu, Bombay.

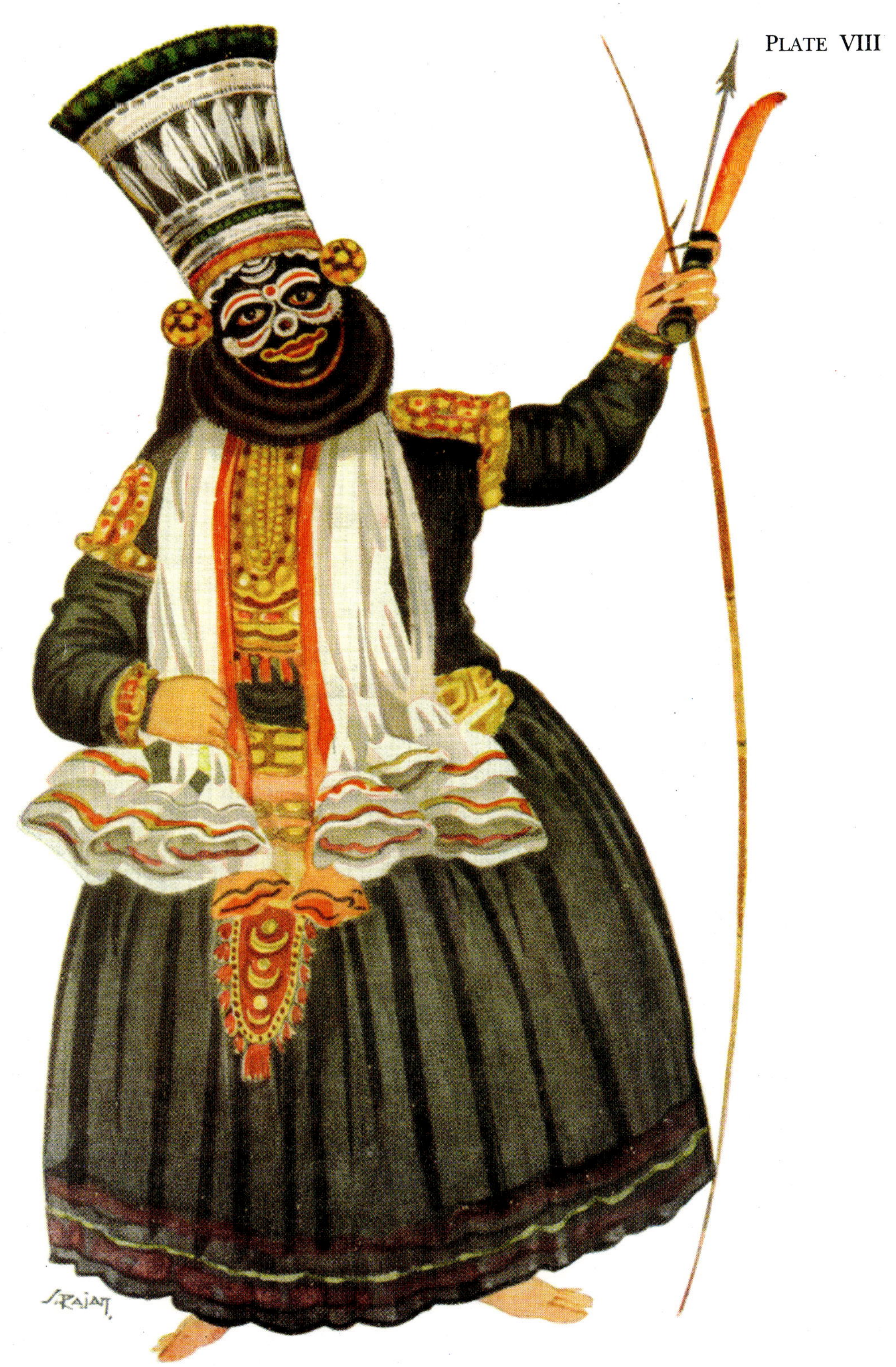

The Black-beard; Kāṭṭāḷan or the Forest-man (p. 49, 51).

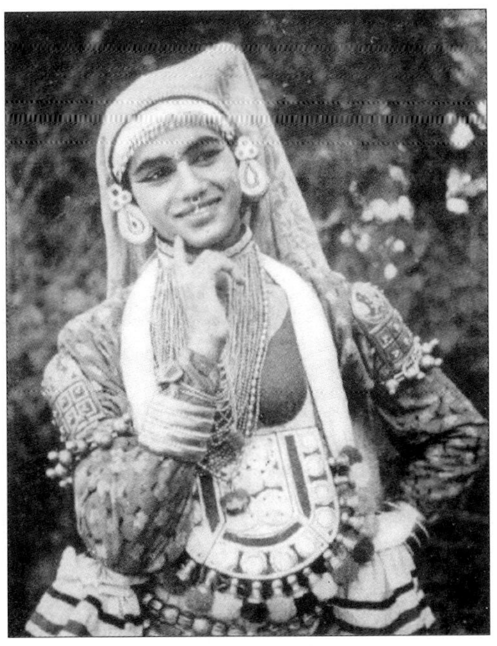

Fig. 1. The *Minukku* type (p. 49).
Mohini tempting King Rugmāngada (p. 39).

Photo courtesy of S. Jepson.

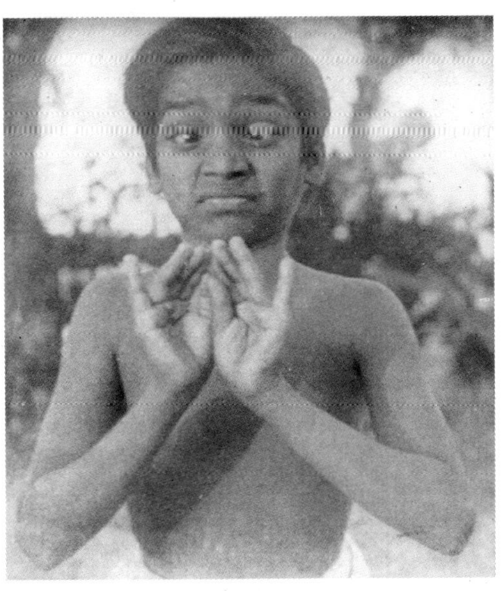

Fig. 3. With hands and eyes the young actor is trying to picture a snake (p. 78).

Fig. 2-4. Colliāṭṭam, pupils rehearsing in the class room (p. 29).

Photos 2 to 4 courtesy of A. Janta.

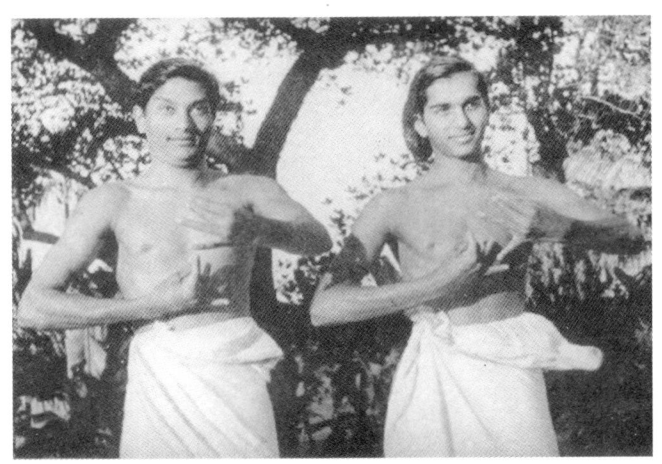

Fig. 2. Suggesting *prema* (love).

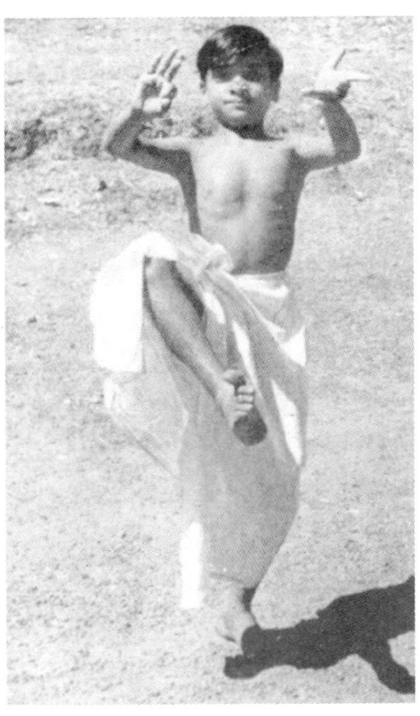

Fig. 4. An initial movement in dancing, particularly in *Kalāsās*.

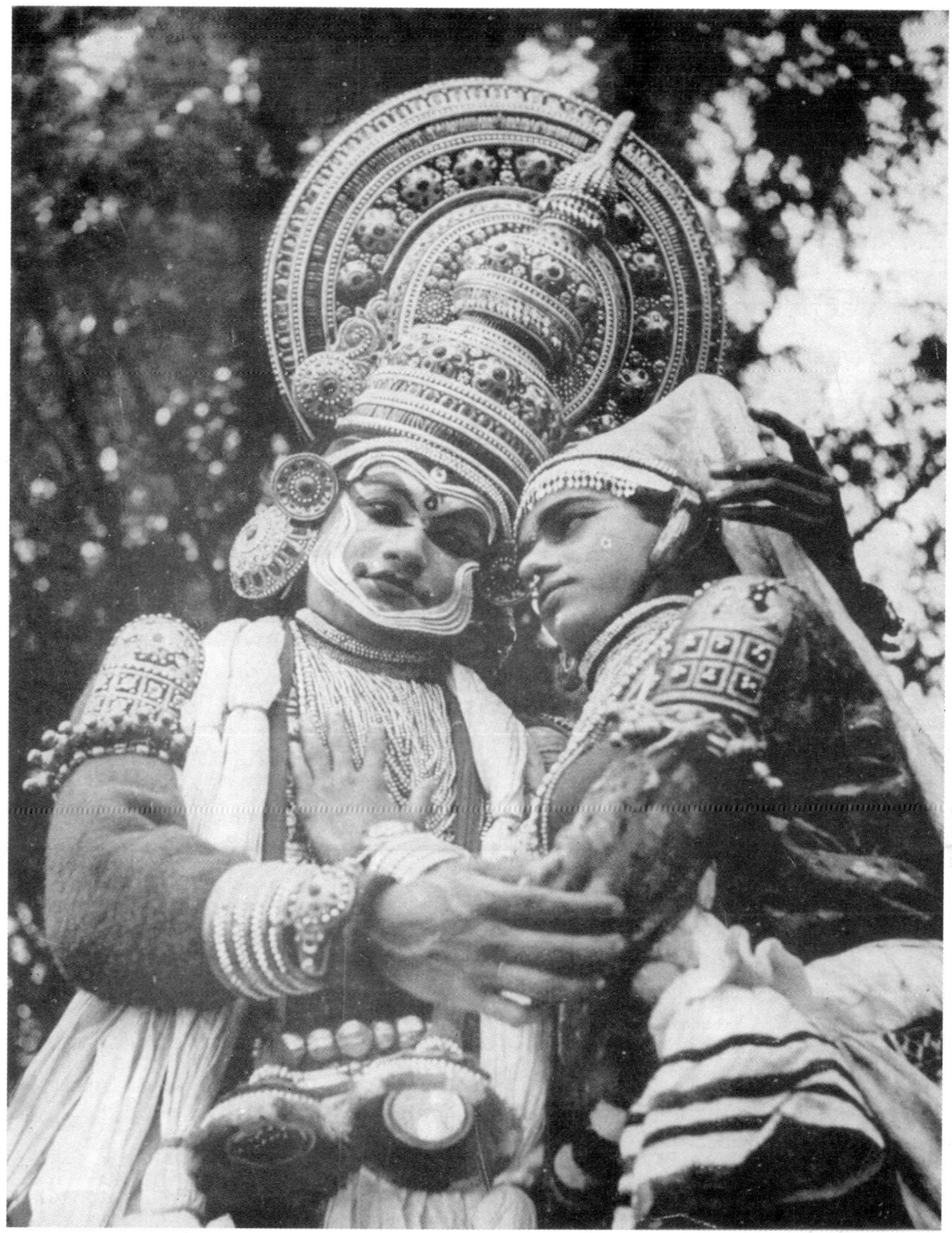

Nala and Damayanti in a love scene (*Patinjattam*) (p. 84). Kalāmandalam Krishnan in the role of Nala.

Photo: Paul Popper, London.

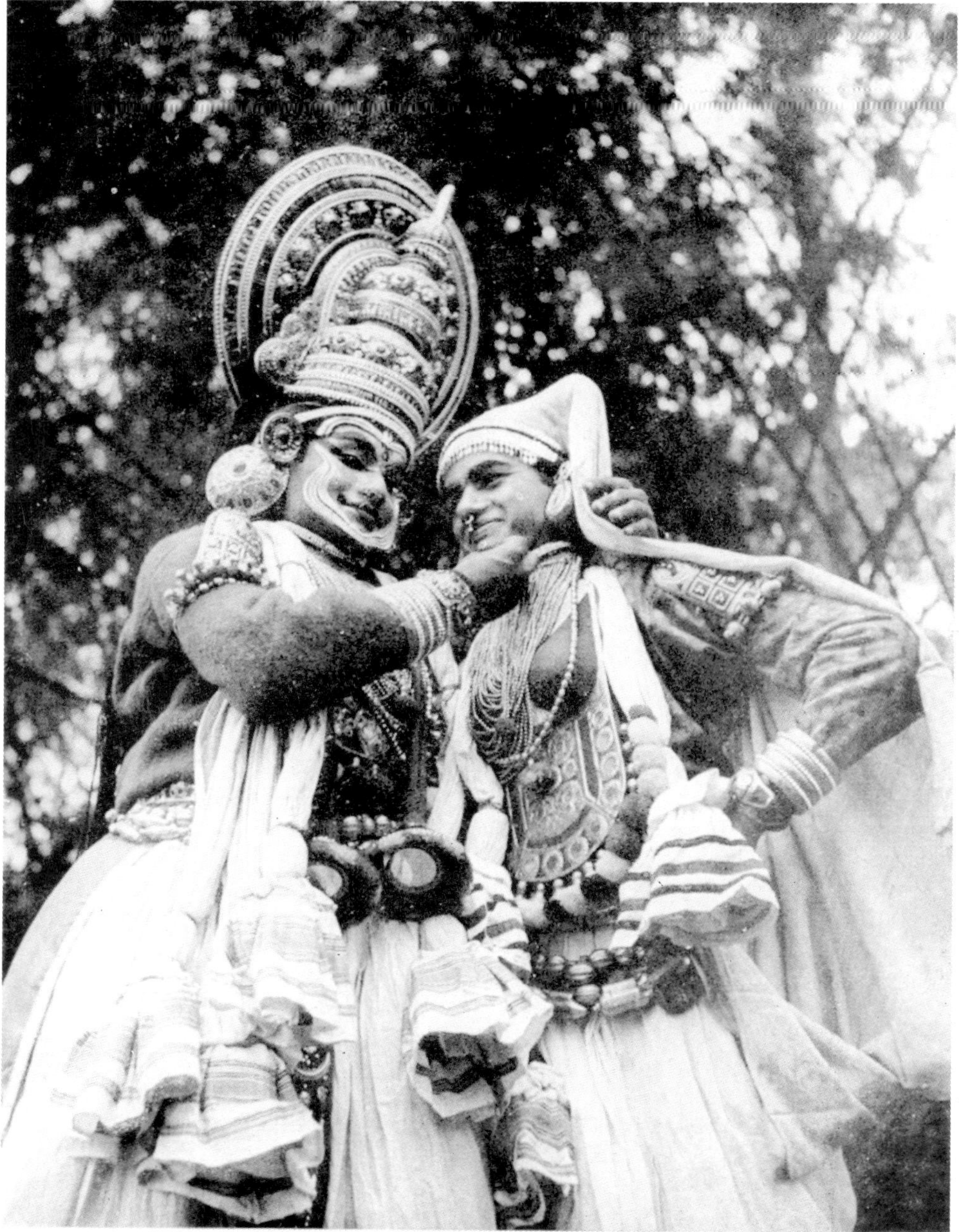

Nala and Damayanti. Another moment in the love scene (p. 85).
Photo: Paul Popper, London.

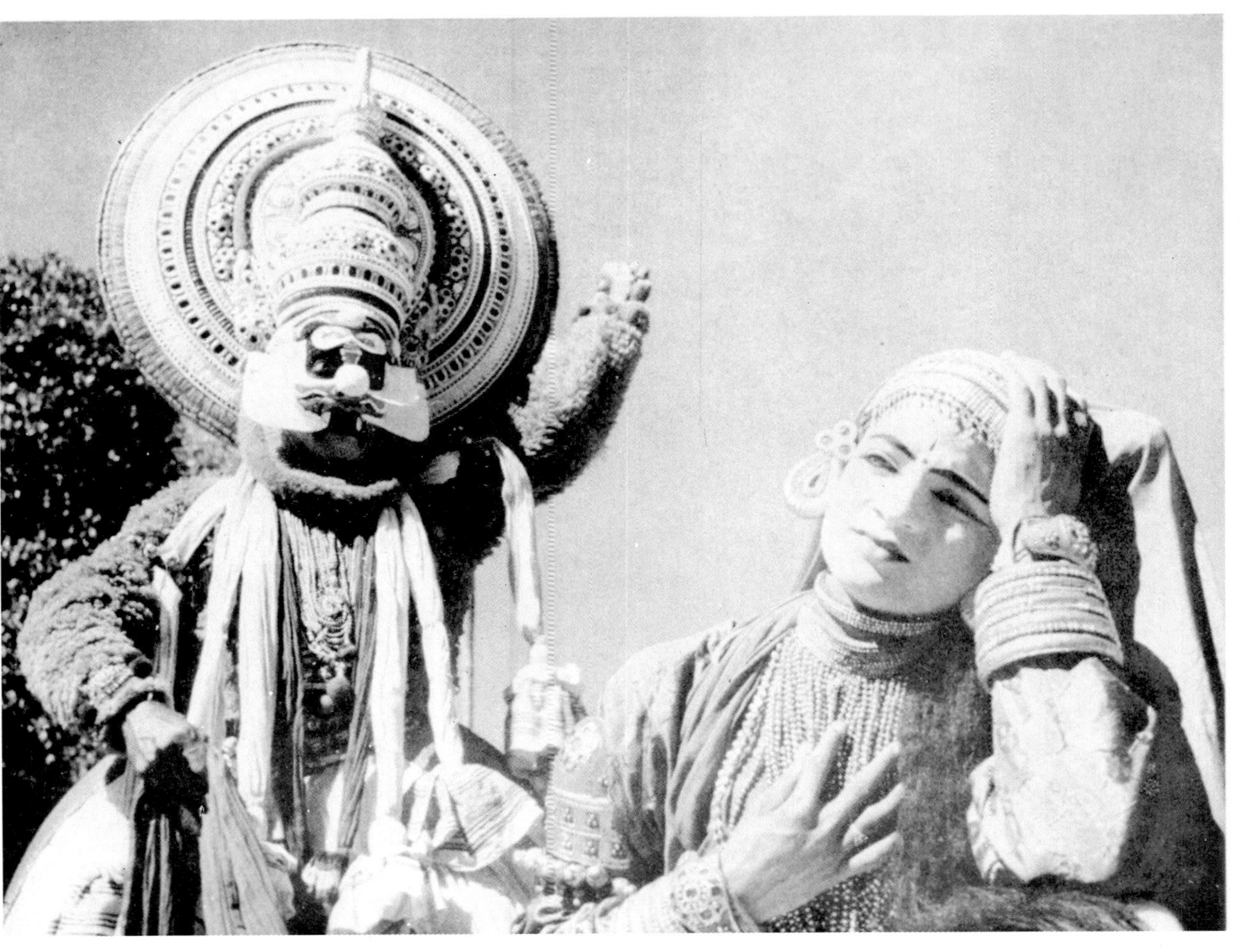

Wicked and vicious Duśśāsana disrobing queen Draupadi (p. 90).

Photo: R. R. Prabhu, Bombay.

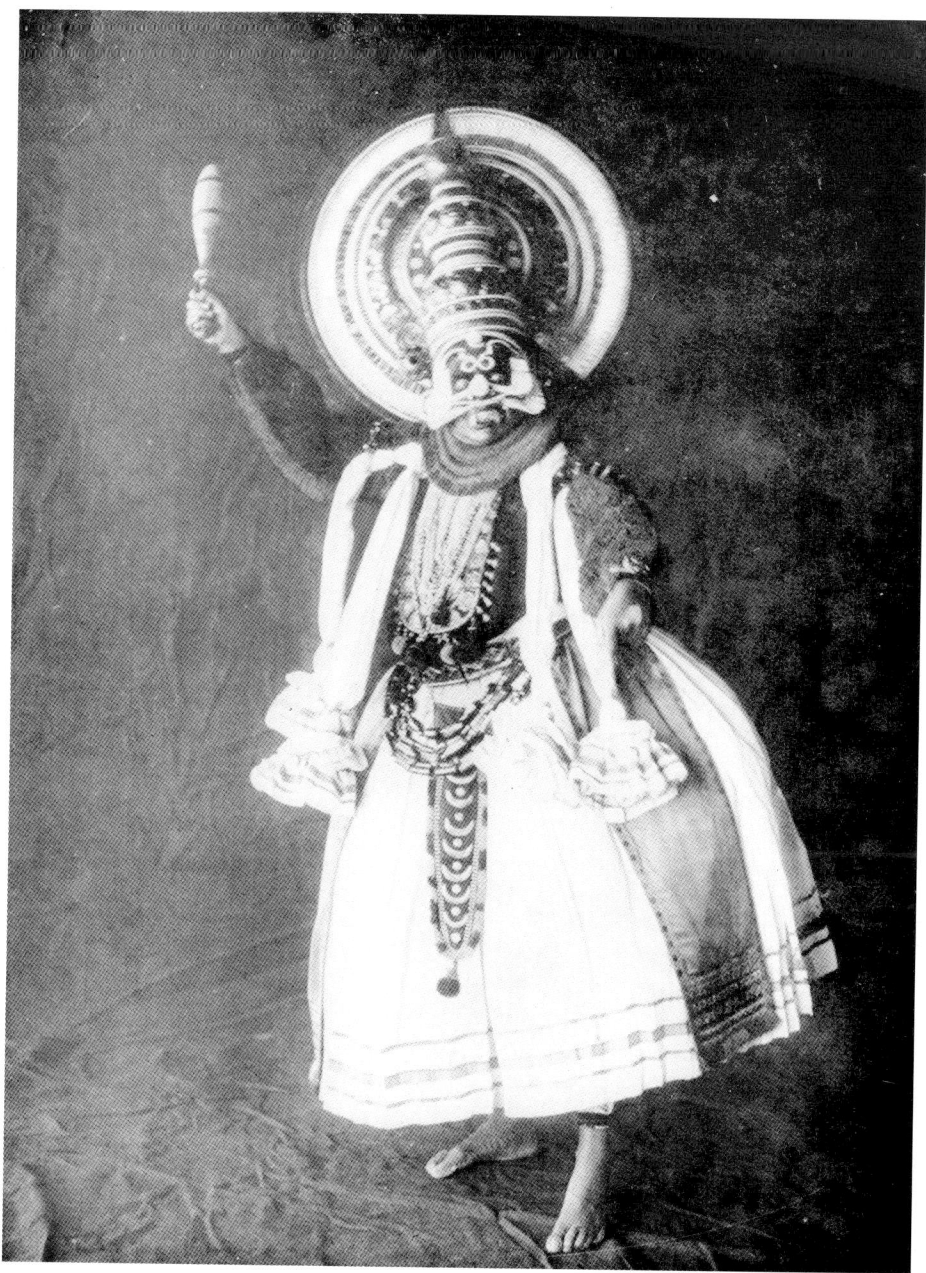

Duśśāsana challenging Bhima (p. 51 & 89).
Photo: Krishnan Nair Bros., Trichur.

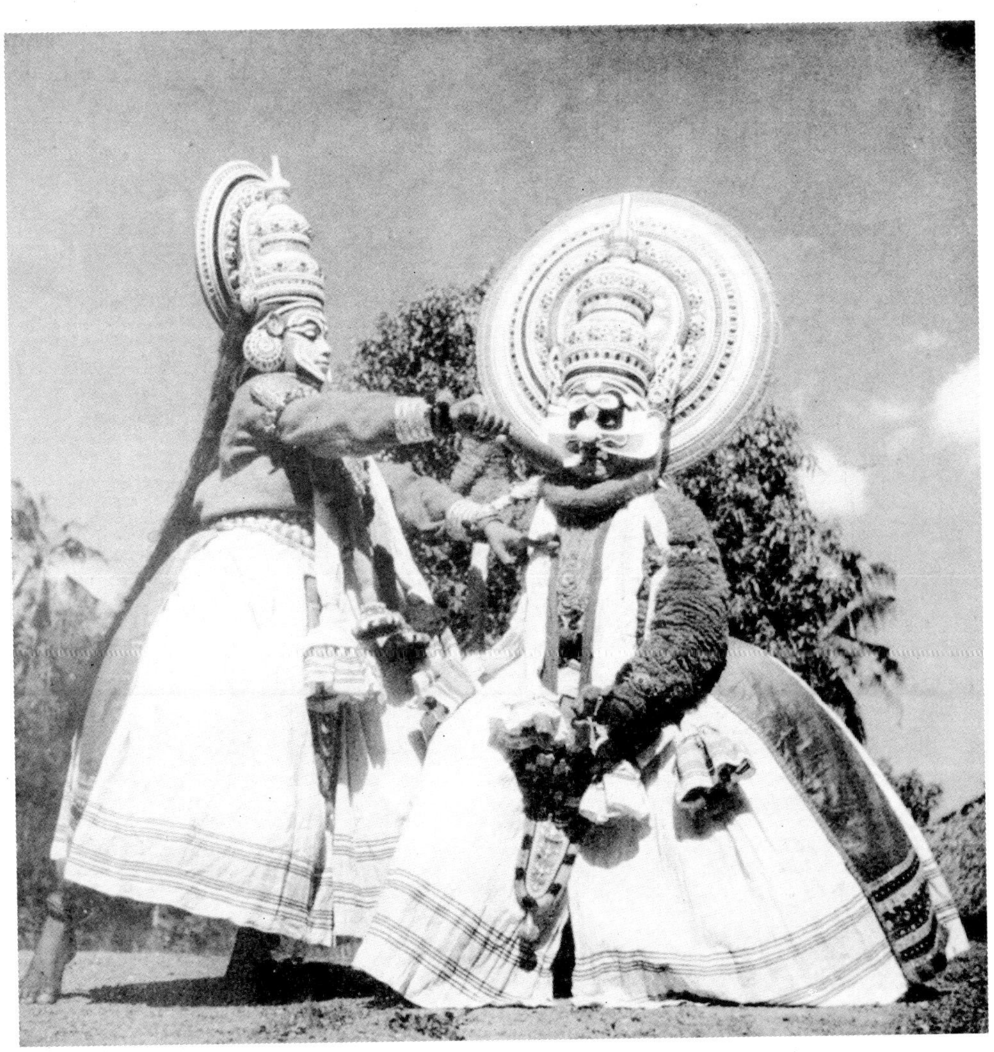

After a great fight Bhima slaying Duśśāsana (p. 89).

Photo: R. R. Prabhu, Bombay.

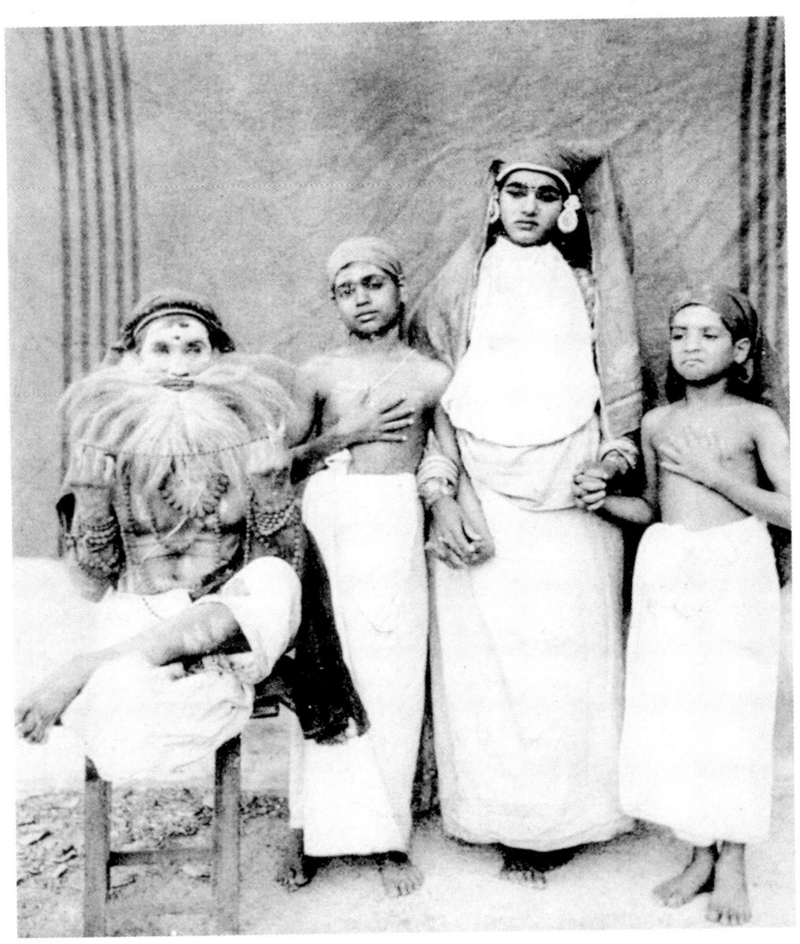

The pious Brahmin Sudāma and his hungry and miserable wife and children.
Kunju Kurup is seen here in the role of Sudāma (p. 39 & 102).

Photo: Royal Studio, Ernakulam.

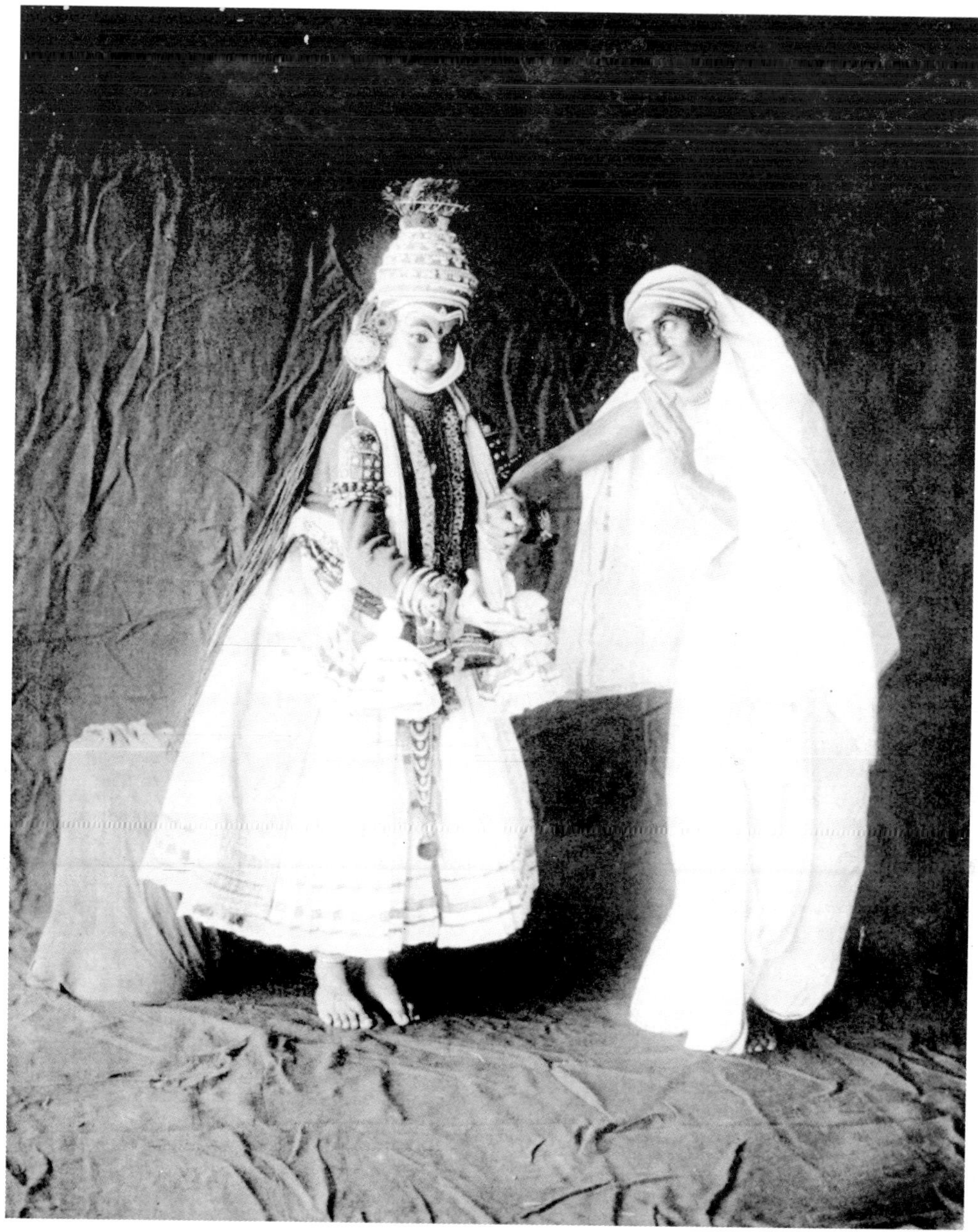

Kunju Kurup (right) is seen here in another of his famous roles as the trusted and astute Brahmin messenger from princess Rukmini bearing her message of love.
Kriṣṇa welcoming the Brahmin (p. 39 & 46).

Photo: Krishnan Nair Bros., Trichur.

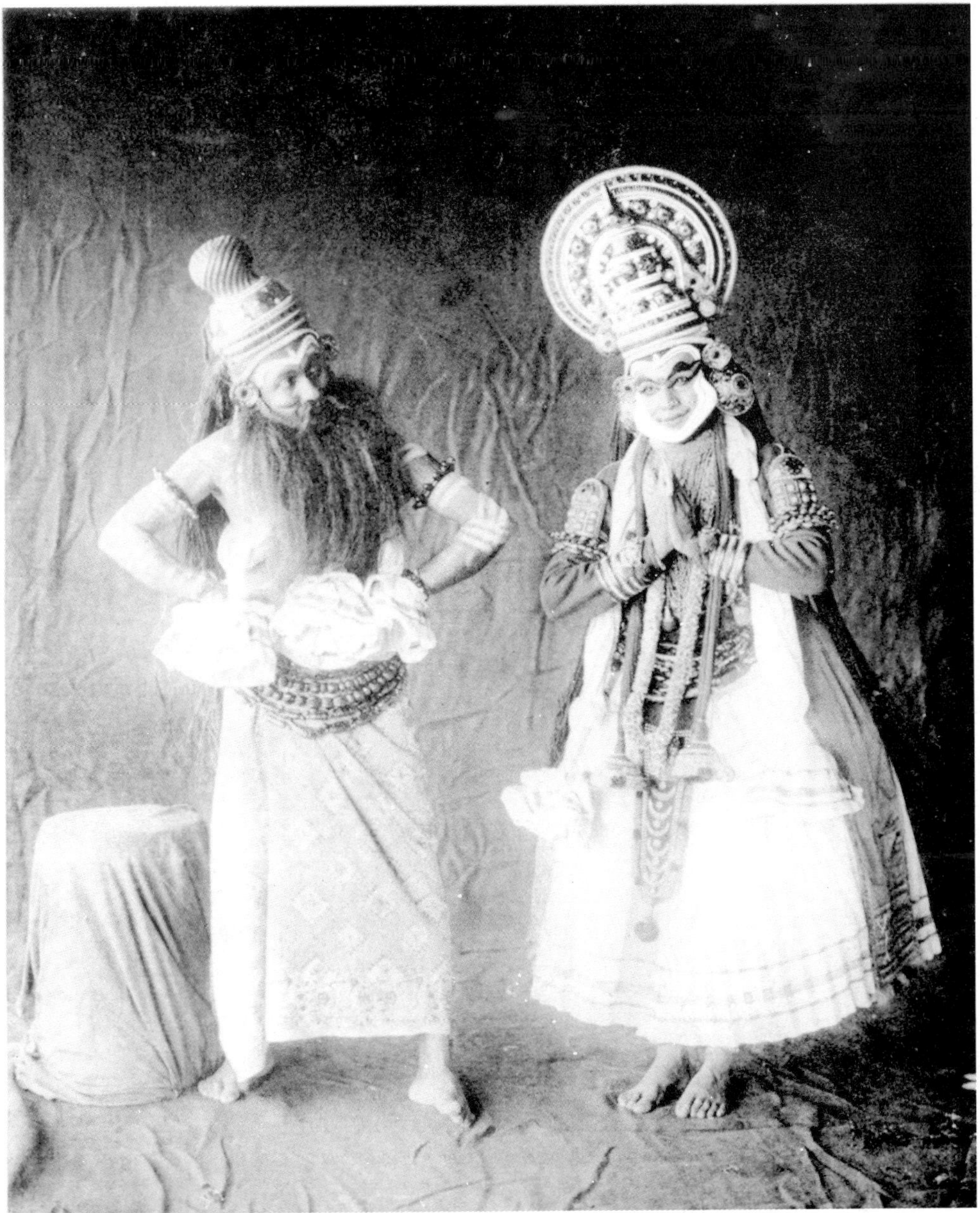

King Naḷa salutes the sage Nārada. A scene from Naḷa Carita.
Nārada belongs to the Minukku type (p. 49 & 127).

Photo: Krishnan Nair Bros., Trichur.

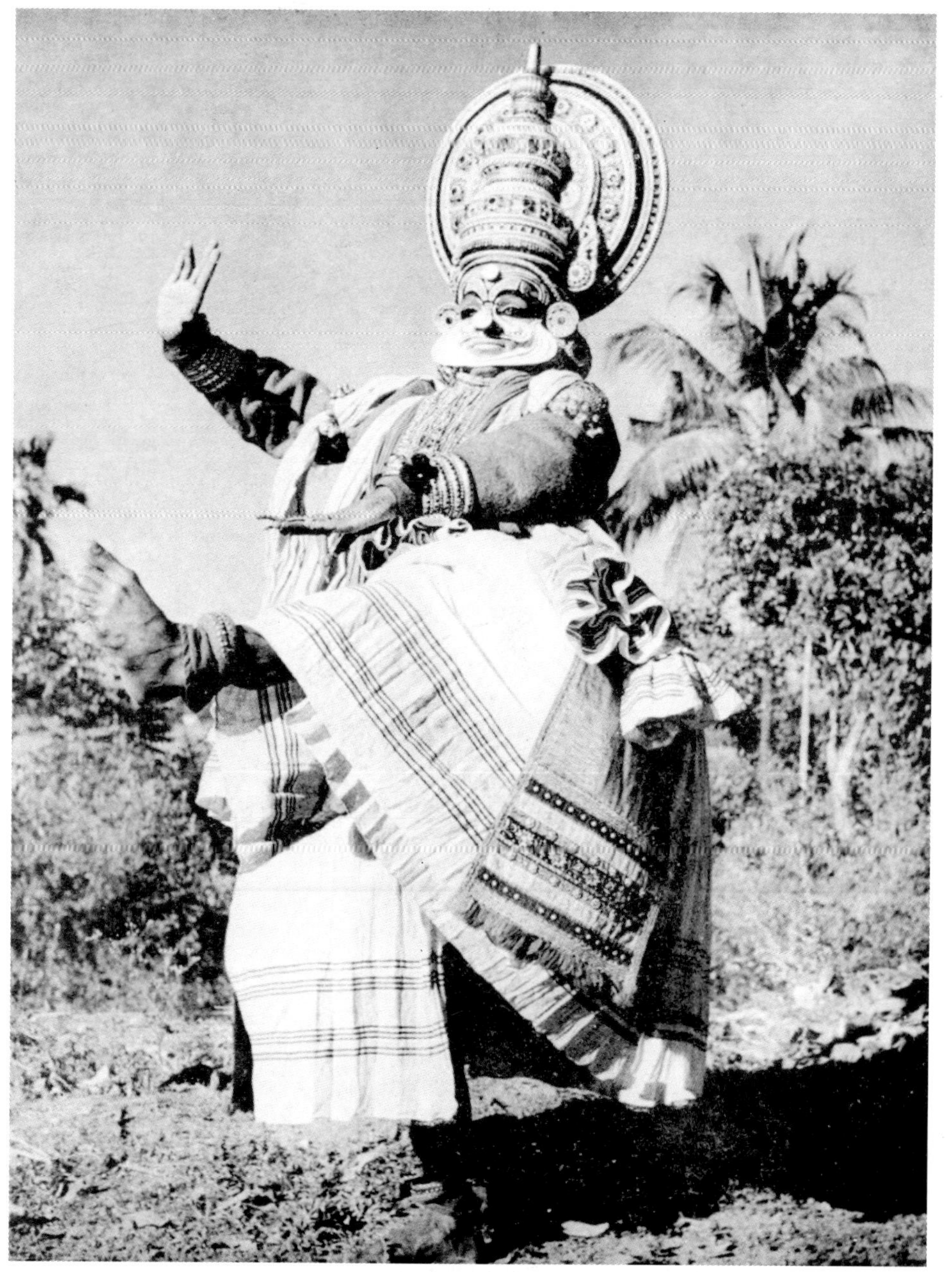

Rāvaṇa in a dynamic pose, suggestive of majesty and the might of an elephant (p. 46).
Photo: R. R. Prabhu, Bombay.

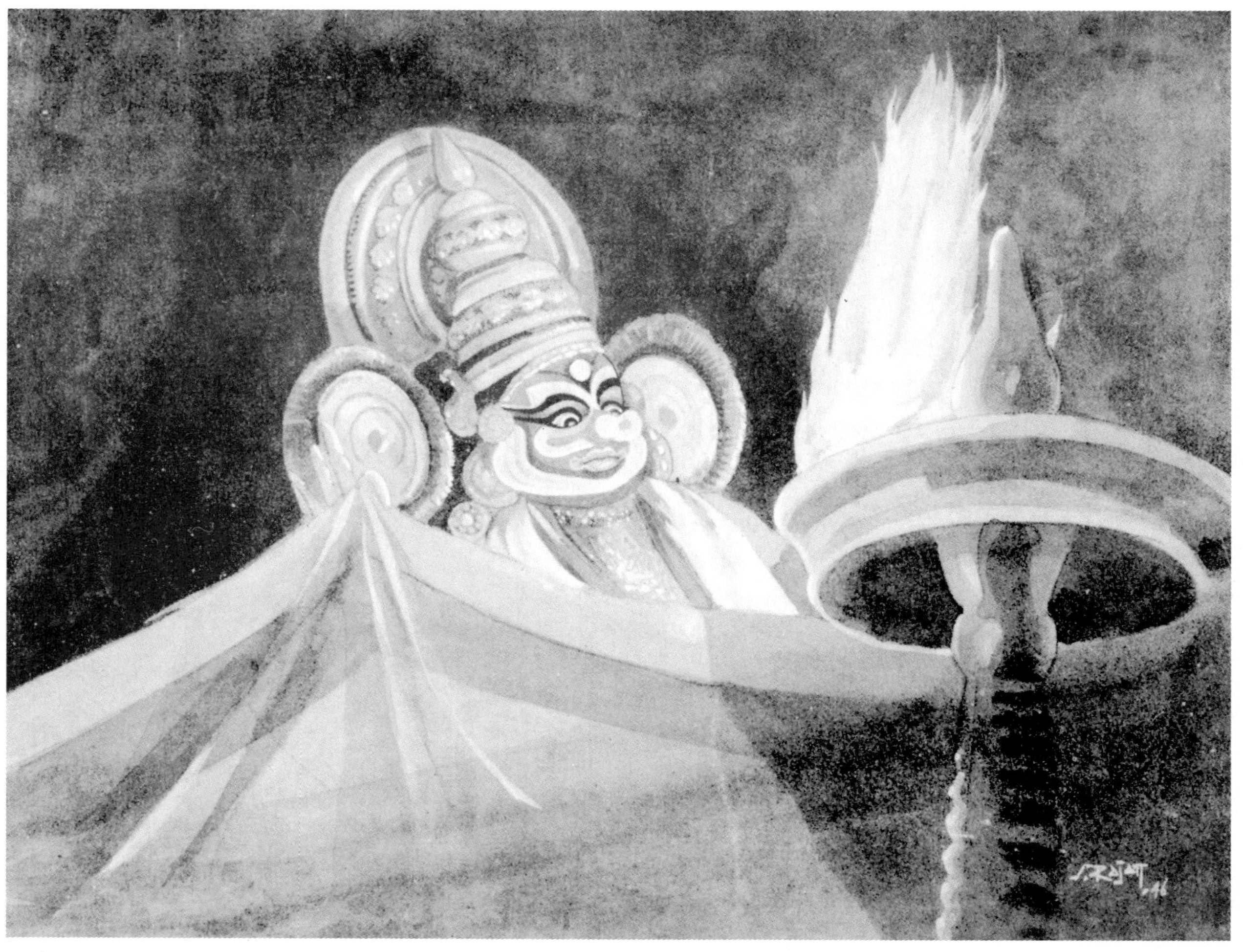

Ravana's Curtain-look (*Tiranōkku*) (p. 36 and 110).

Painting by S. Rajam (Madras).

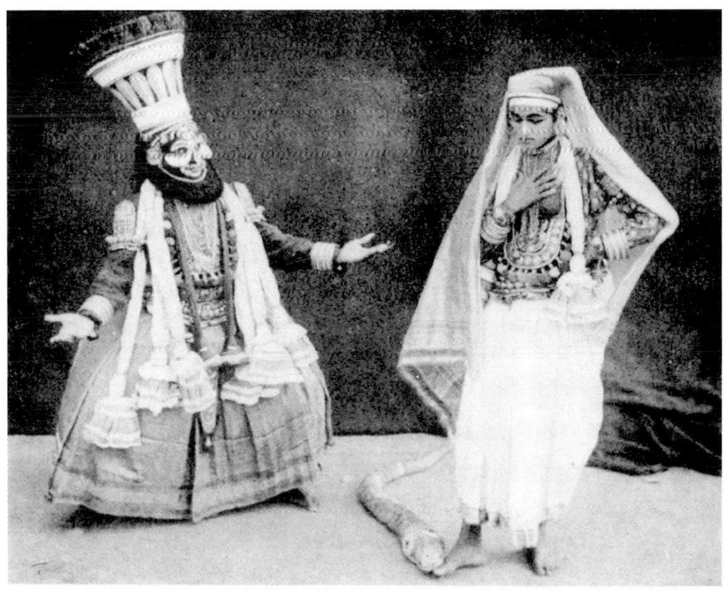

Fig. 1. Deserted by Nala and wandering in the forest Damayanti was caught by a python. Hearing her cries the Kāṭṭāḷan (Forest-man) came to her rescue. But struck by her celestial beauty he gazes at her in undisguised astonishment.

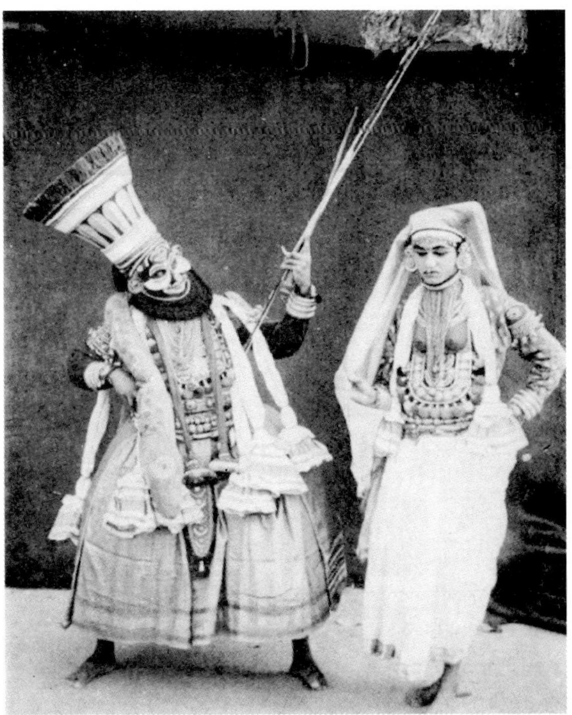

Fig. 2. Having killed the python, he urges his love, assures her protection and all the joys of forest life. He is intrigued and puzzled that she remains un-impressed and unresponsive, even wrathful. The role of the Forest-man is played by Kunju Kurup.

Photo's: Royal Studio, Ernakulam.

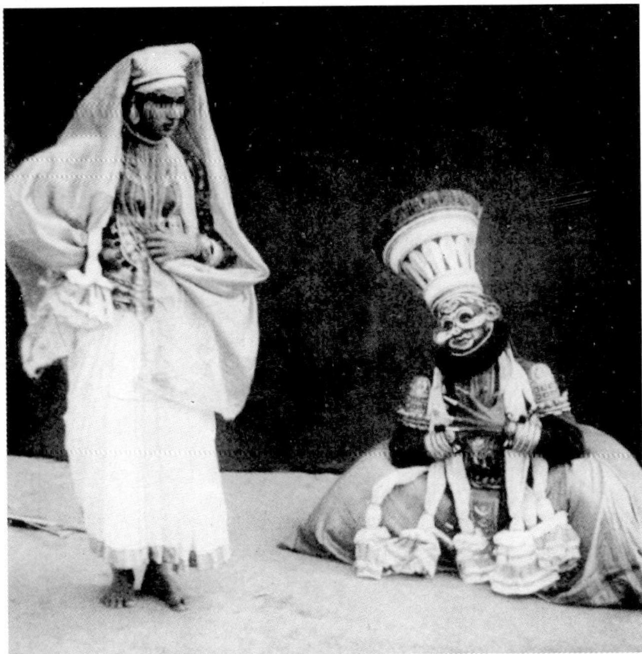

Fig. 1. The Forest-man is frankly miserable and so falls at her feet and piteously pleads for mercy on him whose heart was riven with the cruel darts of *Kāma* or Eros.

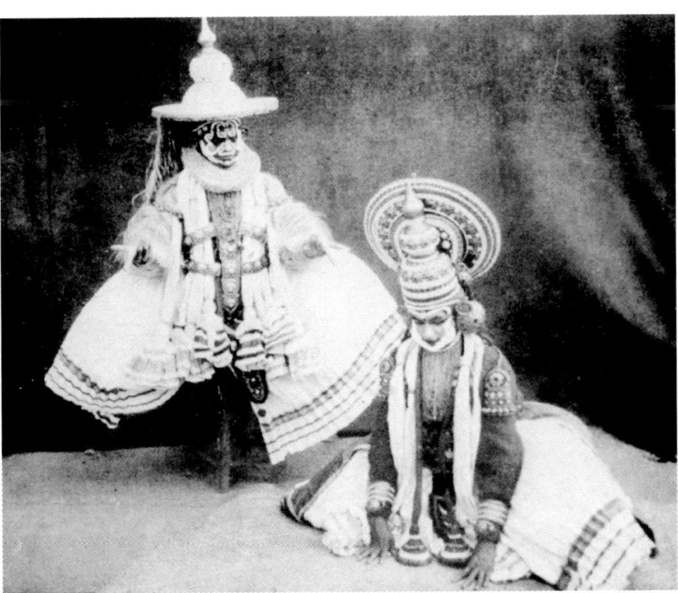

Fig. 2. The top figure is Hanumān, White beard (p. 48). The crest-fallen and humbled figure at his feet is Bhīma the Indian Hercules. A scene from the drama *Kalyāṇa Saugandhika.* Bhīma is worsted in a trial of strength with Hanumān whom he takes for an aged monkey. When he learns later on that it is Hanumān (his own elder brother being a son of the Wind God—his father—, born of a different mother) he is utterly miserable and begs for his forgiveness.

Photo's: Royal Studio, Ernakulam.

PLATE XXII

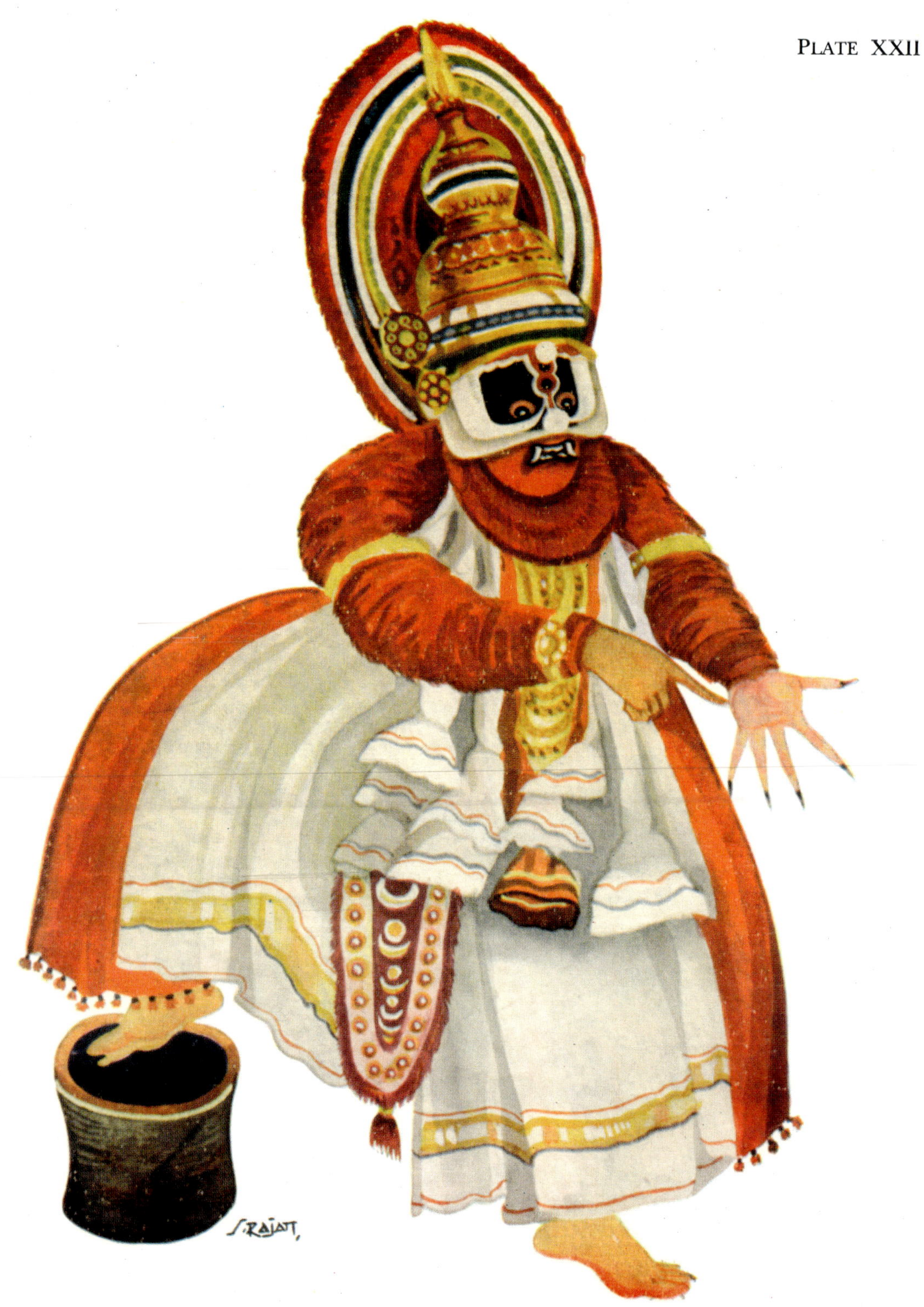

Red-beard type. The enraged demon Baka demands of Bhima to deliver himself up (p. 47, 51 & 52).

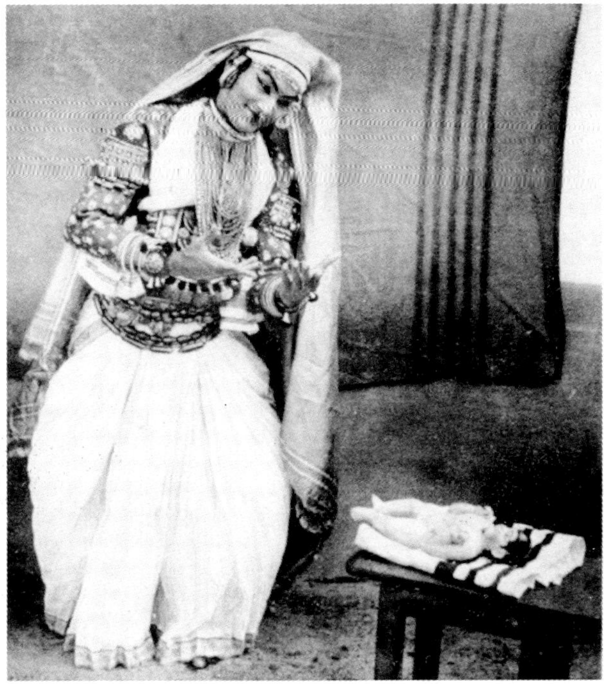

Fig. 1. Stealing into the nursery Pūtana tempts and fondles the divine child Kriṣṇa (p. 103 & 123).

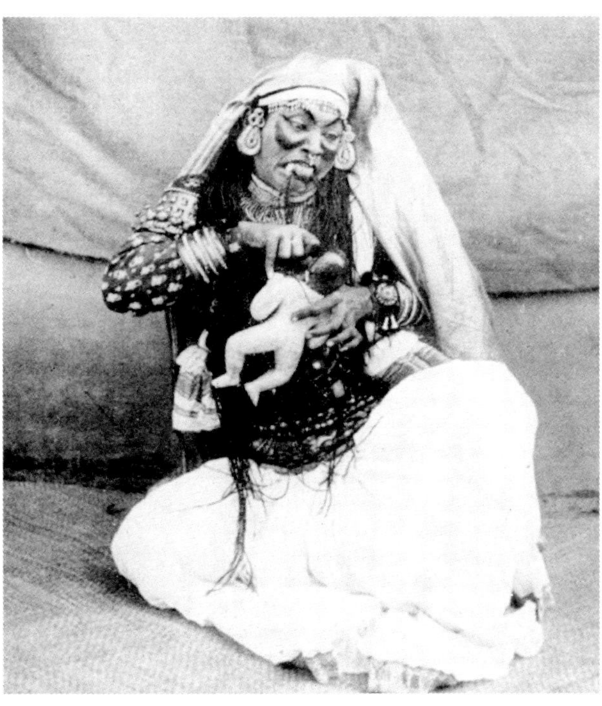

Fig. 2. The divine child feeding at her breast drains Pūtana's life. Her transformation into an ogress is complete (p. 103 & 123).

Photo's: Royal Studio, Ernakulam.

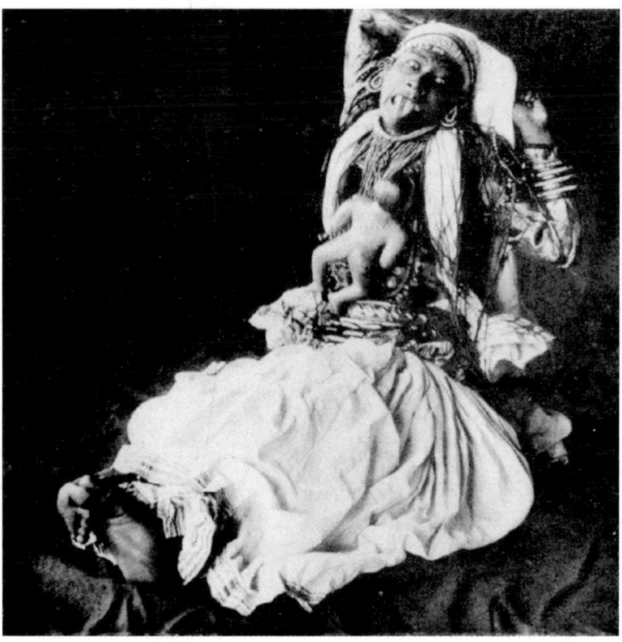

Fig. 1. Insufferable pain seizes her horribly contorting her features (p. 104 & 123).
Photo: Krishnan Nair Bros., Trichur.

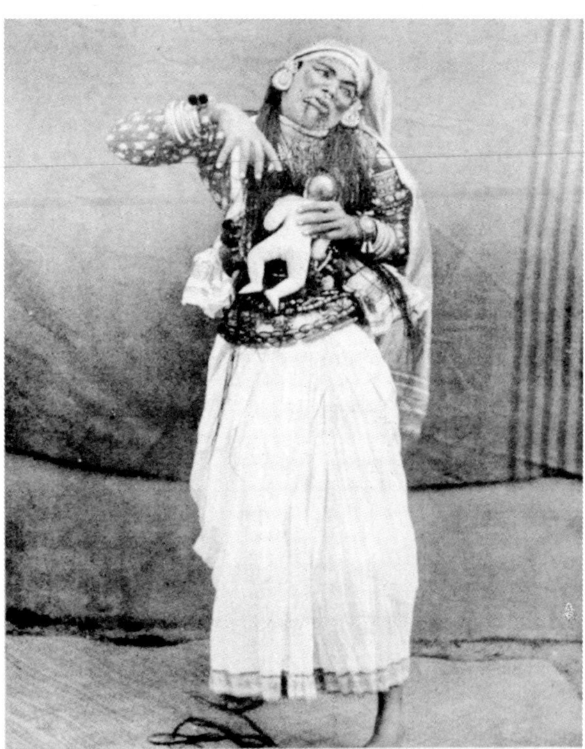

Fig. 2. Unable to free herself from the power that drains her life, fighting, howling and weakening she is collapsing (p. 104 & 123).
Photo: Royal Studio, Ernakulam.

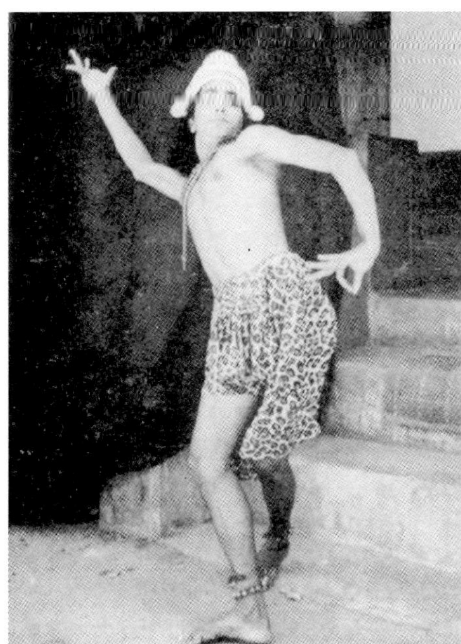

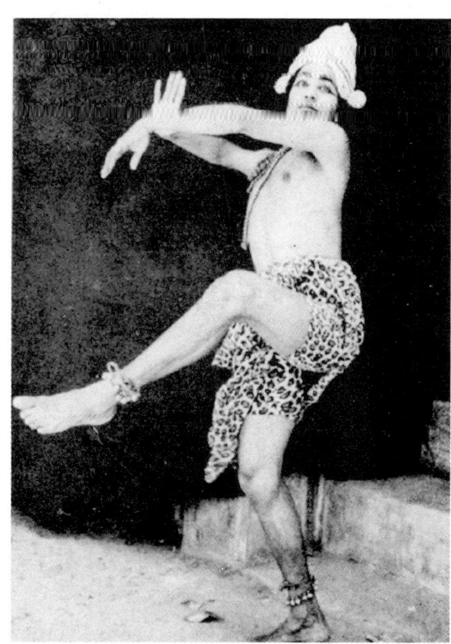

Fig. 1 and 2. Śiva Tandava dance by Madhavan.

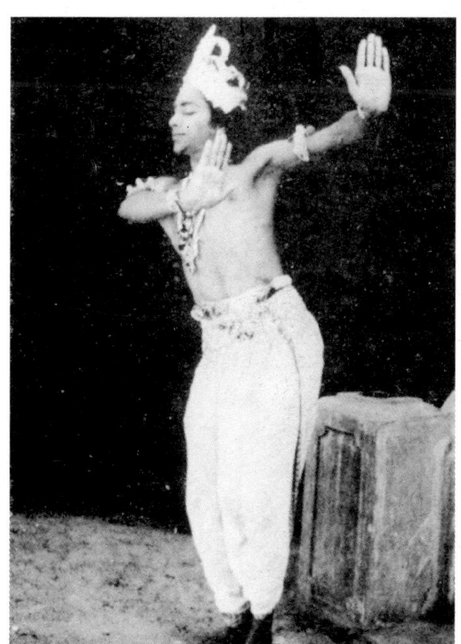

Fig. 3. Aversion and rejection.

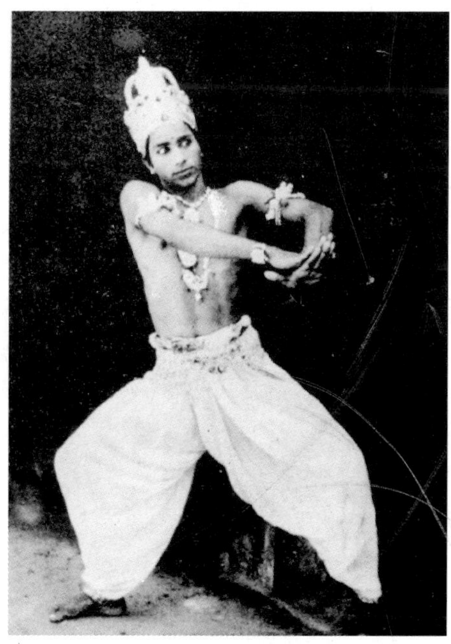

Fig. 4. *Matsya* (fish).

Photo's: Royal Studio, Ernakulam.

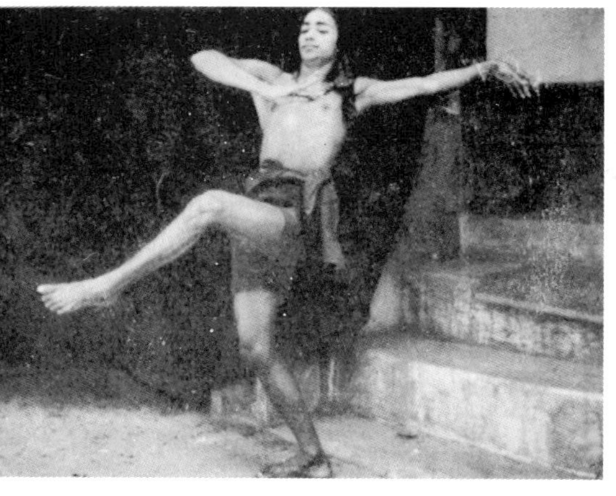

Fig. 1. Madhavan in Hunter dance.

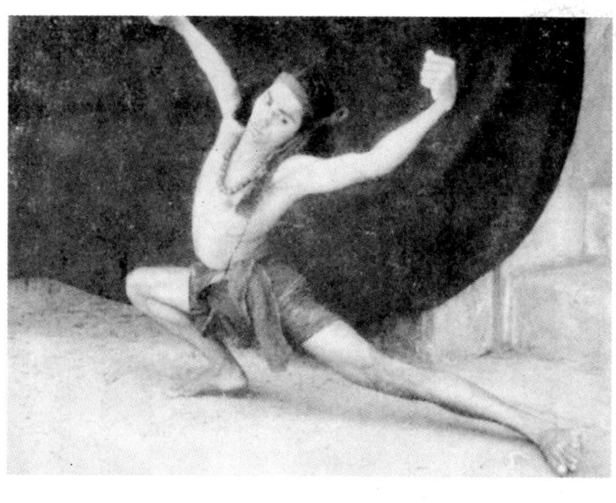

Fig. 2.

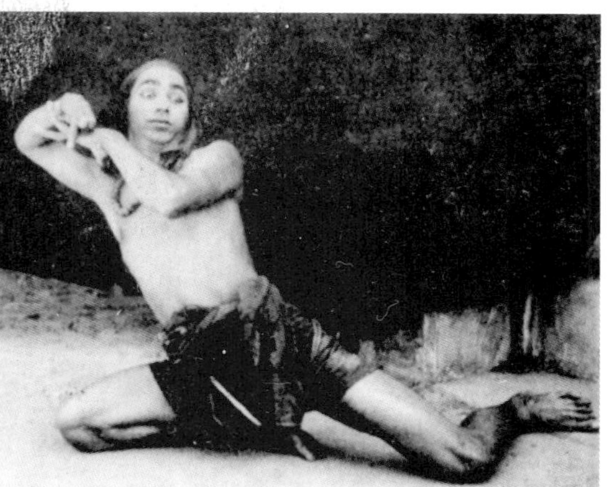

Fig. 3.
Figs. 1-3. Hunter dance.

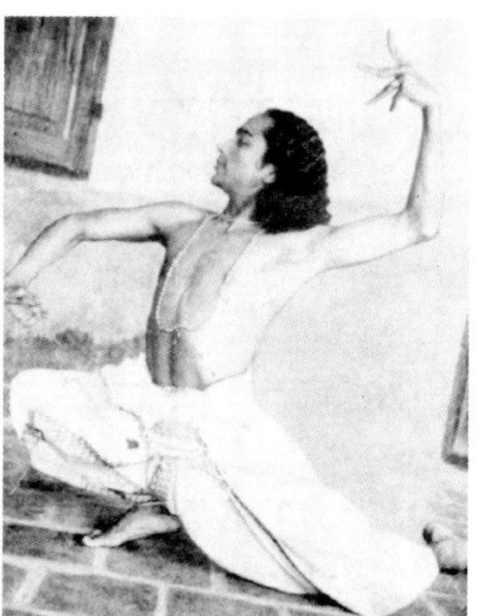

Fig. 4. A Nṛtta pose.